Encountering
the Book of Hebrews

Encountering Biblical Studies
Walter A. Elwell, General Editor and New Testament Editor
Eugene H. Merrill, Old Testament Editor

Encountering the Old Testament: A Christian Survey
Bill T. Arnold and Bryan E. Beyer

*Readings from the Ancient Near East: Primary Sources
for Old Testament Study*
Bill T. Arnold and Bryan E. Beyer, editors

*Encountering the New Testament: A Historical
and Theological Survey*
Walter A. Elwell and Robert W. Yarbrough

*Readings from the First-Century World: Primary Sources
for New Testament Study*
Walter A. Elwell and Robert W. Yarbrough, editors

*Encountering the Book of Genesis: A Study of Its Content
and Issues*
Bill T. Arnold

*Encountering the Book of Psalms: A Literary
and Theological Introduction*
C. Hassell Bullock

Encountering the Book of Isaiah
Bryan E. Beyer

*Encountering John: The Gospel in Historical, Literary,
and Theological Perspective*
Andreas J. Köstenberger

Encountering the Book of Romans: A Theological Survey
Douglas J. Moo

Encountering the Book of Hebrews: An Exposition
Donald A. Hagner

Encountering the Book of Hebrews

An Exposition

Donald A. Hagner

Baker Academic
Grand Rapids, Michigan

Published by Baker Academic
a division of Baker Publishing Group
P.O. Box 6287, Grand Rapids, MI 49516-6287
www.bakeracademic.com

Printed in the United States of America

Library of Congress Cataloging-in-Publication Data
Hagner, Donald Alfred.
        Encountering the book of Hebrews : an exposition / Donald A.
    Hagner.
            p.   cm.
        Includes bibliographical references and indexes.
        ISBN 10: 0-8010-2580-X (pbk.)
        ISBN 978-0-8010-2580-8 (pbk.)
        1. Bible. N.T. Hebrews—Criticism, interpretation, etc. I. Title.
    BS2775.2 .H34 2002
    227'08707—dc21   2002018258

Contents in Brief

List of Sidebars   9

Editor's Preface   11

Publisher's Preface   12

To the Student   14

Author's Preface   16

Abbreviations   17

Introduction   19

1. The Most Important Thing God Ever Said   39

2. The Full Humanity of the Son of God   53

3. Christ Is Superior to Moses   63

4. The Remaining Promise of Rest   71

5. The High Priesthood of Christ   81

6. Apostasy and Divine Faithfulness   89

7. The Priesthood of Melchizedek   97

8. The New and Better Covenant   109

9. Christ the Definitive Sacrifice   117

10A. Moving from the Imperfect to the Perfect: 10:1–18   127

10B. Faithfulness, Apostasy, and Endurance: 10:19–39   133

11. Supreme Examples of Faith   141

12. A Call to Faithfulness   157

13. Concluding Exhortations and Benediction   169

Conclusion: The Place of Hebrews in the New Testament and Its Contribution to Theology, the Church, and the Christian   179

Excursus: The Entry of Hebrews into the New Testament Canon   191

Select Bibliography   197

Glossary   201

Scripture Index   205

Subject Index   211

Contents

List of Sidebars   9

Editor's Preface   11

Publisher's Preface   12

To the Student   14

Author's Preface   16

Abbreviations   17

Introduction   19
Outline
Objectives
The Origin and the
   Historical Setting
   of Hebrews
 • Author
 • Readers
 • Date
 • Purpose
The Structure of Hebrews
The Literary Genre
   of Hebrews
Heavenly Archetypes
   and Earthly Copies
The Use of the
   Old Testament
The Relation of the Old
   and the New
Hebrews' Attitude toward
   Judaism and the
   Problem of Anti-
   Semitism
Study Questions
Key Terms

1. The Most Important
   Thing God Ever
   Said   39
Supplemental Reading
Outline
Objectives
Opening Statement
   (1:1–2a)
Seven Phrases Describing
   the Son (1:2b–3)
 • Phrase 1
 • Phrase 2
 • Phrase 3
 • Phrase 4
 • Phrase 5

 • Phrase 6
 • Phrase 7
The Superiority of Christ
   to the Angels (1:4)
Chain of Seven Old
   Testament Quotations
   (1:5–13)
 • Quotations 1 and 2
 • Quotations 3 and 4
 • Quotation 5
 • Quotation 6
 • Quotation 7
The Role of Angels (1:14)
Study Questions
Key Terms
Further Reading

2. The Full Humanity
   of the Son of God   53
Supplemental Reading
Outline
Objectives
Parenthetical Application
   to Readers (2:1–4)
The Full Humanity
   of the Son (2:5–9)
The Goal of Incarnation:
   the Death of the Son
   (2:10–18)
Study Questions
Key Terms
Further Reading

3. Christ Is Superior
   to Moses   63
Supplemental Reading
Outline
Objectives
Christ as Son over
   God's House (3:1–6)
Admonition Concerning
   Unbelief and
   Hard-Heartedness
   (3:7–19)
Study Questions
Key Terms
Further Reading

4. The Remaining Promise
   of Rest   71
Supplemental Reading

Outline
Objectives
The Sabbath Rest That
   Remains for the
   People of God (4:1–11)
The God Who Discerns
   the Intentions
   of the Heart (4:12–13)
Jesus Our Great High
   Priest (4:14–16)
Study Questions
Key Terms
Further Reading

5. The High Priesthood
   of Christ   81
Supplemental Reading
Outline
Objectives
The Duties of the
   High Priest (5:1–4)
Jesus as High Priest
   in the Order
   of Melchizedek
   (5:5–10)
An Exhortation
   to Maturity (5:11–6:3)
Study Questions
Key Terms
Further Reading

6. Apostasy and Divine
   Faithfulness   89
Supplemental Reading
Outline
Objectives
The Danger of Apostasy
   (6:4–12)
The Fixed Character
   of God's Purposes
   (6:13–20)
Study Questions
Key Terms
Further Reading

7. The Priesthood
   of Melchizedek   97
Supplemental Reading
Outline
Objectives

Abraham and
Melchizedek (7:1–10)
The High Priesthood
of Jesus in the Line
of Melchizedek
(7:11–22)
The Perfect and Perma-
nent Priestly Work
of Christ (7:23–28)
Study Questions
Key Terms
Further Reading

8. **The New and Better
Covenant   109**
Supplemental Reading
Outline
Objectives
The High Priest of the
True Tent (Tabernacle)
(8:1–6)
The Promise of
a New Covenant
and Its Implications
for the Old (8:7–13)
Study Questions
Key Terms
Further Reading

9. **Christ the Definitive
Sacrifice   117**
Supplemental Reading
Outline
Objectives
The Sacrificial Ritual
of the First Covenant
(9:1–10)
The Definitive Work
of Christ the High
Priest (9:11–14)
Christ as Mediator
of the New Covenant
(9:15–22)
The Single Sacrifice
of Christ as the
Final Answer to Sin
(9:23–28)
Study Questions
Key Terms
Further Reading

10A. **Moving from
the Imperfect to the
Perfect: 10:1–18   127**
Supplemental Reading

Outline
Objectives
What the Old Covenant
Sacrifices Could Not
Do (10:1–4)
The Old Replaced
by the New according
to Psalm 40 (10:5–10)
The Perfect Offering
That Establishes and
Fulfills the New
Covenant (10:11–18)
Study Questions
Key Terms
Further Reading

10B. **Faithfulness, Apostasy,
and Endurance:
10:19–39   133**
Supplemental Reading
Outline
Objectives
Drawing Near to God:
The Grounds for
Faithfulness (10:19–25)
The Danger of Apostasy
and Judgment
(10:26–31)
Exhortation to Endurance
(10:32–39)
Study Questions
Key Terms
Further Reading

11. **Supreme Examples
of Faith   141**
Supplemental Reading
Outline
Objectives
The Nature and
Importance of Faith
(11:1–3)
The Faith of Abel, Enoch,
and Noah (11:4–7)
The First Example
of Abraham's Faith
(11:8–10)
The Faith of Abraham
and Sarah (11:11–12)
A Parenthesis Concerning
Hope for What Lies
beyond the Present
and the Earthly
(11:13–16)

The Supreme Example
of Abraham's Faith
(11:17–19)
The Faith of Isaac, Jacob,
and Joseph (11:20–22)
The Faith of Moses
(11:23–28)
The Faith of the Israelites,
Rahab, and Many
Others (11:29–38)
All the Saints Together
Brought to the Goal
(11:39–40)
Study Questions
Key Terms
Further Reading

12. **A Call to
Faithfulness   157**
Supplemental Reading
Outline
Objectives
Fix Your Gaze upon Jesus,
the Peerless Example
of Faith (12:1–3)
The Role of God's
Discipline in the
Christian Life
(12:4–11)
A Call to Holiness and
a Further Warning
(12:12–17)
The Glory of the
Christian's Present
Status (12:18–24)
A Final Warning to
Readers (12:25–29)
Study Questions
Key Terms
Further Reading

13. **Concluding Exhortations
and Benediction   169**
Supplemental Reading
Outline
Objectives
Various Ethical
Exhortations (13:1–9)
The True Sacrifices
(13:10–16)
Obedience to Church
Leaders (13:17)
A Prayer Request and
a Personal Note
(13:18–19)

Contents

Concluding Prayer and
Doxology (13:20–21)
Postscript with Personal
Information (13:22–23)
Greetings and Final
Benediction (13:24–25)
Study Questions
Key Terms
Further Reading

**Conclusion: The Place
of Hebrews in the New
Testament and Its
Contribution to
Theology, the Church,
and the Christian   179**
Outline

Objectives
What Are the Special
Theological
Emphases of
Hebrews?
What Does Hebrews Offer
to New Testament
Theology?
What Does Hebrews Offer
to the Church?
What Does Hebrews Offer
to the Individual
Christian?
Study Questions
Key Terms

**Excursus: The Entry of
Hebrews into the New
Testament Canon   191**
Key Terms

**Select
Bibliography   197**

Glossary   201

Scripture Index   205

Subject Index   211

Sidebars

John Calvin on Hebrews   21

Hebrews and the Pauline Epistles   21

Proposed Authors for Hebrews Other Than Paul   22

Alternating Discourse and Application in Hebrews   26

Midrashic Interpretation in Hebrews   27

An Outline of Hebrews   28

Sensus Plenior in the Interpretation of the Old Testament   32

Pesher Interpretation in Hebrews   33

Seven Phrases Describing the Son in Hebrews 1:2b–3   41

Wisdom Christology   42

The Importance of Psalm 110 in the Early Church   44

Jesus as Prophet, Priest, and King   45

The Word "Better" in Hebrews   46

Chain of Seven Old Testament Quotations in Hebrews 1:5–13   47

The Importance of Psalm 2 in the Early Church   47

Psalm 110 in Hebrews   49

Comparison of Angels with the Son in Hebrews 1:4–14   50

The Word "Perfect" in Hebrews   57

Jesus as the Pioneer of Our Salvation   58

The Identification of Jesus with YHWH in the New Testament   59

Anti-gnostic Elements in Hebrews   60

Jesus as High Priest in Hebrews   61

The Word "Heavenly" in Hebrews   65

Titles of Christ in Hebrews   65

Sabbath Rest: Psalm 95 in Hebrews 3–4   66

The Rest Offered to the People of God   72

The Importance of the Word "Today"   73

"Jesus" as the Greek Translation of "Joshua"   74

The "Word of God" in Hebrews 4:12   76

The Sinlessness of Christ   77

Drawing Near to the Presence of God in Hebrews   77

The Word "Grace" in Hebrews   78

The Verb "Offer" in Hebrews   82

In What Sense Was Jesus' Prayer Heard?   85

The Word "Eternal" in Hebrews   86

"The Elementary Doctrine of Christ"   86

Apostasy and the Question of the Eternal Security of the Believer   91

Postbaptismal Sins   92

Melchizedek in Jewish Literature   98

Melchizedek in Hebrews   100

Motifs of Discontinuity with the Old Testament in Hebrews   101

The View of the Law in Hebrews Compared to Paul's View   103

The Word "Covenant" in Hebrews   104

The Qualities of Jesus as High Priest   104

"Once for All" in Hebrews   105

Why Does Hebrews Refer to the Tabernacle Rather Than the Temple?   111

Dualism in Hebrews: Metaphysical or Temporal?   112

Jeremiah 31:31–34 in Hebrews   114

The New Covenant in the New Testament   115

The Tabernacle, the Priesthood, and the Sacrifices: Lessons on God's Holiness   118

The Mercy Seat of the Ark of the Covenant as the Place of Atonement   119

The Contrast between the New and the Old in Hebrews   122

The Emphasis on the Eternal in Hebrews   122

Christ as the Mediator of the New Covenant   123

The Meaning of "Many" as Those Benefiting from Christ's Work   124

The Insufficiency of the Temple Sacrifices according to the Old Testament   129

Exhortations in Hebrews   135

The Temptation of the Readers to Abandon Their Christian Faith   136

The Christian's Future Inheritance   137

9

Habakkuk 2:4 in Hebrews and in
    Paul   138
Faith according to Hebrews 11:1   143
The Catalog of Supreme Examples of
    Faith in Hebrews 11   144
The Controlling Reality of the Unseen in
    Hebrews 11   146
Sarah's or Abraham's Faith in Hebrews
    11:11?   148
The Binding of Isaac (the Akedah) and
    Hebrews 11:17–19   150

The Examples of Faith in Hebrews
    11:32–38   153
The Positive Results of Suffering as
    God's Discipline   160
A Contrast of the Old and New Cove-
    nants: Mount Sinai and Mount
    Zion   162
The City in Hebrews   163
Realized Eschatology in Hebrews   164
The New Covenant in Hebrews   165
Exhortations in Hebrews 13   170
The Quintessence of Hebrews   188

Editor's Preface

The strength of the church and the vitality of the individual Christian's life are directly related to the role Scripture plays in them. Early believers knew the importance of this and spent their time in fellowship, prayer, and the study of God's Word. The passing of two thousand years has not changed the need, but it has changed the accessibility of many of the Bible's ideas. Time has distanced us from those days, and we often need guidance back into the world of the Old and New Testaments.

To that end, Baker Book House is producing an innovative series of biblical textbooks. The design of this series is to put us back into the world of the biblical text, so that we may understand it as those early believers did and at the same time see it from and for our own day, thus facilitating the application of its truths to our contemporary situation.

Encountering Biblical Studies consists of undergraduate-level texts, and two surveys treating the Old and New Testaments provide the foundation for this series. Accompanying these survey texts are two collateral volumes of readings that illuminate the world surrounding the biblical text. Built on these basic survey texts are upper-level college texts covering the books of the Bible that are most frequently offered in the curriculum of Christian colleges.

Complementing the series is a set of standard reference books that may be consulted for answers to specific questions or more in-depth study of biblical ideas. These reference books include *Baker Commentary on the Bible, Baker Topical Guide to the Bible, Baker Encyclopedia of the Bible, Baker Theological Dictionary of the Bible,* and *Evangelical Dictionary of Theology.*

The Encountering Biblical Studies series is written from an evangelical point of view, in the firm conviction that the Scripture is absolutely true and never misleads us. It is the sure foundation on which our faith and life may be built because it unerringly leads willing readers to Jesus Christ.

Walter A. Elwell
General Editor

Publisher's Preface

Bible courses must be considered the heart of the curriculum for Christian colleges and evangelical seminaries. For Christians, the Bible constitutes the basis for both spiritual life and intellectual life—indeed for *all* of life. If these courses are fundamental to Christian education, then the textbooks used for these courses could not be more crucial.

Baker Book House is launching a series of volumes for college-level Bible courses. The textbooks for the basic college survey courses and for the more advanced college courses on individual Bible books will not be written for laypeople or pastors and seminarians, nor will they be primarily reference books. Rather, they will be pedagogically oriented textbooks written with collegians in mind.

Encountering the Book of Hebrews attempts to build on the basic survey text, *Encountering the New Testament: A Historical and Theological Survey* (Walter A. Elwell and Robert W. Yarbrough). While the survey text is written for college freshmen, this volume is intended for upper-level collegians.

Rather than providing a sustained exegetical analysis of each verse in the Book of Hebrews, this volume surveys the entire book with an emphasis on drawing out its theological message and its practical significance for collegians. It consists of appropriate introduction and survey material with the necessary critical, historical, literary, hermeneutical, and background concerns woven into the exposition of the biblical text.

Guiding Principles

As part of the development of this volume, the series editors, author, and publisher established the following principles:

1. It must reflect the finest in evangelical scholarship of our day.
2. It must be written at a level that most of today's upper-level collegians can understand.
3. It must be pedagogically sound. This extends not only to traditional concerns such as study and review questions, and objectives and summaries for each chapter, but also to the manner in which the material is presented.
4. It must include appropriate illustrative material such as photographs, maps, charts, graphs, figures, and sidebars.
5. It must seek to winsomely draw in the student by focusing on biblical teaching concerning crucial doctrinal and ethical matters.

Goals

The goals for *Encountering the Book of Hebrews* fall into two categories: intellectual and attitudinal. The intellectual goals are (1) to present the factual content of the Book of Hebrews, (2) to introduce historical, geographical, and cultural background, (3) to outline primary hermeneutical principles, (4) to touch on critical issues (e.g., why people read the Bible differently), and (5) to substantiate the Christian faith.

The attitudinal goals also are fivefold: (1) to make the Bible a part of students' lives, (2) to instill in students a love for the Scriptures, (3) to make them better people, (4) to enhance their piety, and (5) to stimulate their love for God. In short, if this text builds a foundation for a lifetime of Bible study, the author and publisher will be amply rewarded.

Overarching Themes

Controlling the writing of *Encountering the Book of Hebrews* have been three essential theological themes: God, people, and the gospel as it relates to individuals. The notion that God is a person—one and three—and a transcendent and immanent Being has been woven into the text throughout. Moreover, God has created people in the divine image, people who, though fallen, are the objects of God's redemptive love. The gospel is the means, the active personal power that God uses to rescue people from darkness and death. But the gospel does more than rescue—it restores. It confers on otherwise hopeless sinners the resolve and strength to live lives that please God, because they walk in the love that comes from God.

Features

The publisher's aim has been to provide a resource that is unique but not trendy. Some of the distinguishing features that we hope will prove helpful to the professor and inspiring to the student include the following:

- liberal use of illustrations—photographs, figures, tables, charts
- sidebars and excursuses exploring exegetical, ethical, and theological issues of interest and concern to modern-day collegians
- chapter outline and objectives presented at the opening of each chapter
- study questions at the end of each chapter
- a glossary of key terms
- a bibliography to guide further study

To the Student

The purpose of this book is simply to help you to understand one of the richest texts of the New Testament, the wonderful Book of Hebrews. In particular, my main goal is to help you follow the author's arguments and trace the logic of the book. This sometimes can be challenging, since Hebrews often takes us into an unfamiliar world.

The heart of the present book, in keeping with the intent of the series it belongs to, is to assist you in your encounter with Hebrews. The main text, therefore, presents a chapter-by-chapter exposition of Hebrews. This is not a commentary, and it leaves many details untouched and many questions unanswered. It focuses on the main themes and significant issues. Thus, you will want to supplement this book with a commentary or two that you keep within easy reach.

The exposition that I present presupposes not only that you will have read the pertinent portion of Hebrews, but also that you will have the biblical text before you for reference as you read. I therefore repeat little of the biblical text in my exposition. We must remember that what is ultimately important is *the text of Hebrews itself*. Secondary literature, including the present book, can be useful, of course, but is not what really matters. The present book is significant only as a servant to a master, only as an aid to understanding the biblical text. Keep your eyes on the text that matters!

One helpful feature of the Encountering Biblical Studies books is the sidebars—the material contained within boxes. Some of these provide distillations and lists, which I hope are useful, while others provide detailed discussion of specific points. For some of these latter sidebars I have included a few references for further reading.

General bibliographical suggestions can be found at the end of the book, where you will also find some recommended commentaries. In my chapter-by-chapter exposition I deliberately avoid interacting with secondary literature, and, mercifully, you will find no footnotes there. The purpose of the exposition, as I have already indicated, is to focus on the argument of Hebrews, and I have resisted becoming engaged, not to say bogged down, with the scholarly discussion of particular issues. Nevertheless, I have included some important bibliography entries at the end of each chapter as a help to those who wish to go deeper. For any who may be interested, I interact with some of the secondary literature in my commentary on Hebrews (see recommended commentaries). The present book is a complement to my commentary and is a totally fresh work, although obviously I agree with myself amazingly often!

At the end of the volume you will find a glossary to assist you with understanding the more technical jargon. Words that appear in bold type can be found in the glossary. At the beginning of each chapter you will find objectives and study questions to help you focus on the important matters.

To begin to understand Hebrews requires a knowledge of some information about the book, especially its origin and historical setting. You will find this kind of information in the introduction. There, I also devote considerable space to the author's distinctive method of interpreting the Old Testament, particularly his habit of quoting a text and then commenting using words drawn from the quotation, in the manner known as midrash. In my exposition of such passages, I have italicized the words that the author draws from the quoted text and uses within his own commentary on the material in the following verses. If you have difficulty comprehending the theoretical discussion of the author's manner of interpreting the Old Testament that I have provided in the introduction, be patient. After you have worked your way through the first chapter or two, you should have a much firmer grasp on the subject. Then return and re-read the pertinent material in the introduction.

In all study, the more you invest yourself, the more rewards you receive. I assure you that the study of Hebrews is well worth the time and energy you invest in it, and that your study of this book will be wonderfully rewarding, both for your understanding of the Christian faith and for your living of the Christian life. I have found this to be true in my life. May God bless you in your study of Hebrews, just as God has blessed many others throughout the history of the church.

Author's Preface

I am grateful to the folks at Baker Books for the invitation to contribute this volume on Hebrews to the Encountering Biblical Studies series. For me, it has been a rewarding experience to return to the study of Hebrews after having published a commentary on the book nearly twenty years ago (republished in a new edition by Hendrickson [1990] in the New International Biblical Commentary). The present book is completely independent from that commentary. I have, however, made use of material from an earlier article, "Interpreting the Epistle to the Hebrews," in *The Literature and Meaning of Scripture*, edited by Morris A. Inch and C. Hassell Bullock, published by Baker Book House in 1981. I am grateful to the publisher for the permission to do this.

I have attempted to make this book accessible to college and university students without compromising the underlying quality of its scholarship. This book is not a commentary, but rather, an exposition—a tracing of the line of thought from section to section. Its main purpose is to assist students in their encounter with Hebrews and the strange new world it presents. In addition to the exposition there are various sidebars, which I hope will be particularly useful. Although I do not interact with secondary literature on Hebrews, I have provided some bibliographical suggestions that will help students to deepen their knowledge of the main issues.

Through God's grace and the inspiration of the Holy Spirit, the author of Hebrews has presented to the church a masterful account of the atoning work of Christ, who is presented as the uniquely qualified priest of the order of Melchizedek and who fulfills the sacrificial ritual of the Old Testament, presenting himself simultaneously as priest and offering. In so doing, the author not only has given us a wonderfully rich theological document, but also has continually drawn out the practical significance of this theology for the life of the Christian. My prayer is that the present book may provide some assistance to readers as they seek to understand and apply the Book of Hebrews to their own lives. Reading Hebrews with an open mind and a receptive heart will make that experience a true encounter.

There are many to whom I owe thanks in the writing of this book. I think first of my Manchester mentor, Professor F. F. Bruce, commentator par excellence, whose lectures on Hebrews first introduced me to its treasures and whose own commentary on the book remains one of the very best. I am grateful to Fuller Theological Seminary for the generous sabbatical program that enabled me to find time to work on this book. I am also grateful for the ongoing friendship and encouragement of my faculty colleagues. I think gratefully too of the several churches where I have taught the Book of Hebrews to adult education classes; members of these classes often have helped me gain insight into the meaning of particular texts. I also thank my Ph.D. student and assistant, Chris Spinks, for helping to produce the study questions, lists of key words, and supplementary Scripture readings, and for compiling the glossary and the indexes. As always, I owe the most thanks to my wife, Beverly, who so beautifully balances her career as a psychologist with being a wife and friend, and whose love and encouragement remain unfailing.

Abbreviations

Old Testament

Genesis	Gn
Exodus	Ex
Leviticus	Lv
Numbers	Nm
Deuteronomy	Dt
Joshua	Jos
Judges	Jgs
Ruth	Ru
1 Samuel	1 Sm
2 Samuel	2 Sm
1 Kings	1 Kgs
2 Kings	2 Kgs
1 Chronicles	1 Chr
2 Chronicles	2 Chr
Ezra	Ezr
Nehemiah	Neh
Esther	Est
Job	Jb
Psalms	Ps(s)
Proverbs	Prv
Ecclesiastes	Eccl
Song of Songs	Sg (Song)
Isaiah	Is
Jeremiah	Jer
Lamentations	Lam
Ezekiel	Ez
Daniel	Dn
Hosea	Hos
Joel	Jl
Amos	Am
Obadiah	Ob
Jonah	Jon
Micah	Mi
Nahum	Na
Habakkuk	Hb
Zephaniah	Zep
Haggai	Hg
Zechariah	Zec
Malachi	Mal

New Testament

Matthew	Mt
Mark	Mk
Luke	Lk
John	Jn
Acts of the Apostles	Acts
Romans	Rom
1 Corinthians	1 Cor
2 Corinthians	2 Cor
Galatians	Gal
Ephesians	Eph
Philippians	Phil
Colossians	Col
1 Thessalonians	1 Thes
2 Thessalonians	2 Thes
1 Timothy	1 Tm
2 Timothy	2 Tm
Titus	Ti
Philemon	Phlm
Hebrews	Heb
James	Jas
1 Peter	1 Pt
2 Peter	2 Pt
1 John	1 Jn
2 John	2 Jn
3 John	3 Jn
Jude	Jude
Revelation	Rv

Introduction

This is the way, beloved, in which we found our salvation, Jesus Christ, the high priest of our offerings, the defender and helper of our weakness. Through him we fix our gaze on the heights of heaven, through him we see the reflection of his faultless and lofty countenance, through him the eyes of our hearts were opened, through him our foolish and darkened understanding blossoms towards the light, through him the Master willed that we should taste the immortal knowledge, who being the brightness of his majesty is by so much greater than angels as he hath inherited a more excellent name.

—*1 Clement 36:1–2*

Outline

- **The Origin and the Historical Setting of Hebrews**
  Author
  Readers
  Date
  Purpose
- **The Structure of Hebrews**
- **The Literary Genre of Hebrews**
- **Heavenly Archetypes and Earthly Copies**
- **The Use of the Old Testament**
- **The Relation of the Old and the New**
- **Hebrews' Attitude toward Judaism and the Problem of Anti-Semitism**

Objectives

1. Identify the various sides of the debate surrounding the author and date of Hebrews.
2. Compare and contrast Hebrews and the letters of Paul.
3. Show how the author of Hebrews uses the Old Testament.

Hebrews is not exactly what most of us would regard as a user-friendly book. Our immediate reaction to the book is that it is deep and rich, and that it deals with fundamentally important matters, but that for the average reader it is tough going, perhaps even inaccessible. Nevertheless, Hebrews has always been popular among Christians. Surely among our favorite passages in the New Testament is Hebrews' opening christological text, which begins with the majestic words "In the past God spoke to our forefathers through the prophets at many times and in various ways, but in these last days he has spoken to us by his Son." We have been excited by the extended arguments concerning the superiority of Christ, his office as incomparable high priest, his definitive sacrificial work, and the astounding fact that in this unique instance the offerer and the offering are identical. We have found the repeated exhortations in Hebrews challenging, and the models of faith in chapter 11 encouraging, if humbling.

Yet undeniably, Hebrews remains one of the most difficult books of the New Testament, second perhaps only to Revelation. The reasons for this are clear. The book depends heavily on the Old Testament for its argument, more so than any other New Testament book, and this in itself evokes feelings of unfamiliarity. In part this is due, no doubt, to our poor knowledge of the Old Testament, but there are other reasons too. The Old Testament is repeatedly quoted to support the arguments of Hebrews, and often it is difficult to bridge the apparent meaning of the Old Testament text and its use by the author of Hebrews. Many of the arguments, not only those dependent on Old Testament quotations, employ typological similarities, whether between old and new, temporal and eternal, or earthly and heavenly. Furthermore, although based on what

seems to be careful reasoning, the arguments themselves are often rather elaborate and extensive. It can be difficult to see how the author moves from one argument, or one stage of an argument, to the next. The continuity of the overall argument, moreover, is frequently interrupted by the repeated insertion of exhortations to the readers. Finally, the meaning of some parts of Hebrews is uncertain because the book's exact historical background and origin are unknown to us. All this together explains why Hebrews appeals to so many not only as a book worth studying, but also as one that requires diligent study.

The Origin and the Historical Setting of Hebrews

Given the central importance of **grammatico-historical interpretation,** the starting point for the interpretation of any book of the Bible is the determination of its situation in history: its author, approximate date, and place of origin, its addressees and their background, its intended purpose, its dependence upon literary and oral sources, and so on. Unfortunately, we are in a remarkably poor position to answer these questions for Hebrews, and this inevitably has an effect on the interpretation of the book at several key points. We turn now to look at the specific questions.

Author

The superscription "The Epistle of Paul the Apostle to the Hebrews," found as the title of the book in the King James Version, is not a part of the original text of Hebrews but a later ecclesiastical addition. It has been challenged on all three points: it is almost unanimously agreed that

John Calvin on Hebrews

"Since the Epistle addressed to the Hebrews contains a full discussion of the eternal divinity of Christ, His supreme government, and only priesthood (which are the main points of heavenly wisdom), and as these things are so explained in it, that the whole power and work of Christ are set forth in the most graphic way, it rightly deserves to have the place and honor of an invaluable treasure in the Church." (*Commentary on Hebrews*)

Paul did not write Hebrews; the document is more a homily-treatise than an epistle; and some have even challenged whether it was written to Hebrews, that is, to Jewish Christians.

The Pauline authorship of Hebrews was not accepted in the Western church (Rome) until late in the fourth century. Although Hebrews was attributed to Paul much earlier in the Eastern church (Alexandria), not everyone could agree. It was the great scholar Origen who, after surveying the possible authors, uttered the famous words "But who wrote the epistle, in truth God knows."[1] If this was Origen's conclusion already in the third century, we can hardly expect to find ourselves in a much better position today. Nevertheless, the authorship of Hebrews is a subject that intrigues the public, and speculation has continued into modern times.

The apparent eagerness of many in the early church to ascribe Hebrews to Paul was motivated by concerns to insure its canonical status within the developing New Testament. Without going into the matter in detail, the more important reasons why Pauline authorship is improbable must be mentioned.

1. According to Eusebius, *Ecclesiastical History* 6.25.

Hebrews and the Pauline Epistles

Hebrews	Paul's Epistles
gospel "attested to us by those who heard him" (2:3)	"I did not receive it from man, nor was I taught it, but it came through a revelation of Jesus Christ" (Gal 1:12)
elegant Greek	standard Greek
Jesus as high priest	not found in Paul
not found in Hebrews	justification by faith
Habakkuk 2:4 refers to faithfulness of believer (10:38)	Habakkuk 2:4 refers to justification by faith (Gal 3:11; Rom 1:17)
not found in Hebrews	polemic against the law
emphasis on exaltation to God's right hand	emphasis on resurrection

John Calvin: "I can adduce no reason to show that Paul was its author." (*Commentary on Hebrews*)

William Tyndale: "It is easy to see that he [the author of Hebrews] was a faithful servant of Christ's and of the same doctrine that Timothy was of, yea and Paul himself was, and that he was an apostle or in the apostles' time or near thereunto." (*Preface to Hebrews*)

Proposed Authors for Hebrews Other Than Paul

Clement of Rome (so Eusebius, *Ecclesiastical History* 3.38): 1 Clement evinces very close agreement in wording at points.

Barnabas (so Tertullian, at the end of the second century): described in Acts 4:36 as a "son of encouragement" (or "exhortation," the same word used in Heb 13:22), he was associated with Paul, and was a Levite who would have been thoroughly familiar with the sacrificial ritual of the temple (he was not the author of the very different epistle [*Pseudo-Barnabas*] in the Apostolic Fathers).

Apollos (Martin Luther's brilliant suggestion): the description in Acts 18:24–28 of this Hellenistic Jew from Alexandria fits the apparent profile of the author perfectly.

Luke: stylistic similarities of Greek (Clement of Alexandria was of the opinion that Luke translated Paul's letter from Hebrew into Greek); similarity of perspective to Stephen's speech in Acts 7.

Silas (Silvanus): stylistic similarities with 1 Peter (see 1 Pt 5:12), and he was a member of the Pauline circle.

Epaphras: similar (gnostic) concerns in Colossians (see Col 1:7; 4:12–13).

Priscilla (so A. von Harnack at the end of the nineteenth century): accounts for anonymity, since a treatise written by a woman would not be accepted as authoritative; but she was an instructor of Apollos (Acts 18:26), so if Apollos is a possible author, how much more so Priscilla! (The masculine participle at Heb 11:32 presents no obstacle, because presumably she would have been clever enough not to give herself away.)

Others (but with little reason): Philip, Mary the mother of Jesus.

Origen (in the third century): "But who wrote the epistle, in truth God knows" (according to Eusebius, *Ecclesiastical History* 6.25).

All the epistles of Paul in the New Testament begin with the explicit identification of the author; Hebrews, by contrast, is anonymous. Moreover, our anonymous author disassociates himself from those who heard the Lord (2:3), quite unlike Paul (Gal 1:12). The Greek of Hebrews—the most elegant in the New Testament—is unlike Paul's. This alone, of course, is by no means an insuperable objection to Pauline authorship, since the unusual literary style could be attributed to Paul using a secretary (cf. Paul's use of Tertius [Rom 16:22]). Perhaps the most significant argument against Pauline authorship involves a number of important theological differences between Hebrews and the Pauline Epistles (see the sidebar "Hebrews and the Pauline Epistles"). The authors clearly seem to be at home in two different universes of discourse.

At the same time, however, as Origen himself noted about Hebrews, "Not without reason have the men of old time handed it down as Paul's."[2] For despite the differences that can be noted, there is also much in the book that sounds like Paul. In addition, the personal note at the end of the book about the release of "our brother Timothy," who will accompany the author when he visits the readers (13:23), identifies the author as a member of the Pauline circle. Unquestionably, in many places our author makes statements that we recognize as identical with Paul's perspective. It would therefore seem probable that the author was a member of the Pauline circle, and was influenced by Paul's thinking.

Numerous suggestions have been made as to the author of Hebrews:

2. Ibid.

hermeneutic

Platonic
idealism

Luke, Barnabas, Silas, Clement of Rome, Apollos, Philip, and Priscilla. There are reasons for (and against, in some instances) each of these possibilities (see the sidebar "Proposed Authors for Hebrews Other Than Paul"). What we can say for sure about the author must be drawn from the book itself: he or she (Priscilla remains a candidate)[3] was exceptionally well acquainted with the Old Testament, employed an obviously christocentric **hermeneutic** in interpreting the Old Testament, probably was familiar with the language of **Platonic idealism** popular in Alexandria, shared the universal perspective of the early Hellenistic Christians, and probably was acquainted with the teaching of Paul. It is almost certain, although not strictly necessary, that the author was a Jew. Exactly for these reasons Apollos has been an attractive candidate (see Acts 18:24–25). But this is only a good guess. (For more information on the authorship of Hebrews and the story of its entry into the canon, see the excursus, "The Entry of Hebrews into the New Testament Canon," at the end of the book.)

Readers

The traditional title "To the Hebrews" is first encountered toward the end of the second century.[4] Strictly speaking, there are no addressees, since the document lacks the usual epistolary opening. No-

3. Hebrews 11:32 is the one instance where the author uses a participle with a masculine ending (*diēgoumenon*, "telling about") in self-reference. This one point does not establish that the author was male. Priscilla would have been wise enough not to give herself away by using a feminine participle there!

4. In Papyrus 46, the earliest complete manuscript of the Pauline letters, dating from about 200, Hebrews occurs as the second writing—that is, between Romans and 1 Corinthians. The heading "To the Hebrews" is attested also by Clement of Alexandria [according to Eusebius] and Tertullian.

where does it tell us that the original readers were Hebrews, nor does it tell us where they lived. That the letter was written to Jewish Christians was universally assumed by scholars on the basis of church tradition until the end of the nineteenth century. Since that time, a number of scholars have argued that the addressees were Gentiles rather than Jews.[5]

These scholars have insisted that nothing in the work requires that the original readers were Hebrews. Gentile Christians would have recognized and been committed to the authority of the Greek Old Testament, they rightly argue. Furthermore, the lapse against which the author warns is described as a turning away "from the living God" (3:12), which seems more appropriately spoken to Gentiles returning to paganism than to Jews returning to Judaism. Similarly, the description of the readers' earlier situation as one of "acts that lead to death" (6:1; 9:14) seems to suggest paganism rather than Judaism. Not many, however, have found these arguments compelling. Without pursuing the matter in further detail, we may say that the very thrust of the book's sustained argument clearly seems to suggest readers of Jewish background. They, far more than any others, would find pressing upon them the question of the relation between the old and new covenants, and they, more than any, might be attracted to their previous mode of life.

Assuming that the readers were Jewish Christians who seem to have been attracted back to their Judaism, we cannot conclude much more about them. A specific community, or perhaps a cluster of communities, of Jews is clearly in view. For whatever reason, they had not begun to achieve the maturity that was expected of them. Rather than being capable of teaching

5. For example, von Soden, Zahn, Moffatt, Windisch, E. F. Scott, Käsemann, Geerhardus Vos.

St. Peter's Basilica in Rome, probably the city to which Hebrews was written

others, they themselves needed to be fed with milk (5:12–14). Some have argued that the addressees were converted priests,[6] and since the discovery of the Dead Sea Scrolls, a number of scholars have been inclined to identify the addressees as converts from, or at least influenced by, the Essene community at Qumran.[7] Indeed, some striking similarities exist between the addressees and the Qumran community, but careful scholarly investigation does not support a facile identification of the two groups.[8]

6. Acts 6:7 refers to a great number of priests accepting the faith. This identification of the addressees is argued extensively by Ceslaus Spicq in *L'Epître aux Hébreux* (Paris: Gabalda, 1952), 1:226–31.

7. For example, F. M. Braun, H. Kosmala, J. W. Bowman, Y. Yadin, D. Flusser, C. Spicq, G. W. Buchanan, P. E. Hughes.

8. See especially the thorough discussion by F. F. Bruce, "'To the Hebrews' or 'To the Essenes'?," *New Testament Studies* 9 (1962–63): 217–32.

Where this group of Jewish Christians lived remains uncertain. It does not follow that because they were Jews they lived in Palestine, since Jews and Jewish Christians dwelled throughout the Roman Empire. The words at the end of the letter ("Those from Italy send you their greetings") could mean that the author is writing from Italy; on the other hand, they could indicate that the letter was addressed to a community or communities in Rome and that those from Italy who were with the author wished to be remembered to their compatriots. The latter conclusion seems more natural, and when combined with other arguments, has led the majority of scholars to locate the readers in Rome.[9]

9. The earliest evidence of knowledge of Hebrews comes from *1 Clement*, written in Rome around 95. See D. A. Hagner, *The Use of the Old and New Testaments in Clement of Rome* (Leiden: Brill, 1973), 179–95.

Two items in Hebrews fit well with a Roman destination: (1) the generosity of the readers (6:10; 10:32–34), known to be true of the Roman church, and practically impossible for the impoverished Jerusalem church; (2) the persecution of former days (10:32), which may refer to Claudius's expulsion of the Jews from Rome in 49, or Nero's persecution in the 60s.

Date

Establishing the date of Hebrews depends in part upon the identification of the persecution mentioned in 10:32–34. This persecution is referred to as taking place in "earlier days"; how much earlier we do not know. We do know that it involved abuse, public insult, and the loss of personal property, but apparently not the loss of life (see 12:4). The prospect of continued or renewed persecution, on the other hand, also seems clear from the tone of chapter 12. All this seems to point to Claudius's persecution of the Jews in 49 rather than Nero's persecution in 64, in which many were martyred for their faith.

It is important to note, moreover, that the author does not seem to know of the destruction of Jerusalem (A.D. 70). This is evident not so much from the use of the present tense in describing the temple cultus (Clement of Rome and Justin Martyr, to name two, do this long after its demise), but rather from the fact that the author makes no reference to its actual end, which would have provided a fitting capstone to his argument (e.g., in 8:13, where our author writes, "What is becoming obsolete and growing old is ready to vanish away"). The implication of 2:3 that the author and addressees were second-generation Christians does not necessitate an excessively late date. With all the data in mind, a date in the 60s seems relatively certain, and one just prior

to the beginning of Nero's persecution probable.

Purpose

One's understanding of the purpose of Hebrews depends to a considerable extent on one's conclusion concerning the original readers. Clearly, a major purpose, if not the sole purpose, of the letter is to warn and to exhort, as the frequently inserted exhortations testify.

But what specifically is the danger in which the readers stand, and how do the specific arguments of the letter apply to their situation and needs? Is the potential lapse from Christianity a lapse into Judaism or into Gentile paganism? More specifically, does the danger involve a retreat into the heresy that we may call "proto-Gnosticism," with its angel worship (cf. 1:5–14; 2:5–9), its "strange teachings," and its concern with foods (13:9; cf. 9:10)? T. W. Manson went so far as to identify the addressees as members of the church at Colossae, who were subject to the heretical, gnostic teachings countered by Paul in his letter to the Colossians (see Colossians 2).[10]

Regardless of the identity of the addressees, however, the following remains clear. Hebrews intends to set forth *the incomparable superiority, and hence finality, of God's work in Jesus Christ.* Christianity is thus *absolute in character and universal in scope.* It is nothing less than the fruition of God's intended purposes from the beginning and is indeed the fulfillment of what God spoke "through the prophets at many times and in various ways." This means that turning away from this teaching to *any* other is unthinkable. The answer to any such tendency is an understand-

10. T. W. Manson, "The Problem of the Epistle to the Hebrews," *Bulletin of the John Rylands Library* 32 (1949): 1–17 (= *Studies in the Gospels and Epistles* [Philadelphia: Westminster, 1962], 242–58).

Alternating Discourse and Application in Hebrews

Although Hebrews in its connected arguments is very much like a treatise, it was not intended to be abstract or theoretical. Its literary genre is best described as a sermon-treatise. The author has a very specific and practical purpose: to keep readers from falling back into the Jewish faith they held before they became Christians. Thus, he sprinkles sections of application throughout his exposition. The argument of Hebrews is, of course, cogent in itself and could stand alone. But the author repeatedly applies it to the situation of his readers. For him, argument and application are inseparable. Or to put it differently, the argument he sets forth has important ramifications. This accounts for the alternation of discourse and application. In some passages application and discourse are mixed. Application is never far from the author's mind. Indeed, he describes his letter as "my word of exhortation" (13:22).

1:1–14, discourse	6:13–10:18, discourse
2:1–4, application	10:19–39, application
2:5–3:6, discourse	11:1–40, discourse
3:7–19, application	12:1–17, application
4:1–16, mixed	12:18–24, discourse
5:1–10, discourse	12:25–13:6, application
5:11–6:12, application	13:7–21, mixed

yield confident conclusions on the questions of author, addressees, date, and purpose. Yet insofar as these matters affect interpretation, one ought always to keep the options in mind, and proceed tentatively wherever necessary. Fortunately, most of the teaching of Hebrews is clear even with the uncertainty that remains on these questions.

When we turn directly to the contents of Hebrews, we encounter several distinctives that make interpretation a demanding task: the structure of the argument itself; the genre of literature; reference to heavenly **archetypes** and earthly copies; the use of the Old Testament; and the relation of the old and the new. To these matters we now turn.

The Structure of Hebrews

Although the central theses of Hebrews are evident, the actual structure of the book and the sequence of the argument are difficult to discover. One reason for this is the author's tendency to interrupt the discourse with exhortations pertinent to the situation of the readers (see the sidebar "Alternating Discourse and Application in Hebrews"). But since Hebrews exists for the sake of the exhortations, it is incorrect to call them interruptions. The fact is that "the expositional material serves the hortatory purpose of the whole work."[11] Exactly for this reason, Hebrews provides an exceptionally rich field for **rhetorical criticism.** In the ancient world, rhetoric was the skill of persuasion. Since our author desires nothing more fervently than to persuade the readers, he makes use of

archetypes

rhetorical criticism

ing of the true significance of Jesus Christ and what he has accomplished, which is precisely what our author seeks to convey. While it is probably correct to conclude that the original readers were Jewish Christians, the argument of the letter, by its nature, is capable of a wider application. Thus, the document is profitable for both Jewish and Gentile Christians, and indeed for Christians of every era.

For most of these questions, then, we have surprisingly little to go on in the case of Hebrews. An inductive examination of the letter does not

11. G. H. Guthrie, *The Structure of Hebrews: A Text-Linguistic Analysis* (Grand Rapids: Baker, 1998), 143.

Midrashic Interpretation in Hebrews

One of the favorite interpretive devices of the author is midrash, which is the quotation of a passage of Scripture followed by an interpretation that deliberately picks up the very words of the passage in the explanatory comments. This textually linked interpretation was already practiced in Second Temple Jewish literature. It is typical of our author's style to quote a passage and then comment on the clauses most appropriate to his argument (see especially 3:12–4:10; 7:11–28; 10:8–18), making use in the explanation of the actual words of the quotation, much in the fashion of a modern commentary.

The noun "midrash" derives from the Hebrew verb *darash*, which means "to seek, investigate, interpret." Midrashic interpretation is a Jewish method based on the unique authority of the Scriptures down to each and every word. It is not based on exegesis as we know it, which is the attempt to arrive at the meaning intended by the original author for the original readers. Rather, employing *sensus plenior*, midrashic interpretation often builds on the sense of the passage for contemporary readers, a drawing out of its interpretation and application, especially in light of recent developments.

The midrashic interpretation in Hebrews is fascinating. The fullest appreciation of it is gained by using the Greek text or a very literal translation (such as the ASV or the NASB), and in the explanatory words immediately following a quotation, marking those drawn from the quotation—that is, identical words or words of the same root. In the exposition of Hebrews in the present book, these words are italicized.

Midrashic commentary occurs together with the majority of Scripture quotations in Hebrews (most conspicuous are 2:5–9; 3:7–4:11; 10:5–14; 12:5–11). Exceptions are the quotations in chapter 1, which themselves carry the argument without the need of exposition. Even there, however, one might compare the words of 1:14 with the quotation in 1:7 (from Ps 104:4). Much of the argument of Hebrews, as we will see, is carried out by means of midrashic exposition.

midrash

many rhetorical devices familiar to us from the ancient world.[12]

What further makes the argument of Hebrews frequently difficult to follow are the quotations and use of Old Testament material in the manner known as **midrash** (see the sidebar "Midrashic Interpretation in Hebrews"); the bridging of one section to another by means of catchwords; the repetition of arguments, often with only slight variations;

12. See the excellent discussion in David A. deSilva, *Perseverance in Gratitude: A Socio-Rhetorical Commentary on the Epistle "to the Hebrews"* (Grand Rapids: Eerdmans, 2000), 35–58. For a fine discussion of the author's style, and in particular his use of rhetorical devices, see A. H. Trotter Jr., *Interpreting the Epistle to the Hebrews* (Grand Rapids: Baker, 1997), 163–84.

and periodic recapitulation. Careful study has shown that although initially the style of the author seems ordinary and straightforward, it in fact often reveals an impressive artistry and sometimes employs a chiastic structure or concentric symmetry. For example, the section 3:1–4:13 is introduced (3:1) and recapitulated (4:14) in nearly symmetrical form; upon close examination, 2:1–4 reveals a symmetrical shaping; the chiastic sequence Christ/angels/angels/Christ in 1:5–8 is repeated in 1:13–2:3. This kind of subtle stylistic device abounds in Hebrews.

Of fundamental importance to the structure of Hebrews is the quotation of the Old Testament and the extent to which this governs much of the content of the book itself. Indeed, as we

An Outline of Hebrews

I. God's definitive revelation in the Son (1:1–4)
II. Discourse: Christ is superior to the angels in his deity (1:5–14)
  • Application: a call to faithfulness (2:1–4)
III. Discourse: Christ is superior to the angels despite his humanity (2:5–9)
  • The benefits of Christ's humanity (2:10–18)
IV. Discourse: Christ is superior to Moses (3:1–6)
  • Exhortation inspired by the exodus (3:7–19)
V. Discourse: the remaining promise of rest (4:1–13)
  • Exhortation (4:14–16)
VI. Discourse: the high priesthood of Jesus (5:1–10)

• Application: the importance of maturity (5:11–6:3)
  ○ the seriousness of apostasy (6:4–12)
VII. Discourse: the faithfulness of God (6:13–20)
  • The priesthood of Melchizedek (7:1–10)
  • The legitimacy and superiority of Christ's priesthood (7:11–28)
VIII. Discourse: the true high priest (8:1–6)
  • The promise of a new covenant (8:7–13)
  • The sacrifices of the old covenant (9:1–10)
IX. Discourse: the definitive nature of Christ's work (9:11–10:18)
  • Application: the grounds for faithfulness (10:19–25)
  ○ The danger of apostasy (10:26–31)

  ○ Exhortation to endurance (10:32–39)
X. Discourse: faith and a catalog of examples (11:1–40)
  • Application: call to faithfulness, endurance, and holiness (12:1–17)
XI. Discourse: the glory of the Christian's present status (12:18–24)
  • Application: various exhortations (12:25–13:17)
XII. Closing remark and a concluding prayer and doxology (13:18–21)
  • Postscript and final benediction (13:22–25)

will see, the argument is carried on to a large extent through the midrashic treatment of Old Testament material.[13] In chapter 1 the argument about the superiority of the Son to the angels is based upon a string of seven quotations, with little comment. In 2:6–8 a long quotation is given, followed by a midrashic commentary on, and application of, certain phrases drawn from the quotation, using the actual words of the quotation. More impressive is how the argument of 3:12–4:11 consists of an exegesis of the quotation of Psalm 95:7–11, again along midrashic lines. The next major section of the book depends upon the quotation of Psalms 2:7 and 110:4 in 5:5–6. The argument about the priesthood of Melchizedek is interrupted by a long digression (5:11–6:12). It resumes in chapter 7, where the Genesis 14 narrative about Abraham and Melchizedek is brought into play, and where Psalm 110:4 is cited two more times. The argument of chapter 7 is a skillful elaboration of the Old Testament texts. Chapter 8, with its argument about the excellence of the new covenant that has now replaced the old, depends on the long quotation of Jeremiah 31:31–34. Chapter 9 is a midrashic presentation of pentateuchal material, but with little explicit quotation. The opening section of chapter 10 presents Psalm 40:6–8 with a brief

13. See G. B. Caird, "The Exegetical Method of the Epistle to the Hebrews," *Canadian Journal of Theology* 5 (1959): 44–51.

commentary; this is followed by a second citation of Jeremiah 31:33–34, and a long exhortation capped by a quotation of Habakkuk 2:3–4. Chapter 11 is the famous chapter on the heroes of faith in the Old Testament. Again in chapter 12 we have exhortation, but not without midrashic treatment of Old Testament material (Prv 3:11–12, pentateuchal material, and Hg 2:6). In short, Old Testament material is pervasive.

Chapter 13 is regarded by some as not belonging strictly with the original document. It contains an assortment of unconnected ethical injunctions, an elaborate doxology, and personal information, including salutations and a benediction. However, it too contains a midrashic treatment of pentateuchal material (13:10–15), and there is no compelling reason to deny that it belongs with the preceding twelve chapters.[14]

However we finally perceive the structure of Hebrews, George Guthrie surely is correct that any adequate outline of the book must give due place to the two major kinds of material—exposition (discourse) and exhortation—and their interrelation throughout. He writes,

> The concept of the two genres moving in concert, but not exact correspondence, makes sense. They move along different lines but hasten toward the same goal. Each in its own way builds toward the goal of challenging the hearers to endure. The expositional material builds toward the goal by focusing on the appointed high priest as a superior basis for endurance. The hortatory passages move toward the goal by reiteration of warnings, promises, and examples used to challenge the hearers to endure.[15]

14. For a brilliant demonstration that chapter 13 belongs with the preceding twelve chapters, see F. Filson, *"Yesterday": A Study of Hebrews in Light of Chapter 13*, Studies in Biblical Theology 2.4 (Naperville, Ill.: Allenson, 1967).

15. Guthrie, *Structure of Hebrews*, 146.

The Literary Genre of Hebrews

Hebrews, as we have already noted, does not begin as epistles normally do. There is no identification of author or addressees, and no opening salutation. Nevertheless, the body of the document clearly suggests that a specific community (or communities) is being addressed. Hebrews, moreover, ends as a letter, with personal information, greetings, a doxology, and a benediction.[16]

The author himself depicts his writing as a "word of exhortation" (*logos tēs paraklēseōs* [13:22]). Hebrews can effectively be described as a carefully argued exposition, employing the midrashic treatment of Scripture, repeatedly punctuated by exhortatory passages. George W. Buchanan goes so far as to describe the letter as "a homiletical midrash based on Psalm 110."[17] Hebrews is much more a homily or sermon than a typical letter, although it is also a letter. This phenomenon is not unique in the New Testament. First John has neither epistolary beginning nor ending, resembling Hebrews in its purpose of exhorting its readers. James has an epistolary beginning, but ends very abruptly. Romans has both epistolary beginning and ending, but is as much a treatise on Paul's gospel as it is a letter. A reasonable conclusion is that Hebrews, which includes a brief but appropriate epistolary ending, is in essence a carefully constructed, trea-

16. W. G. Doty (*Letters in Primitive Christianity* [Philadelphia: Fortress, 1973]) describes Hebrews as a "letter-essay" form. Doty inadvertently says that Hebrews has "only an epistolary opening" (p. 68).

17. George W. Buchanan, *To the Hebrews*, Anchor Bible 36 (Garden City, N.Y.: Doubleday, 1972), xix. Although perhaps overstated, Buchanan's assertion is not without some truth.

prima facie

eschatological

prototypes

Septuagint

Masoretic Text

tiselike exhortatory sermon written by the author for, and sent to, a specific community or communities facing serious crisis.

Heavenly Archetypes and Earthly Copies

Many have discerned a possible influence of the Alexandrian Jew Philo (ca. 20 B.C. to A.D. 50) upon the exegetical methodology of Hebrews. Even more common, however, is the allegation that in his reference to earthly copies of heavenly realities, our author was influenced by Alexandrian Hellenism, whether through the medium of Philo or not. What we are speaking about here traces back in Greek philosophy to the idealism of Plato, who taught a dualism consisting of the phenomena of perception and the ideal: for every object that we experience there is a perfect, changeless "idea" or "form" in heaven that serves as the archetype of what we perceive in our world, and that can be known only through the intellect. To be sure, this has a **prima facie** similarity to what the author of Hebrews argues in several places (see 8:1, 5; 9:11, 23–24; 10:1; 11:1, 3). The language of 8:5 may seem Platonic in tone, yet it must be noted that the concept of God's earthly sanctuary as a copy of the heavenly sanctuary antedates the age of Plato and is even to be found in Old Testament times (e.g., Ex 25:40). Just for this reason Philo could make Moses into a Platonist long before the time of Plato!

More importantly, the dualism in Hebrews is not oriented toward the metaphysical questions of philosophy. Instead, consistent with the author's intended purpose, it is basically a temporal or, better, an **eschato**logical dualism.[18] Despite all the surface similarity between our author's language and that of Plato as mediated by Philo, a huge difference separates the two worlds of discourse.

The heavenly realm has been entered by Christ (something impossible in the Platonic scheme), and there he has accomplished what the earthly **prototypes** pointed toward. The earthly copies and heavenly realities in Hebrews thus relate as promise (the shadow) and fulfillment (of the good things to come). Because of its glorious nature, the fulfillment is expressed in *the exalted language of the spiritual realm, the language of eternal reality*. As always, the author focuses our attention on the work of Jesus Christ as the climax of God's purposes.

The Use of the Old Testament

Hebrews, as we have noted, is filled with Old Testament quotations, and to a large extent the author builds his argument upon them. The text of these quotations generally follows that of the **Septuagint**[19] (the pre-Christian Greek translation of the Old Testament) rather than the Hebrew text (the **Masoretic Text**), and this in itself often accounts for the differences between how the quotation appears in Hebrews and in our English Old Testaments (all of which are translations of the Hebrew text).

More interesting than the question of the text of the quotations, however, are the interpretation and the use of the quotations in the writer's argument. Many have been bothered

18. See R. Williamson, "Platonism and Hebrews," *Scottish Journal of Theology* 16 (1963): 415–24.

19. See K. J. Thomas, "The Old Testament Citations in Hebrews," *New Testament Studies* 11 (1964–65): 303–25.

sensus plenior

pesher

by how the author interprets the Old Testament. Often, it is not clear how he gets from the apparent meaning of the Old Testament text to his own understanding of it in his argument. The exegetical method of the author is therefore frequently maligned.

Much of Hebrews may be described as christological in content—that is, it centers on the person and work of Jesus Christ. The author's interpretation of the Old Testament may also be designated as christocentric. Very simply, this means that the ultimate or final meaning of the Old Testament is to be found in its *telos* (goal), Christ. It is the Jesus Christ of history who stands as the goal, the achieved purpose of all that God has said and done in the Old Testament. In one way or another, virtually all of the Old Testament may therefore be understood as ultimately pointing to Christ. This view of the Old Testament obviously goes beyond what the original writers themselves were able to grasp, given their early position in the history of salvation. Yet God's salvific work is not fragmented; rather, it is a unified whole that finds its culmination in the Lord of the church. Christ thus provides our author (as he does all the New Testament authors) with a point of orientation from which he is able to read the Old Testament with new understanding.

Given the fulfillment that has come to God's people in Jesus Christ, the Old Testament is seen to possess a fuller or deeper sense, a *sensus plenior* (see the sidebar "Sensus Plenior in the Interpretation of the Old Testament"). The recognition of this fuller meaning of the Old Testament that goes beyond the intention of the original authors does not open the door to arbitrary and frivolous exegesis (or "eisegesis"), as is sometimes alleged. To employ a christocentric hermeneutic in interpreting the Old Testament is not to import some foreign element into the picture, as in the case of allegorizing.

On the contrary, it is to press through to the ultimate intention of the divine Inspirer of Scripture and to recognize the underlying unity of God's work in history. Before Christ, there was no key to that ultimate intention and unity, but now in Christ, God has fully disclosed his purposes. All Scripture is thus seen to be anticipatory of the present reality experienced by the community. One is able to compare the Old and New Testaments and repeatedly say, "This is that." This type of interpretation is called *pesher,* and is found also in the Qumran community, which (wrongly) understood itself to be on the verge of eschatological fulfillment, and which, of course, lacked Christ as the key to the Scriptures. The Dead Sea Scrolls' Teacher of Righteousness was not the Messiah. Jesus, the Lord of the church, was the Messiah, the *telos* toward which the Old Testament pointed.

This same perspective is held not only by the author of Hebrews, but also by the New Testament writers generally.[20] What we have described can be illustrated by looking at some of the major Old Testament quotations in Hebrews. The question to be asked is this: What is the meaning of the Old Testament passage in its original context, and what is the meaning as understood by our author in his use of it in the epistle? The opening chain of seven quotations includes three from well-known "messianic" passages: Psalm 2:7; 2 Samuel 7:14 (both in 1:5); Psalm 110:1 (in 1:13). Already we are dealing with a deeper meaning or fuller sense, which the Jews themselves recognized, than is to be found in the original historical reference (an enthroned king in the two psalms; Solomon in 2 Samuel 7).

In Psalm 45:6–7 (quoted in 1:8–9)

---

20. For very helpful discussion of first-century hermeneutics, see R. N. Longenecker, *Biblical Exegesis in the Apostolic Period,* 2d ed. (Grand Rapids: Eerdmans, 2000).

Sensus Plenior in the Interpretation of the Old Testament

In the vast majority of Old Testament quotations in Hebrews, as throughout the New Testament, we encounter an understanding of texts that does not grow out of grammatico-historical exegesis—that is, out of the actual meaning intended by the original authors for the original readers. Because of this, the use of these quotations in Hebrews often has been questioned or even rejected by scholars as arbitrary and frivolous. These texts, it is alleged, simply do not mean what the New Testament authors take them to mean.

It is a fact that the New Testament writers find more meaning in texts than the original authors intended, or even could have known. In this they follow an already established Jewish practice wherein certain texts were regarded as having more meaning than was realized in their particular historical contexts, as, for example, in the so-called messianic psalms. These texts pointed beyond themselves to the future. The first Christians, all of them Jews, read their (Old Testament) Scriptures differently after they had encountered the risen Christ and the fulfillment he brought. From that time on, Christ was the hermeneu-

tical key that unlocked the meaning of the Old Testament—their interpretation became christocentric. Many texts (not all!) were now seen to point to Christ and what had happened, was happening, and would happen through him in the future.

The meaning of texts now seen retrospectively through the new prism of Christ often is called *sensus plenior*, a fuller or deeper sense. Here, the original author alluded unconsciously to things beyond his purview, the ultimate meaning of which could be known only at a later time by those who experienced the fulfillment brought by Christ.

Sensus plenior very often involves a correspondence between what was originally referred to and its counterpart in the era of fulfillment. Such a correspondence might ordinarily be thought to be a matter of mere coincidence, but here the relationship is regarded as divinely intended. It is important to realize that *sensus plenior* has its foundation in the following presuppositions: the sovereignty of God; the inspiration of the Scripture; the unity of God's plan of salvation; and, most importantly, Christ as the *telos*, the goal, of God's plan to

redeem the created order from its fallenness.

In almost every instance the correspondence is apparent, substantial, and discernable. Generally, there are controls at work: the analogies involve historical patterns and they concern significant, not peripheral, matters. If one attempts to step into the shoes of these authors and to understand their use of these texts, it becomes clear that their practice is neither arbitrary nor subjective. There is an underlying rationale to *sensus plenior* that guides our author and that makes his use of Old Testament texts intelligible and convincing.

Further reading:

Ellis, E. E. *The Old Testament in Early Christianity.* Tübingen: Mohr Siebeck, 1991.
Goppelt, L. *Typos: The Typological Interpretation of the Old Testament in the New.* Grand Rapids: Eerdmans, 1982.
LaSor, W. S. "Prophecy, Inspiration, and *Sensus Plenior*." *Tyndale Bulletin* 29 (1978): 49–60.
Longenecker, R. N. *Biblical Exegesis in the Apostolic Period.* Rev. ed. Grand Rapids: Eerdmans, 2000.

and Psalm 102:25–27 (quoted in 1:10–12), God is the addressee. In the first passage, after the initial address, a shift occurs in which the king whom God has anointed is addressed (1:9). Since for our author the Messiah (i.e., "Anointed One") may indeed be addressed as God, the shift is seen not as fortuitous, but as intentional and specially befitting the reality of the incarnation. The second quotation addresses God as

Pesher Interpretation in Hebrews

At the root of most, if not all, midrashic interpretation is what has been called a *pesher* hermeneutic. This approach notes correspondences between what the text of Scripture says and present (or recent) realities. *Pesher* interpretation thus employs the logic of "this is that" in understanding current realities as the fulfillment of Scripture—indeed, as being the very things that Scripture pointed toward.

Obviously, *pesher* interpretation depends on an appreciation of *sensus plenior*, the deeper meaning of a text that can be perceived retrospectively in the light of recent events. Thus, what has happened, or what is happening, is shown to be the ultimate meaning of the Scripture passage in question. Several other New Testament writers engage in this form of *pesher* midrash. A well-known example occurs in Ephesians 4:8–10.

The frequent use of midrashic *pesher* interpretation that we encounter in Hebrews is similar to that of the commentaries on Scripture produced by the Qumran community (see the Qumran commentaries on Habakkuk, Micah, Nahum, and Psalm 37). Familiarity with this method is vitally important to understanding the use of the Old Testament in Hebrews.

Christology

the Creator. The author's **Christology** includes Christ's instrumental role as Creator (1:2), and thus he may apply the passage to Christ, aided by the Septuagint's insertion of the title *kyrios* ("Lord," the primary title ascribed to Jesus in the New Testament). The quotation of Deuteronomy 32:43 in 1:6 is bound to cause readers some difficulty because it is not found in the Hebrew Bible (and hence, not in our English Old Testaments), but only in the Septuagint.[21] Here, the one to be worshiped is the

God of Israel, again called *kyrios* in the Septuagint. If the angels are to worship Israel's *kyrios*, they are to worship the Son of God, who is *kyrios* of all.[22] (For the early church's equation of Jesus with YHWH, see the sidebar "The Identification of Jesus with YHWH in the New Testament" in ch. 2.)

Equally interesting are the quotations in 2:12–13. The first is from Psalm 22, which describes the sufferings of a righteous Israelite. So remarkable, however, are the parallels with the crucifixion—not to mention that from the cross, Jesus quotes the opening verse of the psalm—that the psalm soon was applied to the suffering of Jesus (see especially Matthew 27 and John 19–20). If the deeper meaning of the psalm is realized in Jesus' own experience, so also may he be understood to be the speaker of Psalm 22:22, thus further identifying him with humanity.

Rather more difficult are the succeeding two quotations in 2:13, drawn from Isaiah 8:17–18. In the Hebrew Old Testament, Isaiah speaks of himself in the first person. How can words spoken by Isaiah that refer to his own personal situation be ascribed to Jesus? The common explanation proceeds along the lines of typological correspondence. Just as in the case of the psalmist, Isaiah's experience foreshadows the experience of Jesus. In his suffering and rejection, Jesus, like Isaiah, placed his trust in God. In his identification with humanity, which is the point of 2:13b, he stood with his children as the remnant that was to become God's new community. The similarity between Isaiah's experience and that of Jesus is not regarded as merely

---

21. This verse is found in a Hebrew manuscript of Deuteronomy discovered in Cave 4 at Qumran, indicating that it probably was in the text used by the Septuagint translators. See F. M. Cross Jr., *The Ancient Library of Qumran* (New York: Doubleday, 1958), 135–36.

22. The application of the passage to Christ may have been facilitated by a rabbinic tradition about the angelic worship of Adam. The reasoning would be this: If the first Adam deserved such worship, how much more so the second Adam!

typology

coincidental. In Jesus, who is *the* eschatological prophet and represents corporate Israel, the fullest expression of the content of this passage is realized.

While all of this is possible, the real explanation of the attribution of these words to Jesus is probably much simpler. In the Septuagint, which our author prefers to use, the quoted words are introduced with the formula "He will say," words lacking in our Hebrew Old Testament. Since in the preceding passages of Isaiah, which are highly messianic in content, the Lord is the speaker (Is 8:11: *kyrios;* Heb., YHWH), it is only natural to see the Lord as being the speaker in Isaiah 8:17–18. Apparently, the Septuagint translators, all Jews, had the introductory formula in their Hebrew manuscripts and also understood the passage in this way. The Lord (*kyrios*) who spoke in Isaiah 8:17–18 was the Lord (*kyrios*) of the church.

In 2:6–8 we encounter the important quotation of Psalm 8:4–6. The psalm itself clearly is speaking about humankind, which, although apparently insignificant, paradoxically has been crowned with glory and honor, with everything in creation subject to it (referring back to the divine commission in Gn 1:26, 28). If the passage refers to humans in general, then it refers also to the archetypal human being, Jesus Christ. This identification is strengthened by the occurrence of "son of man" in the quotation, a term understood by the psalmist as synonymous with "man," but for our author and his readers inevitably echoing the title that Jesus regularly used of himself (and that would have been known to them through the oral tradition of the words of Jesus). In the Hebrew Old Testament, Psalm 8 says that humankind was created a little lower than God; the Septuagint, however, reads "angels" instead of "God," which fits our author's argument very nicely.

Even as humankind was made lower than God/angels, so Jesus was made lower than the angels for a time. Our author adds that everything is not yet subject to humankind (2:8b). Perhaps the same may be said of Jesus, although the time of his humiliation is over and he has now in these last days been crowned with glory and honor, being about to express his sovereignty in the eschatological realization of his kingdom.

These few examples indicate the great resource our author found in the Old Testament, as well as his high view of the Old Testament as a repository of timeless, divine oracles. His understanding and exegesis of the Old Testament are governed by his christocentric perspective and involve the recognition of interconnections and correspondences (i.e., **typology**) with the New Testament through *sensus plenior*. Contrary to what is sometimes claimed, we do not find in Hebrews an allegorical exegesis of the Old Testament such as that encountered in Philo, despite some occasional, superficial similarities. Unlike Philo, exegetically our author moves not so much between the real and the ideal, but rather, between the earlier and the later, the foreshadowing and the fulfillment.

Unfortunately, many modern scholars have found it impossible to regard the author's method of interpreting the Old Testament as anything other than arbitrary and unconvincing. If, however, we enter the author's world and share his presuppositions and perspective, we see that this kind of interpretation, found throughout the New Testament, is neither irresponsible nor indefensible. On the contrary, it is coherent, reasonable, and convincing. But this becomes apparent only if, with the author, we accept the sovereignty of God, the inspiration of the Scriptures (so that the recorded correspondences are not coincidental), the unity of God's saving purposes, and most importantly, Christ as the *telos,* or goal, of those purposes.

The Relation of the Old and the New

The relation of the old and the new is, of course, closely connected with the preceding subject. Hebrews manifestly stresses the fulfillment brought by Christ. But now that the new has come, what is the status of the old? The answer is not a simple one, and the whole question bears on the interpretation of Hebrews.

The issue resembles that of Jesus and the law as addressed in Matthew 5:17. There, Jesus says that he has come not to destroy the law and the prophets, but to fulfill them. Our author of Hebrews would concur with this stress on fulfillment. His repeated appeal to the Old Testament as the very oracles of God, through which God continues to speak, shows that the old has not simply been done away with. Yet, the old order is intrinsically incomplete. It has, as George B. Caird puts it, a "self-confessed inadequacy."[23] The Old Testament is an unfinished story; it cannot be made to stand entirely on its own legs. It remains valid in itself as indispensable preparation, but, as Jeremiah saw, something new was needed. Already within the old order, the old was seen as inadequate. Speaking through Jeremiah, God declared the first covenant old and soon to disappear (cf. Heb 8:13). The coming of the new has involved fundamental changes of the old. One of the remarkable things about Hebrews is the courage with which the Jewish author writing to Jewish readers marks out the discontinuity of old and new (see the sidebar "Motifs of Discontinuity with the Old Testament in Hebrews" in ch. 7). Yet,

23. Caird, "Exegetical Method," 47.

for our author the new is ever to be regarded as the fulfillment of the old. For this reason he treasures the prophecy of Jeremiah concerning the new covenant. The new is what the old had promised! Since what Jeremiah had prophesied has now come, the old takes on not less meaning but more meaning; always, however, the old finds meaning not in itself, but as if it were a great arrow pointing to God's definitive revelation in his Son.

Hebrews' Attitude toward Judaism and the Problem of Anti-Semitism

The very strong emphasis on the discontinuity between the old and the new that we encounter in Hebrews raises difficult problems with regard to the Christian perception of Judaism. For our author Judaism is outmoded. It has performed its necessary task in preparation for the universal work that God had always intended to do through Israel, from the promise that in Abraham all the nations of the earth would be blessed to Isaiah's repeated stress on the calling of Israel to be a light to the nations. Israel is a blessing and light to the Gentiles through the Christian church. From our author's perspective Judaism finds its fulfillment in Christianity.

It is crucial to note that neither the author nor his readers believed that they had become disloyal to their Jewish heritage or had stopped being Jews in becoming Christians. On the contrary, the Christian faith was the flowering of Israel's hope. Thus, there is a strong continuity between Judaism and Christianity. But with the coming of the Messiah, the Son of God and High Priest, Judaism had

The plaza directly in front of St. Peter's, with the obelisk from Nero's circus

the harshest critics of the faith they left, and the ensuing polemic often can become bitter. Hebrews is not bitter or harsh in its critique of Judaism, but it is very direct, and does not shy away in the least from the conclusions that must be drawn in the new situation brought about in these last days, now that the Messiah has come.

The point to be emphasized here is that the arguments we encounter in Hebrews (or elsewhere, for that matter) concerning the new and decisive turning point of Christianity that necessarily makes Judaism outmoded *must never be understood as providing even the slightest pretext for anti-Semitism.* We must constantly remind ourselves that Christian faith is the outgrowth of Judaism. As the Gospel according to John puts it, "Salvation is from the Jews" (Jn 4:22). If Judaism is in some sense the "mother" of Christianity, then the persecution of the Jews amounts to nothing short of matricide.

Of the many things to be ashamed of in the history of the church, the most shameful is the Christian persecution of the Jews. For this reason Jesus, who was meant to be "a light for revelation to the Gentiles, and *for glory to your people Israel*" (Lk 2:32), has become a scandal to the Jews. This is the fault of Christians, even if only nominal Christians. And the supreme irony is that the Jesus who is the centerpiece of Hebrews and whose death provides the very basis of Christian salvation—the one whom Christians gladly affirm as Lord—is himself Jewish: "To them belong the patriarchs, and of their race, according to the flesh, is the Christ" (Rom 9:5). How can Christians persecute the very people from whom Jesus is descended? Ought we not to be grateful to them, to value them, and to love them?

As in the first century, so also today, theological disagreement with Judaism will continue. But that dis-

reached its goal. And thus we also confront the strong motifs of discontinuity in Hebrews. That discontinuity cannot be denied, even if "anti-Judaism" is not the most appropriate way to describe it. Salvation is no longer to be found in the sacrifices of the temple, but in what they pointed forward to: the all-sufficient sacrifice of Christ. The Jewish Christian readers, therefore, must not contemplate returning to their earlier Judaism.

Clearly, the sharpness of the stress on discontinuity in Hebrews is the result of an internecine Jewish dispute. A well-known sociological principle is that those who depart from one religious faith for another often become

agreement, however strong, must never be allowed to violate the Christian ethic of love. We can resist the present calls for the radical revision of Christian theology in the post-Holocaust era only if we *unconditionally oppose every form of anti-Semitism.* Nothing would please Christ and the author of Hebrews more.

Study Questions

1. Discuss the similarities and differences between Hebrews and the Pauline Epistles.

2. Discuss the two important kinds of material found in Hebrews.

3. How does the author of Hebrews treat the Old Testament?

Key Terms

grammatico-historical interpretation
hermeneutic
Platonic idealism
archetype
rhetorical criticism
midrash
prima facie
eschatological
prototype
Septuagint
Masoretic Text
sensus plenior
pesher
Christology
typology

1 The Most Important Thing God Ever Said

The first paragraph of the Epistle gives a summary view of its main subject, the finality of the absolute Revelation in Christ as contrasted with the preparatory revelation under the Old Covenant.

—B. F. Westcott, *Commentary on the Epistle to the Hebrews*

Supplemental Reading

Proverbs 8:27–31; John 1:1–18; Philippians 2:6–11; Colossians 1:15–20

Outline

- **Opening Statement (1:1–2a)**
- **Seven Phrases Describing the Son (1:2b–3)**
  Phrase 1
  Phrase 2
  Phrase 3
  Phrase 4
  Phrase 5
  Phrase 6
  Phrase 7
- **The Superiority of Christ to the Angels (1:4)**
- **Chain of Seven Old Testament Quotations (1:5–13)**
  Quotations 1 and 2
  Quotations 3 and 4
  Quotation 5
  Quotation 6
  Quotation 7
- **The Role of Angels (1:14)**

Objectives

1. List seven descriptors of the Son.
2. Evaluate the proper role of angels.
3. Describe the centrality of Christ to Christianity's faith and worship.

Ours is a day of many voices saying many things. Nowhere is this truer than in the area of religious claims. Bits and pieces of value and truth seem to be in many places. But is there any comprehensive, unifying truth in the realm of religion that deserves being called truth with a capital *T*? Although it is somewhat unfashionable to talk about truth in an absolute sense, Christians will make such an affirmation and point to Jesus Christ. He alone is the final and full Truth. In him, God has spoken definitively, and has said, and done, the most important thing ever. We will do well, therefore, to pay close attention to the matters that lie before us in these opening lines.

The Colosseum in Rome; the church in Rome was the likely recipient of the Book of Hebrews

Opening Statement (1:1–2a)

The Book of Hebrews begins with just such an unqualified affirmation of the final truth of Jesus Christ. With eloquence impossible to reproduce in English translation, the author's first words indicate a sense of the fragmentary and varied ways that God had spoken in the past to his people. The whole of God's work with Israel is in view. Implicit in this statement is the conviction that the Old Testament Scriptures do not in themselves provide a unified and conclusive word from God. God has spoken often and much through prophetically inspired individuals in the past; that is clear and gladly affirmed. But where all of this ultimately was to lead remained unclear.

In the first part of verse 2 we encounter the primary assertion of the author: "But in these last days he has spoken to us by a Son." Oddly enough, the name "Jesus" does not occur in Hebrews until 2:9. But despite this, and despite the lack of the definite article before "Son" in the Greek of verse 2, no one in the early church would have had any uncertainty concerning the identity of the one referred to here as the Son. The unique status of the Son is the focus of the remainder of the chapter.

In its contrast with the words in verse 1, the statement in verse 2 indicates that the sending of God's Son is *the pivotal point* in the accomplishment of salvation, and that this event holds *the interpretive key* that unlocks the meaning of all that preceded in the history of God's dealings with his people. Indeed, this insight is a part of the illumination that comes with the end of the age. The coming of God's Son is eschatological and definitive: "in these last days." A turning point in the ages has been

The interior of the Colosseum

some sense the beginning of the end of time, a unique era in which God poured out gifts upon his people that were anticipations of the age to come (see 6:5; 12:22).

Seven Phrases Describing the Son (1:2b–3)

What is now said of the Son is nothing short of astounding. The weighty phrases point to a unique majesty resulting from a unique relationship to the Father. It is no coincidence that seven phrases are used and that seven Old Testament quotations follow in the first chapter, since seven was regarded as the number of fullness or perfection.

Phrase 1

The Son is first described as the "heir of all things." Inheritance in Israel was the right of the firstborn son. As the heir, all things already belong to the Son in principle, just as they will actually and finally be his at the end. The emphasis in the present passage is upon the future time when Christ will be recognized and acknowledged as Lord of all (cf. Phil 2:10–11). All things were created "for him," as another New Testament

reached ("he has appeared once for all at the end of the ages" [9:26]). This means that the author, in agreement with all of early Christianity, believed that the present age was in

---

Seven Phrases Describing the Son in Hebrews 1:2b–3

1. "appointed heir of all things"
2. "through whom he made the universe"
3. "the radiance of God's glory"
4. "the exact representation of his being"
5. "sustaining all things by his powerful word"
6. "provided purification for sins"
7. "sat down at the right hand of the Majesty in heaven"

Only the sixth item, the providing of purification for sins, finds a parallel among mortals, in the high priests, yet even here it is only the work of the Son that proves finally effective. All else points to the deity of the Son.

Wisdom Christology

Hebrews	Proverbs	Wisdom of Solomon
1:2 "through whom he made the universe"	8:27–30 "I [wisdom] was there when he set the heavens in place . . . marked out the horizon . . . established the clouds . . . fixed the fountains of the deep . . . gave the sea its boundary . . . marked out the foundations of the earth. . . . I was the craftsman at his side."	9:2, 9 "By your wisdom [you] have formed humankind." "Wisdom . . . was present when you made the world."
1:3 "the radiance of God's glory"		7:25–26 "She [wisdom] . . . is a pure emanation of the glory of the Almighty." "She is a reflection of eternal light."
1:3 "the exact representation of his being"		7:25–26 "She is a breath of the power of God . . . a spotless mirror of the working of God and an image of his goodness."

Further reading:

Hamerton-Kelly, R. G. *Pre-existence, Wisdom and the Son of Man.* Cambridge: Cambridge University Press, 1973.

wisdom Christology

writer puts it (Col 1:16). There is nothing that will not finally belong to him in the fullest sense.

Phrase 2

Furthermore, the Son was instrumental in the creation of all that exists (for "universe" the Greek has literally "the ages"). The key role of the Son in creation is affirmed by Paul (1 Cor 8:6; Col 1:16) and the Gospel of John (Jn 1:3). Probably underlying this idea is a **wisdom Christology,** which identifies Christ with the personified Wisdom who speaks in Proverbs 8:27–31 and in the similar material in chapter 9 of the apocryphal writing *Wisdom of Solomon* (see the sidebar "Wisdom Christology"). The Son thus belongs with God as the fountainhead of creation and is not to be ranked with the creation as a created being. There is nothing that does not owe its existence to the creating work of the Son. All is his, therefore, by right of that creation.

Phrase 3

The first clause of verse 3 states that the Son uniquely manifests "the glory of God." The Greek word *apaugasma*, translated in the NIV as "radiance" (better than the RSV and NRSV translations, which use the idea of "reflection"), is found in the Greek New Testament only here, and it means a "shining forth," as in the rays of the sun. The point is that the brightness of God's glory is seen in the Son. The idea is the same as in

Paul's statement in 2 Corinthians 4:6, where he refers to "the light of the knowledge of the glory of God in the face of Christ." The Son is nothing less than a brilliant revelation of the glory of God (cf. Jn 1:14). Again, wisdom Christology provides the background. *Wisdom of Solomon* 7:25–26 describes Wisdom as "a pure emanation of the glory of God . . . a radiance of eternal light." To see Jesus is to see the glory of God.

Phrase 4

The Son "bears the very stamp of his nature." That is, Jesus exactly represents God's essence. Here the author employs a Greek word that eventually found its way into the English language, *charaktēr*. In Greek the word means "stamp" or "impress," rather than what "character" currently means in English, although one can see how the ideas are related. The idea behind the Greek word is that of the die and the image it stamps on a coin. As the stamped image on the coin exactly represents the image engraved on the die, so the Son is "the exact representation" of the Father. Only here, as the qualifying words "of his being" indicate, it is not the physical image that is in view, but rather, the being or essence of God (hence, NRSV: "the exact imprint of God's very being"). Here again, our author has used a Greek word found nowhere else in the New Testament. The meaning, however, is not far different from either the Pauline notion of Christ as the "image of God" (as in 2 Cor 4:4; Col 1:15) or the Johannine assertion that to have seen the Son is to have seen the Father (Jn 14:9; cf. Jn 1:18). The Son is the unique revelation of God.

Phrase 5

The Son upholds or sustains the whole of the created order. The Greek present participle, *pherōn*, "sustaining," points to the Son's present and ongoing activity in upholding all that exists. This sustaining activity is accomplished by means of the Son's "powerful word." In view here is the Semitic notion of the dynamic word of God, the word that created and the word that by its nature is effective in accomplishing God's will. The idea is not far from Paul's remark that in Christ "all things hold together" (Col 1:17).

In the first five of the phrases we encounter statements that require us to identify Jesus uniquely with God. The Son is put with God at the beginning and the end of time, as instrumental in creation and as the eventual heir of everything at the end of the age. He also functions in a divine capacity throughout all interim time as the one who through an overruling providence makes possible all ongoing existence. These three time frames anticipate what the author will say at the end of his treatise: "Jesus Christ is the same yesterday and today and forever" (13:8).

In the third and fourth phrases (v. 3), the author indicates the unique relationship between Jesus and God that is assumed in the other three phrases. Jesus radiates the glory of God and perfectly exhibits the imprint of the divine being. That the human Jesus, the son of a carpenter in Nazareth, who so recently taught, healed, and was executed as a common criminal, could be described in this striking language is astonishing, to say the least. Along with passages such as Philippians 2:6–11, Colossians 1:15–20, and John 1:1–18, this passage represents a high point in the Christology of the New Testament.

Phrase 6

The Son made "purification for sins." That is, he made a sacrifice of atonement for the removal of sin. Among the seven phrases, this one alone finds a parallel in the activity of other humans, that of the sacrificial work of the priests of the temple. And it is this priestly work of Christ that will be so central to the author's argument later in his sermon-treatise (chs. 9–10). But despite the similarities between the work of Christ and that of the temple's high priests, there are enormous differences between the two, as our author will point out. So on the one hand, the language of sacrifice would have been familiar to the readers, but on the other hand, it took on far deeper significance than it had for previous generations. The main purpose of Christ's coming into the world was to make an offering for sin, but to do so by offering himself. This was a unique offering, an offering of the one described in the accompanying phrases as the unique Son. Only that offering could be efficacious for the salvation of the world (cf. Rom 3:24–26). Thus, this little phrase contains the heart of the gospel, and it would have immediately triggered a host of associations for the initial readers.

Phrase 7

The Son has been exalted to sit at God's "right hand." This last and climactic phrase refers again to the uniqueness of the Son, who, sitting at the right hand of God, shares his sovereign authority. The words constitute an allusion to Psalm 110:1, which was a weighty verse in the early church (see the sidebar "The Importance of Psalm 110 in the Early Church"). The reference to the Son's sitting down points to his work being completed, although those familiar with Psalm 110:1 also would have perceived an allusion to the future victory in the reference to the enemies being put under his feet. In verse 13, our author will quote the verse. For the earliest Christians,

The Importance of Psalm 110 in the Early Church

In the New Testament, certain Old Testament texts are quoted with exceptional frequency, especially texts from Psalms and Isaiah. One of these texts is Psalm 110, which clearly was important for the early church since it found there words that seemed appropriate to describe the ascension (with the resurrection thereby presupposed) of Jesus into heaven as well as his ultimate victory over all his enemies at the end of the present age. Thus, Psalm 110:1 is referred to in the Synoptic Gospels, Acts, Romans, 1 Corinthians, Ephesians, Colossians, and, of course, Hebrews. Only Hebrews, however, makes much of Psalm 110:4, and the reason for this is clear. Through the commonly accepted fact that Psalm 110:1 anticipated the ascension of Jesus to God's right hand (understood metaphorically), our author also was able to relate verse 4 to Christ. The important result was that Christ could be related to Melchizedek's priesthood and in that way be constituted a priest, thus enabling him to carry out the work of a priest. The argument is stated quite explicitly in 7:1–22. So important is Psalm 110 for our author that G. W. Buchanan, in his Anchor Bible commentary, describes Hebrews as "a homiletical midrash [interpretation] based on Psalm 110." Although this is an exaggeration, it does point to the immense importance of the psalm to our author's argument.

Further reading:

Hay, David M. *Glory at the Right Hand: Psalm 110 in Early Christianity.* Society of Biblical Literature Monograph Series 18. Nashville: Abingdon, 1973.
Loader, W. R. G. "Christ at the Right Hand—Ps. CX.1 in the New Testament." *New Testament Studies* 24 (1977–78): 199–217.

Gnosticism

Christ was Lord not only of the past and future, but also of the present. Having completed his earthly work, he has assumed a kingly throne, beside the Father, from which he reigns. The present lordship of Christ has always been not only the affirmation of Christians, but also their comfort and strength.

These seven phrases, then, are like seven facets of a diamond pointing to the brilliance or glory of the Son as the unique manifestation of God. All point to the obviously unique, except for the sixth. But it, too, when understood as referring to the divine necessity of the cross, and in light of the later argument of the book, indicates a unique and definitive accomplishment. The conclusion of the author of Hebrews and his readers concerning the person of Jesus stands in vivid contrast to the estimate of Jesus in contemporary "historical Jesus" studies, where often he is reduced to being merely a teacher of ethics.

Many scholars have seen the special character of the elevated language of the seven phrases, their confessional character, and their form as pointing to an underlying hymn or liturgical piece taken up by the author. Also worth noting is that in this section the Son is described as the one who embodies in himself the three main Old Testament offices of prophet, priest, and king. All the various threads of the Old Testament expectation come together in Jesus. Clearly, our author regards an adequate understanding of who Christ is to be of the highest importance. The weighty argument of the heart of the book depends squarely upon the person of Christ. The way that Hebrews begins is hardly an accident.

The Superiority of Christ to the Angels (1:4)

With the view of Christ just discussed in mind, the author now turns specifically to draw out the implications for a proper evaluation of angels. That he does so may seem strange to the modern reader, despite the widespread contemporary interest in the subject of angels evidenced by numerous recent books on the topic. There is, however, evidence from the first century that some groups worshiped angels (e.g., in the New Testament, Col 2:18). People inclined toward **Gnosticism**—that is, people who regarded materiality as intrinsically evil—might well conclude that angels, as spiritual beings, were superior to Jesus, who had been incarnated in human flesh. Angels were popularly regarded as powerful intermediaries between God and humans, who had to be feared and placated.

Surprisingly, the situation was not much different from that of today. From astrology to "new age" phenomena, even at the beginning of the twenty-first century, one encounters the conviction that fates, powers, or the stars control our lives, and that we must order our lives accordingly, in relation somehow to those realities. But if what our author has said about Christ is true, then Christ is far superior to any created beings, be

---

Jesus as Prophet, Priest, and King

In the opening phrases describing the Son, he is shown to possess the three great Old Testament offices of prophet, priest, and king.

Prophet	God has spoken by his Son, Jesus
Priest	Jesus has accomplished purification for sins
King	Jesus sits at God's right hand

they angels, powers, stars, or whatever else one may care to think of.

In making this clear, the author first articulates a comparison that focuses on Jesus' title "Son." Jesus is as far superior to the angels as his name is to theirs. The Greek word *angelos*, "angel," means literally "messenger." By the "superior name" the author does not mean "Jesus," but rather, "Son," the title already used in verse 2, which, as we have seen, points to the uniqueness of Jesus. This becomes clear from the first two Old Testament quotations in this section (v. 5).

When our author refers to Jesus as having inherited a name "superior" to that of the angels, he probably has in mind the status of the Son now, sitting at the right hand of the Father. For the resurrection/ascension is what serves as the vindication of the unique sonship of Jesus. Also worth noting is that names in Hebraic thinking are more than simple labels. Names reflect somehow the being or character of the person. The comparative "better" is one of the author's favorite words to describe Christ and Christianity in comparison to what had preceded (see the sidebar "The Word 'Better' in Hebrews").

The Word "Better" in Hebrews

The Greek word *kreissōn/kreittōn*, "better," occurs thirteen times. It is used in reference to

the Son	1:4
the readers (i.e., their salvation)	6:9
Melchizedek	7:7
future expectation	7:19; 11:16, 35, 40
covenant	7:22; 8:6
promises	8:6
sacrifice	9:23; 12:24
present possession	10:34

Chain of Seven Old Testament Quotations (1:5–13)

Our author makes his point about the superiority of Christ to the angels by means of seven quotations from the Old Testament (again, a deliberate number for perfection). The first two and the last three contain words that the author understands as either directed to or about Christ. This involves a Christ-centered interpretation wherein a *sensus plenior*, a deeper meaning, can be ascertained in the texts (see the sidebar "Sensus Plenior in the Interpretation of the Old Testament" in the introduction). The third and the fourth quotations concern what God has said about the angels. It is possible that this string of seven quotations had already been collected before our author wrote his sermon-treatise.

Quotations 1 and 2

Jesus is the unique Son of the Father. The first of the two quotations used by the author in verse 5 to make this point is Psalm 2:7, "You are my Son; today I have become your Father." This text was very popular in the early church (see the sidebar "The Importance of Psalm 2 in the Early Church"). Because the psalm was understood as referring to the Messiah, the Anointed One (note the reference to God's "anointed one" in Ps 2:2), it established the unique character of the Messiah as the Son of God. Initially, the psalm probably referred to the coronation of a king of Israel (who as such was designated son of God), but because of its content, it was soon understood to have a deeper fulfillment in the Messiah to come. The word "today" was taken by the early Christians to refer to the

Chain of Seven Old Testament Quotations in Hebrews 1:5–13

1. Psalm 2:7	Hebrews 1:5
2. 2 Samuel 7:14	Hebrews 1:5
3. Deuteronomy 32:43 (LXX)	Hebrews 1:6
4. Psalm 104:4	Hebrews 1:7
5. Psalm 45:6–7	Hebrews 1:8–9
6. Psalm 102:25–27	Hebrews 1:10–12
7. Psalm 110:1	Hebrews 1:13

adoptionist

day of Jesus' resurrection (e.g., Rom 1:4) or his ascension. It should not be understood in the **adoptionist** sense, i.e., that at the resurrection God made Jesus to be something he was not before, but rather, in the sense that God has now openly manifested

and vindicated the identity of the preresurrection Jesus as the unique Son of God.

The second quotation is drawn from the Davidic covenant, articulated in 2 Samuel 7:4–17. Here, in the clearest of terms, the unique relationship between the greater Son of David and God is indicated: "I will be his Father, and he will be my Son" (1:5b; cf. 2 Sm 7:14). Again the context is one of eschatological fulfillment. That is, this Descendant of David will establish a kingdom that will have no end (2 Sm 7:16). Solomon, initially in view in this passage, was not the one who could accomplish this. It is the Descendant of David, the Messiah, who alone would bring this passage to its fulfillment.

With these two quotations, both of them central to the Jewish expectation, the author has demonstrated the unique relationship between the Son of God and his Father. Jesus is the unique Son and thus incompara-

The Importance of Psalm 2 in the Early Church

Psalm 2 was particularly useful to the early church because it was easily recognized as a "messianic" psalm from the specific reference to God's "anointed" in verse 2. It was applied to Jesus in a variety of ways. When the first Christians read the words "The kings of the earth set themselves, and the rulers take counsel together, against the Lord and his anointed," they thought immediately of the trial of Jesus before the authorities. This is exactly the use of the quotation of these words in Acts 4:25–26 (see Acts 4:27). More important, however, are the words of Psalm 2:7, quoted in 1:5 by our author, and again in 5:5 (cf. 7:28). The unique sonship of Jesus the Messiah is in view in the words "You are my son; today I have begotten you." These words are quoted again in Paul's sermon at Pisidian Antioch (Acts 13:33), and are alluded to, together with Isaiah 42:1, in the words spoken to Jesus at his baptism (Mt 3:17; Mk 1:11; Lk 3:22) and again at his transfiguration (Mt 17:5; Mk 9:7; Lk 9:35). The words of Psalm 2:8, "I will make the nations your heritage, and the ends of the earth your possession," support the idea that the Son of God has been "appointed the heir of all things" (Heb 1:2; cf. Rv 2:26). Finally, Psalm 2:9, "You shall break them [the nations] with a rod of iron, and dash them in pieces like a potter's vessel," is quoted in Revelation 2:27 and 19:15 (cf. 12:5), where the words refer to the future judgment to be accomplished by Jesus at the end of the age.

bly superior to the angels—indeed, to any creature of God. Angels are in fact referred to as "sons of God" in the Old Testament (e.g., Jb 1:6; 2:1; 38:7; Ps 29:1; possibly, Gn 6:1–4), but never as the unique Son who possesses a unique relationship with his Father. Thus, the superiority of Jesus to the angels is clear.

Quotations 3 and 4

In these two quotations the focus shifts from the Son to the angels themselves. Here the stress is upon the inferiority of the angels. The first of the quotations (v. 6) is from Deuteronomy 32:43, but consists of words found in the Septuagint (the pre-Christian Greek translation of the Old Testament) and the Dead Sea Scrolls, but not in the Hebrew Bible (which is the basis of all standard English translations): "Let all God's angels worship him." In the introduction to this quotation our author identifies the pronoun in "worship him" with the Son: "When God brings his firstborn into the world, he says . . ." The Greek word *prōtotokos*, "firstborn," here refers not to Jesus being created at the beginning of creation, but to his primacy of rank over all of creation, his superiority or preeminence over it. As the agent of creation (v. 2), Jesus is not himself a part of the creation. In the Deuteronomy text, the pronoun "him" in the quotation refers to the Lord (YHWH—the Tetragrammaton, the personal name of God, "Yahweh"), and by applying these words to the Son, the author in effect affirms the deity of the Son. If the angels are called to worship God, so also are they called to worship the Son, whom God has now sent into the world and through whom he has spoken definitively.

The second of these two quotations (v. 7), drawn from Psalm 104:4, provides a description of angels, God's "servants," as "winds" and "flames of fire." That they are servants will be stressed again in verse 14. The contrast between servant and Son and the subservience of the former to the latter are obvious. Furthermore, the changeability and transitoriness of wind and fire are contrasted with the permanent and unchanging character of the Son, which will be stressed especially by the quotation in verse 12 (cf. 13:8). The angels cannot compare to the Son.

Quotation 5

The words of the quotation from Psalm 45:6–7 in verses 8–9 probably were sung originally in connection with a royal wedding, where the king was apparently addressed as God's representative and hence hyperbolically as "God." They are regarded as finding their fullest meaning, however, in application to the Son of God. It seems clear from verse 8 that God is being addressed: "Your throne, O God, will last for ever and ever." The astounding surprise in these words is that somehow God is regarded as addressing God! Thus, in the next verse, to the one addressed as God it is said, "Therefore God, your God, has set you above your companions by anointing you with the oil of joy." A number of elements come together here to confirm the appropriateness of the application of these words to Jesus: the anointing alludes to Jesus as Messiah; the throne and kingdom that will last forever allude to the kingdom inaugurated by Jesus in fulfillment of the Davidic covenant; righteousness may point to the teaching of Jesus; the elevation above the companions alludes to the incarnation (cf. "companions" with the cognate idea in 2:14 of how Jesus "shared" in human flesh and blood). Thus, here the Son is referred to as "God" by God. This is not unlike the remarkable reference to Jesus as the unique God in the bosom of the Father who is God (Jn 1:18, according to

functional
Christology

ontological
Christology

the best manuscripts). We do not have ditheism here; there are not two Gods, since all of these Jewish Christians, including our author, were ardent monotheists, unalterably opposed to polytheism. What we have is Christians in the first century coming to grips with the uniqueness of Jesus and beginning to make the natural transition from **functional Christology** (emphasis on what Jesus did) to the necessarily implied **ontological Christology** (emphasis on who Jesus was). Eventually, the early church (at Nicea in 325) drew out the implications by stating unequivocally, "We believe in one God . . . and in one Lord, Jesus Christ, the only Son of God, eternally begotten of the Father, God from God, light from light, true God from true God, begotten, not made, of one Being with the Father." The doctrine of the Trinity, not explicitly stated in the New Testament, is an attempt to do justice to the data that the New Testament clearly provides.

The contrast between the Son, who can be addressed as God, and the angels hardly needs emphasis. Angels are categorically inferior to the God who created them.

Quotation 6

The longest quotation of the seven (vv. 10–12), from Psalm 102:25–27, again brings to the fore the instrumental role of the Son of God in creation (cf. v. 2). The insertion of the word "Lord" (*kyrios*) in the first line, found only in the Septuagint version, makes the application of the material to the Son obvious and natural. The Son's role in creation again puts him alongside God and separates him from the creation itself. "In the beginning, O Lord, you laid the foundations of the earth, and the heavens are the work of your hands." The created order of things is not eternal: "they will perish," and "like a garment they will wear out." God the Son, however, *is* eternal and unchangeable:

"you remain the same, and your years will never end" (again, cf. 13:8). The dramatic contrast with the angels again is left implicit, but it cannot be missed.

Quotation 7

The final quotation is from Psalm 110, of key importance in the early church and especially in the Book of Hebrews. The first verse of the psalm was understood as indicating the as-

---

Psalm 110 in Hebrews

Psalm 110:1: "The Lord says to my lord, 'Sit at my right hand until I make your enemies your footstool.'"

1:3	allusion
1:13	quotation
(4:14	possible allusion)
(7:26	possible allusion)
8:1	allusion
10:12–13	quotation
12:2	allusion

Psalm 110:4: "The Lord has sworn and will not change his mind, 'You are a priest forever according to the order of Melchizedek.'"

5:6	quotation
5:10	allusion
6:20	allusion
7:3	allusion
7:11	allusion
7:15	allusion
7:17	quotation
7:21	quotation
7:24	allusion
7:28	allusion

Comparison of Angels with the Son in Hebrews 1:4–14

The comparison is made clear by the chain of Old Testament quotations.

Angels	The Son
	superior to the angels
	a superior name
	"my Son"; "I will be your Father"
worship the Son	
changeable servants (wind and fire)	you remain the same
	addressed as "God"
	set above his companions
	instrumental in creation
	sits at God's right hand, with his enemies as his footstool
ministering spirits who serve the saints	

The Role of Angels (1:14)

The opening chapter of Hebrews concludes with a rhetorical question that defines the role of angels in the current era of salvation. The question, whose form presupposes a positive answer, is in effect a statement: all angels are "ministering spirits sent to serve those who will inherit salvation." In contrast to the Son, who *effects* salvation, the angels are mere assistants or servants (cf. the quotation of Ps 104:4 in v. 7) in attendance to those privileged to receive salvation. Despite verses such as Matthew 18:10 and Acts 12:15, it is not clear from the New Testament that every Christian has a personal or guardian angel. The New Testament is reticent about specifics, and describes the work of the angels in the most general terms. It seems clear only that angels work in the administration of salvation for us on God's behalf. The Christian must regard the current flourishing of interest in angels as at best a curiosity, and at worst a potential danger. Surely, angels are not meant to be the focus of our attention. However wonderful they may be, they pale in significance when compared to the Son, who was God's agent in their creation.

The Book of Hebrews has opened with a powerful and marvelous statement about the absolute uniqueness of the Son of God. These opening lines assert that Jesus is "the radiance of God's glory and the exact representation of his being." The quotations that follow, as we have seen, likewise point to the deity of the Son. Thus, from the first chapter of Hebrews alone, not even to mention the writings of John and Paul, we see the correctness of Christianity in making Christ central to its faith and worship. Contrary to what some have

cension of Jesus, after his death and resurrection, to the right hand of God—a position of incomparable authority and status. The point already was made at the end of verse 3. The exaltation of Jesus to the right hand of God, however, does not yet bring with it the total defeat of his enemies. A new situation exists, but not all is resolved. Christ presently reigns with God at his right hand, until that day when God finally will defeat all evil and make his enemies a footstool for his Son. The kingdom of God is both present and future. Most importantly, Jesus again is put with God in an utterly incomparable position. "To what angel did God ever say anything comparable to this?" asks our author in introducing the quotation.

Study Questions

1. In what ways does the author of Hebrews indicate the unique status of the Son?

2. How is the Son understood as the unique manifestation of God?

3. What does the author of Hebrews establish in the first chapter?

Key Terms

wisdom Christology
Gnosticism
adoptionist
functional Christology
ontological Christology

maintained, the church has not erred in focusing upon Christ, for to do so is to focus on God. Indeed, Christ is God come to us to accomplish our salvation. Hebrews thus begins with the bedrock of our faith and that toward which all of God's previous activity in Israel was directed. "In these last days he has spoken to us by his Son." What glorious truth is enshrined in these few words! Here is the very heart of Christianity, simultaneously the most important thing God ever said and the most important thing God ever did. And what the author establishes here is of fundamental importance for the argument of the remainder of the book, as we will see.

Further Reading

Allen, L. C. "Psalm 45:7–8 (6–7) in Old and New Testament Settings." In *Christ the Lord*, ed. H. H. Rowden. Downers Grove, Ill.: InterVarsity, 1982. Pp. 220–42.

Bateman, H. W. *Early Jewish Hermeneutics and Hebrews 1:5–13.* New York: Lang, 1997.

Black, D. A. "Hebrews 1:1–4: A Study in Discourse Analysis." *Westminster Theological Journal* 49 (1987): 175–99.

Cockerill, G. "Hebrews 1:6: Source and Significance." *Bulletin for Biblical Research* 9 (1999): 51–64.

Harris, M. J. *Jesus as God: The New Testament Use of* Theos *in Reference to Jesus.* Grand Rapids: Baker, 1992. Pp. 205–27.

Helyer, L. R. "The *Prototokos* Title in Hebrews." *Studia Biblica et Theologica* 6 (1976): 3–28.

Hurst, L. D. "The Christology of Hebrews 1 and 2." In *The Glory of Christ in the New Testament: Studies in Christology*, ed. L. D. Hurst and N. T. Wright. Oxford: Clarendon, 1987. Pp. 151–64.

Meier, J. P. "Symmetry and Theology in Hebrews 1,1–14." *Biblica* 66 (1985): 168–89.

Motyer, S. "The Psalm Quotations in Hebrews 1: A Hermeneutic-Free Zone?" *Tyndale Bulletin* 50 (1999): 3–22.

Thompson, J. W. "The Structure and Purpose of the Catena in Heb 1:5–13." *Catholic Biblical Quarterly* 38 (1976): 352–63.

2 The Full Humanity of the Son of God

The end is this: that He, through divine grace, should be found to have tasted death for the good of all and each of us, and that He should thus have entered into the lowliness of our death-subjected humanity, in order to exalt that lowliness to the high estate which the eighth Psalm declares to be our ultimate destination, and into which He is already entered Himself.

—F. J. Delitzsch,
The Epistle to the Hebrews

Supplemental Reading

Psalm 8; Galatians 2:6–14, 26–29

Outline

- **Parenthetical Application to Readers (2:1–4)**
- **The Full Humanity of the Son (2:5–9)**
- **The Goal of Incarnation: the Death of the Son (2:10–18)**

Objectives

1. Describe the alternating pattern of discourse and application.
2. Explain the reason for the incarnation.
3. Elaborate on the meaning of the death of Jesus.

incarnation

It is sometimes said that if Jesus was fully God, then he could not have been fully human; or if he was fully human, then he could not have been fully God. This either/or dilemma is a false one, and it refuses to face the full reality of the miracle of the **incarnation**, which affirms both the deity and the humanity of Christ. This mystery is at the heart of the Christian faith. It is worth noting that two of the New Testament writings that are the clearest on the deity of Christ—the Gospel of John and Hebrews—are also writings that emphasize most the full humanity of Jesus. The first chapter of Hebrews, as we have seen, emphasizes the deity of Christ, the unique Son of God. In the second chapter we have an equally strong affirmation of the full humanity of Christ. So here we have an unflinching affirmation of the two sides of the mystery. But why, after all, did God have to come among us as a human being? The answer to that question is vitally important to our author and the argument of Hebrews, as we now will see.

Parenthetical Application to Readers (2:1–4)

Before our author turns to the discussion of the humanity of Jesus, however, he presents a brief exhortation to his readers. The alternation of discourse and application is a conspicuous feature of Hebrews (see the sidebar "Alternating Discourse and Application in Hebrews" in the introduction). The application most often takes the form of exhortation, as in the present passage. The concern of our author is that the readers not "drift away" from the message of the gospel. The point is made by yet another comparison involving the an-

gels and Christ. The "message declared through angels" was the law of Moses received on Sinai (for the same point, see Acts 7:38, 53; Gal 3:19). If this was "valid" and to be taken seriously in light of the "just penalty" for disobedience, how much more seriously should we pay attention to the message of salvation "announced by the Lord" and certified by "signs, wonders and various miracles, and gifts of the Holy Spirit"? Although the specific language is not used, this amounts to a comparison not merely of earlier and later times, but of preparation and fulfillment. The salvation—"such a great salvation," as our author puts it—is not only superior to what Moses brought to Israel, but also has an eschatological character about it, and thus a weight and finality that makes Sinai pale by comparison (on this, see 12:18–24). If there was judgment in the former situation, "how shall we escape if we neglect such a great salvation" as has now come to us in Jesus Christ? Exactly the same argument from the lesser to the greater appears in 12:25. A falling back into Judaism, such as apparently was being contemplated by the readers, is unthinkable.

The Full Humanity of the Son (2:5–9)

The one to whom deity is ascribed in the opening chapter had actually appeared in history as a human being. This fact, however, constitutes a considerable problem for the author's argument concerning the superiority of the Son to the angels. By their very nature, angels are superior to human beings. Furthermore, there are the problems of the suffering and death of Christ, which also would seem to point to the inferiority of

Jesus to the angels. The author addresses the problems head-on. He first remembers a passage in the Scriptures (since it is the word of God, the location is incidental to the author):

> What is man that you are mindful
> of him,
>   the son of man that you care for
>   him?
> You made him for a little while
>   lower than the angels;
>   you crowned him with glory
>   and honor
>   and put everything under his
>   feet.

As our author interprets this passage in the following verses, it is clear that again we encounter here an example of *sensus plenior*, a deeper meaning of the passage that goes beyond what the original writer of Scripture intended. There is no doubt about the latter meaning. Psalm 8 is a poem of praise to the Creator that marvels at the wonders of creation. In comparison with the heavens created by God, the psalmist expresses wonder at God's concern for mere human beings. The second line is an example of **synonymous parallelism**, where the thought of the first line is repeated in different language. The words "son of man" are simply a different way of referring to "man," meaning human beings. The second half of the quotation admits the very objection noted above: human beings were created a little lower than the "angels" (so the Septuagint; the Hebrew has *elohim*, which can be translated as either "heavenly beings" [thus, "angels"] or "God"). Although human beings are lower than the angels, they nevertheless were created in the image of God and were given authority and dominion over the creation (thus, "and put everything under his feet").

It was not hard for New Testament authors to find a deeper meaning

that applied to Christ in these words. The words "son of man" could not but suggest that connection, given the high prominence of that designation for Jesus in the tradition known to the readers, which eventually was incorporated into the four Gospels. But beyond that, other elements of the passage also were seen to fit well with the application of the passage to Christ.

"Made a little lower than the angels" was taken as an allusion to the incarnation. The reference to being "crowned with glory and honor" was easily understood as an allusion to the ascension of the risen Christ to the right hand of God. This is in accord with the understanding of "sit at my right hand" in Psalm 110:1, quoted in 1:13. The last words of Psalm 110:1, "until I make your enemies a footstool for your feet," agree with the last line of the Psalm 8 quotation, "and put everything under his feet." It is easy to see, then, how the two passages could be associated and how Psalm 8 could be taken as referring to Christ. The words from Psalm 8:6, "and put everything under his feet," are quoted in reference to the ascended Christ also in 1 Corinthians 15:27 and Ephesians 1:22.

In the sentences immediately following the quotation, our author provides an interpretation of the passage that deliberately employs specific words from the quotation. This procedure is rather like the practice of modern commentaries, where in the commentary words from the text are put in bold type. This practice, much favored by the author of Hebrews, is a Jewish practice given the name "midrash" (see the sidebar "Midrashic Interpretation in Hebrews" in the introduction). To help make this clear, I will use italics in my exposition whenever words drawn directly from the quotation are used by our author.

We see it immediately in verse 8b, where the author begins his com-

Entrance to the Church of the Nativity in Bethlehem, the traditional site of the birth of Jesus

mentary with the words "*putting everything under* him" and interprets them as meaning that "God left nothing that is not *subject* to him." To this he adds the complicating fact that "at present we do not see *everything subject* to him." At this point he has said nothing, however, that indicates that he understands the passage, via *sensus plenior*, as referring to Christ. The three occurrences of the pronoun "him" in verse 8b are ambiguous. But in light of the interpretation in verse 9, which explicitly mentions Jesus, we are probably justified in also taking verse 8b as referring to him. The point then would be that despite the present reign of Christ at the right hand of God, we do not yet see all things in subjection to Christ. This

would tie in with the "until" in the quotation of Psalm 110:1 in 1:13. Thus, although the Son of God already sits at God's right hand, the time is yet future when God will make his enemies "a footstool for your feet." That this is a future time, and that the words are to be understood as referring to Christ, become evident from the words used to introduce this quotation in verse 5: "It is not to angels that he has subjected the world to come." The unmistakable implication is that God will subject the world to come to the Son. But that time and world have not yet come, and in the present we do not see the ultimate fulfillment of the promise.

In verse 9 the author makes it clear that he understands the passage to refer to Christ: "But we see Jesus, who was *made for a little while lower than the angels*" ("little while" is the translation preferable to "a little lower," since our author's argument is concerned not with the degree of the subordination of the Son to the angels, but with its temporary character). Obviously, our author was aware of the natural objection to his argument in chapter 1 concerning the superiority of the Son to the angels. By their nature, angels are superior to human beings. They are not subject to the weaknesses and limitations of the human body, nor are they mortal. Our author faces the objection squarely by his interpretation of Psalm 8 as referring to Jesus, and he will soon go beyond this and turn it to his advantage. The application of the quotation to Jesus is furthered by noting the words "now *crowned with glory and honor*," taken as a reference to the exaltation of Jesus to the right hand of God (cf. again 1:3 and Ps 110:1, quoted in 1:13).

The coronation and glory received by Jesus at God's right hand are attributed to his obedience: "because he suffered death." We have here the same sequence as in the Christ hymn of Philippians 2: "And being found in

The Word "Perfect" in Hebrews

The word "perfect," in its adjective, verb, and noun forms, occurs in Hebrews no less than fourteen times. It has a special significance for our author, who uses it not to point to morality or character, but to completeness of God's purposes—as in "bringing to perfection." It is a particularly effective word for our author's argument, as he draws out the contrast between the preparatory character of the old covenant and the fulfillment of the new. What Christ has accomplished in his death brings us to what must be described as eschatological fulfillment, hence perfection.

The root is found in the following passages:

verb form		other forms
2:10	10:1	5:14
5:9	10:14	6:1
7:19	11:40	7:11
7:28	12:23	9:11
9:9		12:2

Further reading:

Carlston, C. "The Vocabulary of Perfection in Philo and Hebrews." In *Unity and Diversity in New Testament Theology*, ed. R. A. Guelich. Grand Rapids: Eerdmans, 1978. Pp. 133–60.
Peterson, D. *Hebrews and Perfection: An Examination of the Concept of Perfection in the "Epistle to the Hebrews."* Society for New Testament Studies Monograph Series 47. Cambridge: Cambridge University Press, 1982.
Silva, M. "Perfection and Eschatology in Hebrews," *Westminster Theological Journal* 39 (1976): 60–71.

human form he humbled himself and became obedient unto death, even death on a cross. Therefore God has highly exalted him and bestowed on him the name which is above every name" (Phil 2:8–9). The reason God made Jesus lower than the angels, then, was "so that by the grace of God he might taste death for everyone." The humanity of the Son of God was indispensable to the fulfillment of God's saving purpose for the world. The incarnation of the Son meant a temporary state of inferiority to the angels, and constitutes a kind of parenthesis followed by the subsequent glorification of the Son. Thus, here we have implicitly a three-stage Christology (as in Phil 2:6–11): initial glory, incarnation, subsequent glorification.

The Goal of Incarnation: the Death of the Son (2:10–18)

Hebrews is fundamentally about the death of the Son of God and how it stands as the fulfillment of the sacrificial ritual of the old covenant. The sacrificial death of Christ ("that by the grace of God he might taste death for everyone") necessitates, and therefore is the reason for, the incarnation. Christ must have a body in order to die for others in fulfillment of the will of God. In short, God became human in order to die (note 10:5: "a body you prepared for me . . . to do your will, O God").

Salvation ("bringing many children to glory") was accomplished by Jesus ("the author of salvation") only through suffering—that is, through death. The notion of Jesus being "made perfect" through suffering should not be pressed to mean that the Son was imperfect before his death on the cross. The word "perfect" here connotes fulfillment of God's will. In accomplishing salvation on the cross, Jesus fulfills the purpose of God, and thus he himself is, so to speak, brought to perfection. The work of Jesus on the cross is responsible for the designation "the pioneer of salvation" (v. 10), the one who first makes salvation a reality.

The full humanity of Jesus is again brought forward in verse 11. Now, salvation is spoken of in terms of its

sanctification

effect: **sanctification**. Jesus, the one who "makes holy," is "of the same family" with "those who are made holy." That is, Jesus is fully human, like those who are the recipients of salvation. They are all of "one origin." Thus, Jesus is not ashamed to call them "*brothers* [and sisters]," a word that anticipates, in midrashlike commentary, the quotation about to be given. Indeed, we now encounter three successive quotations, each of which is an example of christological interpretation of the Old Testament, to establish the solidarity that exists between Jesus and humanity.

The first is drawn from Psalm 22:22. This psalm plays an important role in the passion narrative of the Gospels. Just before his death on the cross, Jesus quotes (in Aramaic) the opening words of Psalm 22: "My God, my God, why have you forsaken me?" Further details of the crucifixion were taken by the early Christians as specifically anticipated in the psalm—for example, the phys-

ical suffering (Ps 22:14–17), the mocking (Ps 22:6–8), the casting of lots for his clothing (Ps 22:18). The way was prepared, then, for our author to understand the words of Psalm 22:22 as being spoken by Jesus: "I will proclaim your name to my brothers and sisters; in the midst of the congregation I will praise you." Here, Jesus in his humanity identifies with the people of God.

The justification of the christological exegesis of the next two short quotations is not so immediately apparent from the English translations, or even from the Hebrew text. In the Septuagint text of Isaiah 8:17–18 used by our author, however, the speaker of these words is assumed to be the Lord (i.e., Yahweh) and thus "God" replaces "Lord" (*kyrios*). Accordingly, the words "I will put my trust in him" refer to the Lord putting his trust in God. Similarly, in the following sentence, it is the Lord who says, "Here am I, and the children God has given me." Reading *kyrios* in the text, it was not difficult for our author to understand Jesus as the speaker. The same identification has already been made in the quotations in 1:6 and 1:10–12. Jesus is understood to stand before God together with those whom he has redeemed. Thus, in these two quotations from Isaiah our author finds Jesus identifying with and standing with the people of God. Similar to this idea is the understanding of the incarnate Jesus as the representative of Israel, as we see, for example, in the Old Testament quotations in Matthew (e.g., Mt 2:15; 4:1–11) and in his identification with the people in his baptism (Mt 3:13–15).

The next paragraph (2:14–18) focuses intensely on the purpose of the incarnation: the death of Jesus as a sacrifice for sin. A midrashic link is made with the preceding quotation by the use of the word "*children*." Jesus shared fully the same physical nature, vividly expressed

Jesus as the Pioneer of Our Salvation

The Greek word *archēgos* can be translated in several ways (thus, KJV: "captain"; RSV, NRSV, REB: "pioneer"; NIV: "author"; NJB and NAB: "leader"). The title is applied to Jesus four times in the New Testament, twice in Hebrews (12:2) and twice in Acts (3:15; 5:31). The root idea of the word is "one who goes first, at the head of," in the sense of "leading the way" or "making a way," and thus in the New Testament references it can connote one who is a pathbreaker, one who goes ahead of us, making possible a new reality.

Further reading:

Johnston, G. "Christ as Archegos." *New Testament Studies* 27 (1980–81): 381–85.
Scott, J. J. "*Archegos* in the Salvation History of the Epistle to the Hebrews." *Journal of the Evangelical Theological Society* 29 (1986): 47–54.

in the words "flesh and blood," common to all humans. The reason for this was not that he might come as an example or a teacher or a wonder-worker in Israel. The explicit reason for Jesus coming in the flesh was that he die, and in so doing overcome the devil and thereby bring the power of death to an end. Here we see the goal and fruit of salvation: the reversal of the fall at the beginning of human history and its effects (sin and death).

Death, the fruit of sin, has been an ever-present reality in human history. It is the opposite of life and a contradiction of God's creation; little wonder, then, that those created to live should quake at the prospect of death. But through the death of Jesus deliverance becomes available to all who have lived their lives in bondage to the fear of death. It is, of course, not yet the case that the devil or death itself has already been destroyed. The devil and death have been delivered a decisive blow, according to the New Testament ("I saw Satan fall like lightning from heaven" [Lk 10:18; cf. Jn 12:31]; Christ "abolished death" [2 Tm 1:10]), yet the full effects of Christ's victory are

The Identification of Jesus with YHWH in the New Testament

A remarkable indicator of the high Christology of the New Testament writers can be seen in the rather comfortable way in which they are able to understand Jesus as the YHWH of certain Old Testament texts. Obviously, this shows that writers of the New Testament thought of Jesus as the manifestation of deity. Thus, he could be equated with YHWH.

Some of the most important New Testament texts in which Jesus is understood as YHWH are Acts 2:21; 2:34–35; Romans 10:13; Philippians 2:9–11; 1 Peter 3:15–16 (Is 8:13); Revelation 19:16.

not yet manifested. Death is, to quote Paul, "the last enemy to be destroyed" (1 Cor 15:26). By the death of Christ, death itself has been done away with in principle. Death no longer holds any terror for the Chris-

Entrance to the Church of the Holy Sepulcher in Jerusalem, the traditional site of the burial of Jesus

atonement

docetic

tian. Its victory and its sting are gone (1 Cor 15:55). Death is out of place in the time following the cross of Christ and can do no harm to those who name Christ as their Lord, for to die is to be with Christ (Phil 1:23).

With the thought of Christ being made lower than the angels (2:9) still in his mind, our author notes, "Surely it is not angels he helps" (v. 16). The Greek verb here for "help," *epilam-banō*, means literally "to take hold of," and this well could allude not merely to taking hold in the sense of helping, but in the sense of taking hold of a nature, human or angelic. That is, Christ did not take upon himself the nature of angels but the nature of humans, and this precisely for the reason that he might redeem the children (literally "seed") of Abraham. By the latter reference the author perhaps has especially in mind his Jewish Christian readers, but no doubt he can, like Paul, think of Gentile Christians also as the seed of Abraham. The initial statement of the Abrahamic covenant includes a reference to the blessing that was to come to the Gentiles through Abraham (Gn 12:1–3).

The clause "made like his *brothers*" again speaks of Jesus' full humanity, and perhaps alludes to the same word in the quotation in verse 12. Now, however, the humanity is stressed as a necessary qualification for Christ to become a "high priest." The office of high priest was well known to our author's readers, and the duties of the specially privileged high priest will be spelled out in 5:1–4 (cf. 8:3; 9:7) as the parallel is drawn with Christ and his work. Whereas a prophet speaks on behalf of God to humanity, a priest speaks on behalf of humanity to God. Thus, a priest is a representative of the people, and as such, must be one of them. Therefore, to accomplish this priestly duty, Christ had to become like us "in every respect"—except, of course,

Anti-gnostic Elements in Hebrews

It seems probable that the reference to "flesh and blood" (2:14) contains a specifically anti-gnostic emphasis. Gnostically inclined Christians were **docetic** in their Christology. This means that because they believed that physical matter was intrinsically evil, they held that Jesus only appeared or seemed (the meaning of the Greek verb *dokeō*) to be human, but in fact was a purely spiritual being. The same anti-gnostic emphasis is familiar from the Johannine literature (e.g., Jn 1:14; 1 Jn 1:1; 4:2). Gnostic teaching probably is also in view in the "diverse and strange teachings" mentioned in 13:9, as well as in the defense of marriage in 13:4.

that he was without sin, a point made explicit in 4:15.

But the particular point that our author wants to stress is the work of the high priest in making "atonement for the sins of the people" (v. 17). It is precisely for this reason that the unique Son had to take upon himself flesh and blood. Here, in short, we have the reason for the incarnation: the **atonement** for sins. The Greek noun for "sin," *hamartia*, occurs more often in Hebrews than in any other New Testament book except for Romans. Both books focus on the significance of the death of Jesus for the forgiveness of sins. The Greek verb translated "make atonement" (*hilaskesthai*) in the NIV is of the same root as the Greek word for "mercy seat" in Romans 3:25 (which also occurs in Heb 9:5). Here, it denotes "expiation of" or "making amends for" sin. Jesus accomplishes the reconciliation of the holy God with sinful humanity. He thereby functions as a high

Jesus as High Priest in Hebrews

It may seem surprising, but Jesus is referred to as "high priest" in the New Testament only in the Book of Hebrews, where the title occurs no less than ten times in describing Jesus. Our author found the analogy compelling, since the work of atonement is central to his argument. What Jesus did through his death on the cross was seen as the goal and fulfillment of the sacrificial ritual performed by the high priest on Yom Kippur, the Day of Atonement (see 9:7). The parallels between the two are brilliantly worked out in the central chapters of Hebrews (8–10). The salvation brought by

Jesus is thus understood fully within the framework of Old Testament religion and Judaism. Indeed, it is the climax of all that preceded it.

Although this vocabulary is unique to our author, the idea of Jesus accomplishing atonement for the sin of the world is common to other New Testament writers. Jesus is referred to as "high priest" in the following references:

the high priest who is of the order of Melchizedek (5:5, 10; 6:20)
the high priest who accomplishes atonement (2:17; 7:26; 8:1)

the high priest who helps those in difficulty (4:14–15)
the high priest who brings good things (9:11)
the high priest of our confession (3:1)
cf. a great priest over the house of God (10:21)

Further reading:

Culpepper, R. H. "The High Priesthood and Sacrifice of Christ in the Epistle to the Hebrews." *Theological Educator* 32 (1985): 46–62.
Powell, D. L. "Christ as High Priest in the Epistle to the Hebrews." *Studia Evangelica* 7 (1982): 387–99.

priest in priestly "service to God," and as such is described as both a merciful and faithful high priest. The two adjectives wonderfully capture two central characteristics of Jesus Christ: his faithfulness to the will of God that took him to the cross (see 3:2, 6), and the mercy displayed to sinners by his death on that cross.

The final verse of chapter 2 makes a parenthetical practical application,

something our author very much likes to do. He does not here, or in the closely parallel 4:15, have in mind general temptation in the ordinary sense of that word. Since he no doubt has the actual situation of his readers in mind, the word "temptation" is probably best understood in the sense of "testing." The REB (cf. too NJB) catches the nuance well: "Because he himself has passed through the test of suffering, he is able to help those who are in the midst of their test." If the readers are suffering for their faith and thereby are inclined to

Study Questions

1. Discuss the importance of the pattern of discourse and application for the writer of Hebrews.

2. How does the author of Hebrews express a three-stage Christology?

3. According to Hebrews, what is the reason for Jesus' incarnation?

Key Terms

incarnation
synonymous parallelism
sanctification
atonement
docetic

Further Reading

Burns, L. "Hermeneutical Issues and Principles in Hebrews as Exemplified in the Second Chapter." *Journal of the Evangelical Theological Society* 39 (1996): 587–607.

Childs, B. "Psalm 8 in the Context of the Christian Canon." *Interpretation* 18 (1969): 20–31.

Dukes, J. "The Humanity of Jesus in Hebrews." *Theological Educator* 32 (1985): 38–45.

Grogan, G. W. "Christ and His People: An Exegetical and Theological Study of Hebrews 2:5–18." *Vox Evangelica* 6 (1969): 54–71.

Hickling, C. J. A. "John and Hebrews: The Background of Hebrews 2.10–18." *New Testament Studies* 29 (1983): 112–16.

Miller, D. G. "Why God Became Man: From Text to Sermon on Heb. 2:5–18." *Interpretation* 23 (1960): 3–19.

return to their Judaism, they may draw strength from Jesus, their high priest. He knows what it is to be tested, and therefore he is in a perfect position to help those who are undergoing testing.

Often, the importance of the full humanity of Jesus is underestimated by Christians who seem more concerned with defending his deity. But as we have seen, without the complete humanity of Jesus there would have been no cross, and hence no redemption. Christianity depends upon the deity *and* the humanity of Jesus. Our author, at the very end of chapter 2, mentions other benefits of the humanity of Jesus: because he knows our human plight, he is all the more able to help us in our frailty. This motif will be explored further by our author, but no aspect of the humanity of Jesus can compare with the importance of his death, for the death of Jesus alone establishes the reality of salvation.

3 Christ Is Superior to Moses

If Moses could have sufficed you for righteousness and salvation, one so great [as Jesus] would never have been sent to you. . . . He surpasses Moses in glory and in merit: for he is the Son, but Moses is a servant; he is the sanctifier, but Moses is one who has been sanctified; he is free from all sin, even as he has been made perfect in all goodness, but Moses was not without sin.

—Lefèvre d'Etaples, quoted in P. E. Hughes, *A Commentary on the Epistle to the Hebrews*

Supplemental Reading

Exodus 17:1–7; Numbers 14:20–25; 2 Corinthians 3:7–11

Outline

- **Christ as Son over God's House (3:1–6)**
- **Admonition Concerning Unbelief and Hard-Heartedness (3:7–19)**

Objectives

1. Identify the way Christ is made superior to Moses.
2. Delineate the midrashic interpretation of Psalm 95.
3. Explain the warning concerning unbelief.

Son

servant

house

The Dome of the Rock, the seventh-century mosque that stands on the traditional site of the Jerusalem temple

We are familiar in our day with claims of superiority. Indeed, the great modern edifice of sports is built on competition to establish the superiority of one team or person over others in the field. In these contests the players are usually more or less equal to one another, the playing field being level. Here, however, as in the earlier argument concerning the superiority of the **Son** to the angels, the players are anything but more or less equal. The comparison is not between members of the same league or level of play, not between two more or less equal religious leaders, but between totally different categories: the difference between son and **servant.**

In this passage the author again returns to the theme of the superiority of Christ, but now, that of Christ to Moses. To the Jews, Moses held an incomparable position among those whom God had used in the history of the people of God. Through Moses the people had been delivered from slavery in Egypt, and through him on Sinai God had given Israel its greatest possession, the law. To argue that Jesus is greater than Moses was to make an astounding claim, especially to the minds of Jewish readers, and that is exactly what our author does here.

Christ as Son over God's House (3:1–6)

Having introduced Jesus as high priest, our author asks his readers, addressed as "holy brothers [and sisters]," to turn their minds to contemplate Jesus, described as "the apostle and high priest whom we confess." Only here in the New Testament is Jesus referred to as "apostle." The word means "one who is sent," and in view here is the mission of Jesus, which he accomplished on the cross in obedience to his Father. It is this Jesus whom we confess, the one who is at once the object and content of our faith. We do well to focus our thoughts upon him, and especially, but not only, when we are in difficult straits.

The comparison with Moses begins with the recognition that Moses, like Jesus (cf. 2:17), was faithful to God. The mention of Moses being faithful in God's **house** recalls Numbers 12:7. Unquestionably, there was a glory that characterized Moses, but it was not at all comparable to the glory of Jesus (cf. 2 Cor 3:7–11). Our author describes the difference as

The Word "Heavenly" in Hebrews

The word "heavenly" occurs six times in Hebrews, more often than in any other New Testament book. In 3:1 it modifies "calling," and in 6:4 it modifies "gift," where the gift is virtually the equivalent of salvation. It is used in describing a "country" (11:16) and "Jerusalem" (12:22), obvious eschatological realities with both present and future dimensions.

The word refers to a "sanctuary" (8:5) and to heavenly "things" (9:23) of which the earthly temple and ritual were but a copy. This has led some scholars to the conclusion that the author was influenced by Platonic dualism. But rather than reflecting a strictly vertical dualism, the word "heavenly," like the word "perfect," is used to point to the fulfillment of eschatological realities, the historical foreshadowings of which pale by comparison.

being like that between a house and its builder, the created and the creator. The honor that distinguishes the latter is far greater than the honor that belongs to the former. That is, a categorical difference exists between Jesus and Moses. Notice that since God is here called "the builder of all things," the comparison involves putting Jesus alongside God, that is, with the Creator over against what is created (cf. 1:2, 10).

But the main comparison between Jesus and Moses is made in terms of son and servant. The difference settles upon rank associated with identity. Moses, for all his greatness, was, after all, but a servant of God. The Numbers 12:7 text, which refers to Moses "being faithful in all my house," explicitly designates him as "my servant," using, in the Septuagint, the same rare word for servant (*therapōn*) that we find here in 3:5.

Titles of Christ in Hebrews

Son	1:2; 3:6; 5:8; 7:28
Son of God	4:14; 6:6; 7:3
heir of all things	1:2
pioneer of salvation	2:10
high priest	3:1 and elsewhere; see the sidebar "Jesus as High Priest in Hebrews" in ch. 2
apostle	3:1
forerunner	6:20
Lord	7:14
surety of a better covenant	7:22
minister in the sanctuary and true tent	8:2
mediator of a new covenant	9:15; 12:24; cf. 8:6
great priest	10:21
pioneer and perfecter of faith	12:2
great shepherd of the sheep	13:20

admonition

Whereas Jesus brought the fulfillment of God's purposes, Moses had what must be described as a preparatory role in the purpose of God, and thus he "testified to what would be said in the future." Jesus, on the other hand, is the unique Son and therefore without equal (cf. esp. ch. 1). The obedience of Jesus marked him out as "faithful over God's house as a son" (cf. 10:21).

Furthermore, our author is eager to add, "We are his house." The house of God is now identified as those who confess faith in Jesus as their apostle and high priest, those who acknowledge Jesus as the unique Son of God, and who thereby "share the heavenly calling" (v. 1). But for those who make up this house, it is vitally necessary that they hold true to their faith, maintaining their courage and confidence (cf. 10:23). Again the situation of the readers is specifically in view in this **admonition** (cf. 2:1), and again our author does not miss an opportunity to apply the material to them.

Sabbath Rest: Psalm 95 in Hebrews 3–4

Psalm 95:7–11 provides the text for our author's midrashic comments on the rest available to his readers. The expository argument is based on the very words of the quotation, which after its initial presentation, is partially quoted again, as summarized in the following:

Hebrews	
3:7–11	initial quotation of Psalm 95:7b–11
3:15	quotation of Psalm 95:7–8a
4:3	quotation of Psalm 95:11
4:5	quotation of Psalm 95:11b
4:7	quotation of Psalm 95:7b–8a

Admonition Concerning Unbelief and Hard-Heartedness (3:7–19)

By means of the quotation of Psalm 95:7–11, our author now begins a long illustration-admonition that will last until the end of chapter 4. The quotation (vv. 7–11) is so important for the argument that it merits presentation here.

> Today, if you hear his voice,
>   do not harden your hearts
> as you did in the rebellion,
>   during the time of testing in the desert,
> where your fathers tested and tried me
>   and for forty years saw what I did.
> That is why I was angry with that generation,
>   and I said, "Their hearts are always going astray,
>   and they have not known my ways."
> So I declared on oath in my anger,
>   "They shall never enter my rest."

After the long initial quotation, certain parts are quoted again by the author: the opening sentence in 3:15, the final sentence in 4:3, 5, and the opening sentence again in 4:7. Here, the experience of Israel, described in Exodus 17:1–7 and Numbers 14:20–25—passages alluded to by the psalmist—is made an example to the church. This use of the Old Testament is quite like Paul's in 1 Corinthians 10:11, where he writes, "These things happened to them as a warning, but they were written down for our instruction, upon whom the end of the ages has come." What happened to Israel could well happen to the readers if

rest

they did not hold to their faith. By means of this exodus typology (historical analogy) our author brings home the seriousness of unbelief. As the author expounds the psalm quotation, we again encounter midrashic interpretation, wherein the actual words from the quotation are used in its explanation and application.

The introduction of the quotation by the words "as the Holy Spirit says" indicates once again that our author views the Scriptures as the timeless oracles of God that find their ultimate reference point, indeed, their ultimate meaning and purpose, in Christ, his work, and his people. The Holy Spirit speaks words that are relevant to Christian readers, and thus the Old Testament speaks directly to the church. The admonition against a "sinful, unbelieving *heart* that turns away" (v. 12) and being *"hardened* by sin's deceitfulness" (v. 13) picks up the language of the quotation concerning the rebellion of hardened hearts that went astray. Less direct, but equally significant, are the words "turn away" (v. 12), which reflect the words "going astray" in the quotation. What was possible for God's people in the wilderness is possible for God's people, the church: "Take care, brothers [and sisters], lest there be in any of you an evil unbelieving heart, leading you to fall away from the living God" (v. 12). The readers are in need of warning and daily encouragement: "Exhort one another every day, as long as it is called *'today'"* (v. 13). Just as the psalmist in his time, centuries after the wilderness wandering, called for faith *"today,"* so too now every day is a "today" in which the readers are called to faithfulness. To be sure, the situation is different in that the readers "have come to share in Christ" and have thus moved into fulfillment. Nevertheless, that fulfillment is not to be regarded presumptuously or taken for granted: "For we share in Christ, if only we hold our

first confidence firm to the end" (v. 14).

The repetition of the beginning of the quotation in verse 15 leads the author to focus attention on the identity of those who rebelled. They were, in fact, the very ones whom "Moses led out of Egypt" (v. 16). That is, they had been the favored recipients of God's saving activity in the exodus. This people whom God had delivered and made his own in the holy covenant of Sinai turned against him and died in the wilderness. Their unbelief, their unfaithfulness, was indefensible because they had every evidence of God's reality and love (cf. 4:2). Again, midrashic interpretation can be seen in phrases picked up from the initial quotation (3:7–11): *"angry for forty years"* (v. 17) and *"in the desert"* (v. 17; cf. Nm 14:29 for a close parallel). Further midrash is apparent in "to whom did God swear [*'declared on oath'*] that they would *never enter* his *rest?"* (v. 18), and in the words *"rebelled"* (v. 16) and *"enter"* (v. 18).

These rebellious people failed to enter what God had prepared for them: "his *rest"*—words that our author will find capable of several applications. In the first place, the **rest** not entered by the Israelites referred to possession of the promised land. Despite all that they had experienced of God's grace in miraculous deliverance under the leadership of Moses, they died in the wilderness, unable to enter because of their unbelief. Nor was that rest experienced by those who finally did enter the promised land, since their hold on the land was insecure until the time of David, and even then they secured it but briefly. For our author, unbelief and disobedience are practically synonymous (vv. 18–19).

The author's implicit application of this passage to the Christians he was addressing is evidence of his familiarity with and use of exodus typology. Thus, the exodus of Israel

The Dome of the Rock, said to be built over the rock on which Abraham nearly sacrificed Isaac and which formed the base of the altar where burnt offerings were made in Solomon's temple

from slavery in Egypt foreshadows God's deliverance of his people from the bondage of sin; the Passover lamb (cf. 1 Cor 5:7) points to the death of Christ. Further parallels may be drawn, such as the present one involving Israel's experience in the wilderness and the time of testing there. The implication here, made specific in the verses to follow, is that what happened to the people of the old covenant may also happen to the people of the new covenant. Hence, the passage issues a warning about the continuing peril of unbelief.

It is sobering to think that those who were so highly privileged to be the recipients of God's grace and power of deliverance could fall so easily into unbelief and disobedience. This is precisely the point our author wants his readers to see. What happened then can happen again; indeed, the original readers apparently were in very real danger of falling away from their Christian commitment. But this danger is one that

Study Questions

1. How does the author compare Jesus to Moses?

2. Discuss the intent of the midrashic interpretation of Psalm 95:7–11.

Further Reading

D'Angelo, M. R. *Moses in the Letter to the Hebrews.* Society of Biblical Literature Dissertation Series 42. Missoula, Mont.: Scholars Press, 1979.
Kaiser, W. C. "The Promise Theme and the Theology of Rest." *Bibliotheca Sacra* 130 (1973): 135–50.

Key Terms

Son	admonition
servant	rest
house	

every generation of Christians needs to ponder. Though our salvation derives from grace and is therefore free and unmerited, we dare not take it lightly. We are called to perseverance and faithfulness.

4 The Remaining Promise of Rest

The apostle assumes that actual experience establishes the reality of the promise and the condition of its fulfillment. "I speak without hesitation" he seems to say "of a promise left to us, *for we enter*, we are entering now, *into the rest* of God, *we that believed. . . .*"

—B. F. Westcott, *Commentary on the Epistle to the Hebrews*

Supplemental Reading

Joshua 22:1–6; Matthew 4:1–11

Outline

- **The Sabbath Rest That Remains for the People of God (4:1–11)**
- **The God Who Discerns the Intentions of the Heart (4:12–13)**
- **Jesus Our Great High Priest (4:14–16)**

Objectives

1. Describe the rest promised to the faithful people of God.
2. Explain the importance of obedience.
3. Relate the implications of Jesus as high priest.

eschatology

Our world, frantic with activity and insecurity, is desperately in need of the peace and well-being that are offered by the Sabbath. And often this is true even of religious people, including Christians. The *shalom*, the "peace," of the Sabbath is that sense of ultimate well-being in every regard that is the fruit of being in covenant relationship with God. It is this Sabbath rest that is presently offered to the readers and to Christians of every era. It is a Sabbath rest that, as our author points out, remains to be entered.

The Sabbath Rest That Remains for the People of God (4:1–11)

The first and major part of this chapter is a continuation of the interpretation of Psalm 95:7–11 from the preceding chapter. Our author begins by stating that "the promise of entering [God's] rest still stands" and is offered to God's people. This "rest" is a kind of spiritual rest, the spiritual counterpart of what possession of the

land was meant to picture: security, contentment, profound satisfaction, and peace. The availability of rest is put before the readers in verses 6–11, but not before the warning motif is resumed. The readers should fear the possibility of failure to enter this rest.

Again our author continues his midrash on the psalm, applying the words *"entering his rest"* to the reality offered to the church. Following the pattern of exodus typology, the promised rest in the land of Canaan becomes a figure or foreshadowing of the spiritual rest available to the Christian. The reason why the author speaks of this rest as continuing to be available is not given until verses 7–9. To interpret this rest in terms of a national-political restoration is to miss the author's dramatic shift away from earlier limited perspectives toward an understanding of Christ as the fulfillment of the promises and the inauguration of **eschatology**.

The Israelites who perished in the wilderness had been the recipients of "the gospel" (cf. also v. 6), that is, the good news of God's redemptive love as manifested in the exodus from Egypt and covenant at Sinai. Yet, that hearing of the gospel had not been combined "with faith." The readers, and we too, have heard the gospel—for us, the climactic, redemp-

The Rest Offered to the People of God

In the Wilderness (Ex 17:1–7; Nm 14:20–25)	At the Time of David (Ps 95:7–11)	For the Readers of Hebrews (Heb 3:7–4:11)
entry into Canaan	"Today" do not harden your hearts	As long as it is called "today"
unable to enter because of unbelief	the rest remains for some to enter it	There remains a *sabbatismos* for the people of God
"They shall never enter my rest"		eschatological blessing

indicative

imperative

tive work of God's Son—and are thus offered "the promise of *entering his rest*." This, however, will be "of no value" to us either unless we demonstrate faith. The actual content of the good news is governed by the historical context. Despite differences due to the progress of revelation in history, a basic continuity exists between what the Old Testament saints experienced in their time frame and what is now experienced in the church.

The ominous closing words of the original quotation are now repeated: "So I declared on oath in my anger, 'They shall never enter my rest'" (v. 3). Having been told that the rest is available and that the people of the wilderness will never enter that rest, the readers are now informed that those who have faith (i.e., "we who have believed") "enter [or 'are entering,' as the Greek present tense may also be translated] that rest." Yet, as so often occurs in the New Testament, the **indicative** statement will

The Importance of the Word "Today"

Because of the reality of eschatological fulfillment brought by the death and resurrection of Jesus, the word "today" took on special significance. Our author has already indicated his conviction that these are the "last days" (1:2). His perspective of realized eschatology can be seen at other points in Hebrews. Thus, for example, in 12:22–24 he notes that the readers *have come* (i.e., already arrived) to the heavenly Jerusalem, and in 6:5 he indicates that Christians have "tasted the powers of the coming age."

The point is similar to that made by Paul in 2 Corinthians 6:2, where he comments midrashically on Isaiah 49:8: "Behold, now is the *acceptable time*; behold, now is the *day of salvation*." The fulfillment already present through the work of Christ makes each day a "today" of special significance, a day of eschatological significance.

be coupled with a complementary **imperative**, here added in verse 11: "Let us, therefore, make every effort to enter that *rest*." The rest referred to is the sure position and possession of the Christian who responds faithfully to the gospel.

Furthermore, and again in keeping with a common New Testament emphasis, this rest is both present and future (in its fullest realization). Especially pertinent to the readers is that at the same time, ongoing faithfulness (note the stress on "have believed") and obedience—the two are closely linked in Hebrews—are necessary if the rest is to be enjoyed. It is a major concern to our author to stress that the rest not entered by the Israelites is explicitly *God's rest*. This, indeed, is the sole purpose of the quotations given in verses 3 and 5 ("my rest").

The author's midrashic procedure is evident in the way he uses the assertion "They shall never enter my rest." Even this negative statement can be shown to have positive import. Since that rest was not entered by the Israelites, it is to be entered by a later people. One reason the rest still remains available is that God's own Sabbath rest continues: "his work has been finished since the creation of the world." This is supported by the brief quotation concerning *"the seventh day"* from Genesis 2:2: "And on the seventh day God rested from all his work" (v. 4).

Since God's rest is a reality, and since the Israelites did not enter that rest, the rest remains for others to enter. This was noted already in the time of David, who "a long time later" spoke of *"today,"* a day set by God for his people to enter that rest. The issue now can be seen as being far more significant than the readers initially might have supposed. That is, the rest not entered by the Israelites refers not simply to literal rest in the land of Canaan, which is but a picture of something greater, but to a

73

"Jesus" as the Greek Translation of "Joshua"

In the Septuagint, the Hebrew name Yehoshua (Joshua) was translated in Greek as "Jesus." While Joshua, the "Jesus" of the Old Testament, was unable to bring the Israelites fully into the realization of the promises made by God, the Jesus of the New Testament did accomplish this. The analogy must have occurred to the minds of the Hellenistic Jewish Christians as they read their Septuagint. Our author must consciously be thinking of this analogy when he goes out of his way to refer to Joshua, an otherwise unnecessary reference. He thereby makes us aware of the rich theological interconnection between the Old Testament and the events of the New Testament as seen in the schema of promise and fulfillment. All of the Old Testament is indeed summed up and finds its culmination in Christ.

The Greek name "Jesus" as the translation of Joshua appears not only in Hebrews 4:8, but also in Acts 7:45. In both places the KJV has "Jesus" in the text, undoubtedly providing confusion to the unsuspecting reader. Context shows that it should be translated "Joshua" in these passages.

today

kind of transcendent spiritual rest enjoyed by God and offered to his people, who now in these last days have the privilege of entering it.

To our author's mind, it is indeed no accident that this language, "a certain day—'today'," was used several hundred years after the exodus ("a long time later") in the appeal of the psalmist to his generation for responsive, faithful hearts. This proves that Joshua had not been able to give this rest (the rest mentioned in Jos 22:4 is hardly the rest of fulfillment). Otherwise, why would God (through David) have "spoken later about another day"? Thus, David contemporized for his own day the narrative of the wilderness rebellion. Our author follows suit in his use of the Old Testament, with the major difference that for our author the word

today has an added, eschatological significance.

In the specific reference to Joshua our author hints at something that surely the readers caught. Since in Greek the names "Joshua" and "Jesus" are identical (*Iēsous*), and given the argument of Hebrews, one may infer that Jesus provides the rest that Joshua, the "Jesus" of the Old Testament, could not provide. That the "certain day" ("another day") is called "today" obviously is significant in extending the application of the argument to the readers. Every day is a new "today" offering the prospect of God's rest.

In a further exposition of the meaning of "entering God's rest" as stated in Psalm 95:11, the rest put before the readers as their portion is in verse 9 specifically called a "Sabbath rest." The use here of the very rare word *sabbatismos* takes us significantly beyond the word for "rest" (*katapausis*) used up to this point. The identification of the promised rest for God's people with God's rest on the seventh day from his work of creation (v. 4; cf. v. 10) thereby is made explicit. God's gift of rest to his people is the gift of his own rest. To put it another way: the enjoyment of the blessings of salvation involves a participation in the Sabbath rest of God. The Sabbath rest of God thus becomes a beautiful picture—one well could say "type"—of the marvelous reality made available through Christ. It puts the Christian in a position of peace that from the world's viewpoint appears to transcend understanding (cf. Phil 4:7).

The aspect of the rest singled out for attention in the text is a resting from one's own "works," as God rests "from his." The sense in which this is to be understood is somewhat unclear. What is the activity from which human beings rest in the experience of salvation? Here, one should not too quickly understand "works" (the Greek word is plural) in the

The Jordan River, crossed by Joshua and the Israelites into Palestine

Pauline sense of "works of righteousness." Nowhere in Hebrews does the author adopt the Pauline polemic against works of righteousness. Perhaps the author is simply drawing out the parallel and does not expect the question to be asked. For him it is the idea of rest itself that is important, not the nature of the work that one no longer needs to do. If he were to answer the question, however, he might well indicate the sacrificial ritual and all that goes with the Judaism to which the readers were attracted. The "people of God," now understood to be the church, have been provided with a Sabbath rest, made possible, the author will go on to establish, by the finished work of Jesus Christ. That great reality of Sabbath rest, with its security, well-being, and peace, is the rightful inheritance of the saints. Though in its fullness Sabbath rest will be realized only in the eschaton (i.e., the final age to come), it can be experienced now (cf. v. 3). Thus, we are encouraged to "make every effort to enter that *rest*" (v. 11), to experience it ever anew in the "to-

day" that God gives us. The author does not shy away from the paradox inherent in energetically pursuing rest. As with eschatological material elsewhere, what is stated by means of an indicative ("we who have believed enter that rest" [v. 3, cf. v. 10]) also can be put before the readers as an imperative. It points to the perseverance required of the readers. The appropriateness of addressing this exhortation to these Jewish Christians is self-evident.

At the end of this passage we find the author characteristically punctuating his argument with exhortation. At the bottom of all his sophisticated argumentation, with its midrashic artistry and overarching grasp of the history of salvation, is a continual concern for the genuine needs of his readers. They are warned lest they "fall by following their example of disobedience." For the author of Hebrews, theology always is immensely practical.

The idea of entering a *sabbatismos*, God's Sabbath rest, is exceptionally appealing, even if conceptually somewhat elusive. In coming to a more adequate concept of the nature of that rest, we can hardly do better than to consider what the Sabbath means as observed in Judaism. There, it means much more than the cessation of work. Rather, it is essentially a day of celebration, a time of happiness, feasting, and spiritual joy, and at the same time a rejoicing in God's creation and an anticipation of final eschatological fulfillment. Thus it points forward to, and tastes in advance, an eschatological *shalom* ("peace"): ultimate well-being in every regard, the time when redemption is fully and finally realized.

The God Who Discerns the Intentions of the Heart (4:12–13)

That these verses are closely related to the material immediately preceding is clear from the strong logical connective "for." These verses provide the reason or grounds for the exhortation in verse 11, and thereby strengthen it.

The "word of God" is the convicting word that God speaks to individuals. Our author has been calling the readers to heed the voice of God through his exposition of Scripture. It is that "living and active" voice that he has in mind rather than the written word as such, although, of course, that voice is often heard through Scripture. The reference here to the "division of soul and spirit" should not be taken as teaching about separate components of the human being, leading to, for example, a trichotomistic view of human beings. The author is not teaching about that subject, but is using analogies to point to the penetrating character of God's word. The word of God in this sense pierces through to the inner being of a person, down to the very "thoughts and intentions of the heart." It thereby calls for authentic response. No one can hide from that voice, nor can anything be hidden from God's penetrating knowledge. All that is in us is "open and laid bare" to God, and to God we ultimately "must give account." When God speaks, the only

The "Word of God" in Hebrews 4:12

Considerable debate has occurred concerning the meaning of the term "the word of God" in 4:12. The majority of patristic writers and commentators up to the Reformation period took it as referring to Christ as the Word (*logos*) of God. But elsewhere in Hebrews we find no indication that the author held to a *logos* Christology similar to that of the prologue to the Gospel of John. Furthermore, on this interpretation Jesus would be likened to a sword, which is rather odd.

A second popular interpretation equates "word of God" with Scripture, meaning the Old Testament. Inasmuch as God speaks to us in Scripture, this interpretation is not wrong, but it is only a secondary meaning. Our author is thinking primarily of God's direct speech to the heart, and the present statement was probably inspired by his repeated reference to hearing God's voice in the preceding verses (3:7, 15, 16; 4:2, 7). The Israelites in the wilderness had no access to Scripture, yet they heard the word of God.

The Sinlessness of Christ

It is sometimes argued that Christ's sinlessness meant not merely that he did not sin, but that because of his divine nature he *could not* sin. Such a conclusion neglects the full humanity of Jesus, which must be held in tension with his deity. It makes a mockery of the temptation narratives of the Synoptic Gospels, or of the struggle in the garden of Gethsemane, issuing in the

submission "Yet not as I will, but as you will." If Jesus did not have the capacity to disobey his Father, then in these passages we see only playacting, which makes little or no sense.

Such a conclusion furthermore undermines completely the argument of our author. If Jesus could not have disobeyed God, then he was not tempted "just as we are," and therefore can-

not really "sympathize with our weaknesses" (see also 2:17–18). This is not the kind of high priest described here.

The problem with the faulty reasoning on Christ's sinlessness is that it fails to face the mystery and paradox of the incarnation head-on. Systematic theology must yield on points such as this if it is to remain faithful to the biblical texts.

appropriate response is faithful obedience, an obedience that is authentic and sincere.

This emphasis may point to an attempt by the readers to disguise a future compromise of their Christian faith so that it appeared to be something less than the actual apostasy that it was. This point emerges with all clarity in the warnings against apostasy in chapter 6.

Jesus Our Great High Priest (4:14–16)

Now that he has completed his lengthy midrashic application of Psalm 95 to the readers, exhorting them to take up the present day and

Drawing Near to the Presence of God in Hebrews

A most remarkable characteristic of the language of Hebrews is the way in which language that originally referred to the temple and its sacrificial ritual is spiritualized and applied to the believer in Christ. Here we call attention to the way in which through Christ the believer enters spiritually and directly into the presence of

God, symbolized by the Holy of Holies.

"with confidence draw near to the throne of grace" (4:16)

"a hope that enters into the inner shrine behind the curtain" (6:19)

"through which we draw near to God" (7:19)

"those who draw near to God through him" (7:25)

"make perfect those who draw near" (10:1)

"we have confidence to enter the sanctuary" (10:19)

"let us draw near with a true heart" (10:22)

"whoever would draw near to God" (11:6)

The Word "Grace" in Hebrews

Although Hebrews does not contain the polemic against works righteousness encountered so often in Paul's letters, it is well acquainted with the concept of grace: the unmerited, merciful favor of God. Thus, the Greek word *charis* as "grace" occurs seven times.

by the grace of God Christ died for all (2:9)
approach the throne of grace to receive mercy and
    grace (4:16 [2x])
outrage of the Spirit of grace (10:29)
failing to obtain the grace of God (12:15)
the heart strengthened by grace (13:9)
grace be with all of you (13:25)

enter the promised rest, our author returns to the notion of Christ as our high priest, which he first introduced in 2:17 and 3:1. The high priesthood of Christ now becomes a major theme to which he will repeatedly return in chapters 5–9.

The high priesthood of Christ is presented here as a motivation to

Original steps into the temple area, approaching from the south

hold "firmly to the faith we profess." In 3:1, Christ was identified as the "high priest of our confession." Several points are made in this connection. Our high priest has "gone through the heavens" (possibly an allusion to Ps 110:1; cf. 7:26), and this points to the efficacy and finality of his atoning work before the very presence of God in the true or heavenly sanctuary (cf. 6:20; 8:1–2; 9:11–12). Through Christ our high priest we are able to "approach the throne of grace with confidence." There, in the presence of God, we can find "mercy" and "grace" to help us "in our time of need." Although the primary application of this truth is to the original readers, it applies to Christians of every era. The God of grace is always ready to provide help to those in need.

Christ as a *human* high priest was, as we have already seen, made like us in every respect (2:17). To that point is added, as it also was in 2:18, that he "was tempted [or, 'tested'] in every way, just as we are," with one important difference now made clear: Christ was "without sin." Christ's full humanness and his sinlessness are not contradictory. Being sinful is not intrinsic or necessary to being fully human, nor, to state the opposite, is being sinless an obstacle to full humanness. In the Genesis account we see that prior to their fall, Adam and Eve were fully human but without sin. So too Christ, "the last Adam" (to use Pauline language [1 Cor 15:45]), was fully human but without sin.

Since Christ has been tempted or tested, he can "sympathize with our weaknesses." The point is not that Christ experienced every specific temptation that we do, but rather, that he experienced every basic type of temptation. He knows well what it is to be in our position of human weakness, and therefore he is able to stand with us and help us when we are in need. Thus, Christ is an ideal

Study Questions

1. Compare and contrast the rest promised to the people of Israel with the rest that remains available for the faithful people of God.

2. How does the author emphasize to his readers the importance of obedience?

3. In what ways is Christ an ideal high priest?

Key Terms

eschatology
indicative
imperative
today

high priest, who represents us before God and whose full humanity makes possible not only the atonement that is the answer to our sin, but also an identification with human plight in situations of testing and pressure.

The author, in his customary fashion, exhorts the readers to turn to God's presence and to receive the mercy and grace that will sustain them in their time of need. With all the strength of his argument, he will not miss an opportunity to apply it to those who are needy—in the first instance the immediate readers, but also Christians of every age.

Further Reading

Attridge, H. W. "'Let Us Strive to Enter That Rest': The Logic of Hebrews 4:1–11." *Harvard Theological Review* 73 (1980): 279–88.

deSilva, D. A. "Entering God's Rest: Eschatology and the Socio-Rhetorical Strategy of Hebrews." *Trinity Journal* 21 (2000): 25–43.

Gaffin, R. B. "A Sabbath Rest Still Awaits the People of God." In *Pressing toward the Mark*, ed. C. G. Dennison and R. C. Gamble. Philadelphia: Orthodox Presbyterian Church, 1986. Pp. 33–51.

Gleason, R. C. "The Old Testament Background of Rest in Hebrews 3:7–4:11." *Bibliotheca Sacra* 157 (2000): 281–303.

Lincoln, A. T. "Sabbath, Rest and Eschatology in the New Testament." In *From Sabbath to Lord's Day: A Biblical, Historical and Theological Investigation*, ed. D. A. Carson. Grand Rapids: Zondervan, 1982. Pp. 177–201.

Lombard, H. A. "Katapausis in the Epistle to the Hebrews." *Neotestamentica* 5 (1971): 60–71.

Trompf, G. "The Conception of God in Hebrews 4:12–13." *Studia Theologica* 25 (1971): 123–32.

von Rad, G. "There Remains Still a Rest for the People of God: An Investigation of a Biblical Conception." In *The Problem of the Hexateuch and Other Essays.* London: Oliver & Boyd, 1966. Pp. 94–102.

Weiss, H. "*Sabbatismos* in the Epistle to the Hebrews." *Catholic Biblical Quarterly* 58 (1996): 674–89.

5 The High Priesthood of Christ

And now, therefore, even because He, as the Representative of all mankind, did not supplicate for deliverance from death, without at the same time an obedient self-submission to everything beforehand which the determinate counsel and foreknowledge of God might demand, God heard and answered Him . . . by temporal death being made for Him the gate of paradise, and the cross of shame a ladder to heaven.

—F. J. Delitzsch,
The Epistle to the Hebrews

Supplemental Reading

Exodus 28; Matthew 26:36–46; 1 Peter 2:1–3

Outline

- **The Duties of the High Priest (5:1–4)**
- **Jesus as High Priest in the Order of Melchizedek (5:5–10)**
- **An Exhortation to Maturity (5:11–6:3)**

Objectives

1. Explain the work of the high priest.
2. Demonstrate Jesus' qualifications to be high priest.
3. Show the results of maturity.

Until one gains an adequate sense of the overwhelming majesty of the thrice-holy God and simultaneously a true sense of one's sinfulness and unworthiness (as Isaiah did [Is 6:1–5]), one is not in a position to understand or appreciate the importance of priests and their work. Our failure on these two points probably is what makes the idea of priesthood unfamiliar and without apparent significance or meaning. One of the reasons that the Old Testament is indispensable to understanding the New Testament is exactly here, since on the one hand, it provides us with a sense of the sovereignty, majesty, and power of God, and on the other hand, it confronts us with the reality of human failures and needs. In the light of these two points, the importance of sacrifices and priests readily emerges.

In chapter 5 of Hebrews we begin to approach the main argument of the book: the interpretation of Christ's work on the cross by anal-ogy with the Old Testament sacrifices of which it is the climactic fulfillment. Through the cross of Christ the sin of the human race is forgiven and the holiness of God is upheld. Indeed, only through that cross could this have been accomplished. It was the work of high priests in the Old Testament and the work of the unique high priest of the New Testament that effected the forgiveness of sins. The argument begun here will be interrupted by the exhortation/warning of 5:11–6:12 and then continued in 7:1.

The Duties of the High Priest (5:1–4)

Our author begins by providing a basic definition of a priest as "one who represents humanity in matters related to God." This representation is done by the offering of "gifts and sacrifices for sins." The high priest is particularly in view here because of the work he alone was able to do each year on the Day of Atonement (see 9:7, 25). The humanity of the high priest is very important because it enables him to work gently with the wayward and the weak, a point already made about Christ as high priest (2:18; 4:15). But since the ordinary high priest is also himself weak (7:28) and sinful, he had to "offer sacrifices for his own sins, as well as for the sins of the people." In this respect, the contrast with our great high priest, who was sinless, is dramatic. As the author will say in 7:27: "Unlike the other high priests, he does not need to offer sacrifices day after day, first for his own sins, and then for the sins of the people."

The next point to be made is that the office of high priest is an office that can be granted to an individual by God alone. The author speaks ide-

The Verb "Offer" in Hebrews

It is not surprising that the verb "offer" (*prospherō*), as in "offer sacrifice," occurs much more often in Hebrews (eighteen times) than in any other New Testament book. The idea of offering sacrifice is central to the author's argument. (What *is* surprising is that the verb does not occur in the Pauline letters, since the sacrificial death of Christ is supremely important for Paul.)

In the majority of instances the verb refers to the work of the priests and the high priest in the temple ritual. But it also refers to the work of Christ, as in 9:14, 25, 28. The point of the repeated references is in the contrast between the futile work of the priests and the effective work of Jesus. Thus, the very heart of the author's thesis is found in the contrast in 10:11–12: "Day after day every priest . . . offers the same sacrifices, which can never take away sins. But when this high priest had offered for all time one sacrifice for sins, he sat down at the right hand of God."

A model of what the Herodian temple may have looked like

ally here, ignoring the illegitimate high priesthood current in his day, which had been appointed by human rulers. This statement prepares for the author's unique and wonderful argument concerning the legitimacy of Christ's priesthood in the following verses. The example given is that of Aaron, who was appointed by God as the prototypical high priest (see Ex 28:1).

Jesus as High Priest in the Order of Melchizedek (5:5–10)

Jesus did not appoint himself to be high priest. The supreme qualification of Jesus to be a high priest is that he is the unique Son. Thus, our author begins again with Psalm 2:7, just

as he did in 1:5. Jesus is the unique Son of the Father. Only the unique Son could be the unique high priest whose one act of atonement would itself become the source of "eternal salvation" (v. 9). In the next quotation we come to what undoubtedly is one of the author's most insightful, and perhaps original, contributions to the understanding of Christ and his work: the use of Psalm 110:4 to establish Christ's priestly credentials.

It is the very important Psalm 110:1 (already cited in 1:13) that enables our author's understanding of Psalm 110:4. Although not quoted here, Psalm 110:1 serves as the bridge between Psalm 2:7 and Psalm 110:4. As we have seen, Psalm 110:1, "Sit at my right hand until I make your enemies a footstool for your feet," was widely understood in the early church as referring to the ascension of Christ. Since just a few verses later in the same psalm we read of a unique priesthood "of the order of Melchizedek," we can readily see

Entrance to the traditional site of the garden of Gethsemane

allusion

perfect

sorrow to the point of death" (Mt 26:38). Our author, writing before the formation of the Gospels, probably knew the oral tradition that eventually became incorporated into the Gospels. The prayers of Jesus were heard, he notes, "because of his reverent submission," which seems to echo Jesus' words in the garden: "Yet not as I will, but as you will" (Mt 26:39). Since Jesus did die on the cross, the prayer that was heard and answered was that his Father's will be done.

The statement that Christ "learned obedience" should not be understood to mean that he came to know something he did not know before. He had already obeyed his Father. Nor should the reference to his being "made perfect" be taken as suggesting that he was imperfect prior to the cross. He was both obedient and **perfect** before the cross. Instead, the notions of learning and perfection have to do with the progressive accomplishment of God's will. That is, Jesus exemplifies his obedience and perfection supremely in going to his death on the cross. Thus, learning obedience and being made perfect both refer to Jesus' own experience of fulfilling the will of God in the accomplishment of salvation. Prior to the cross there was a necessary incompleteness, but now God's plan of salvation is brought to completeness.

Through his obedience and completion of God's purpose—his "being made perfect"—Jesus "became the source [or, 'cause'] of eternal salvation" (cf. 2:10). The description of salvation as "eternal" points to its definitive and final character. This salvation comes to "all who obey" Jesus. Again Jesus is exalted as the one to whom obedience is due. As Jesus obeyed God, so we obey Jesus. This statement does not entail a salvation by works. Rather, for our author (as also for the much misunderstood Paul), faith (see 4:3) and obedience go together, just as unbelief and disobe-

how the author connected this too with Christ. Thus, when he quotes Psalms 2:7 and 110:4 together in verses 5–6, he also implies Psalm 110:1: it is the unique Son of the Father, the one presently at God's right hand, who has been appointed by God as "a priest forever, in the order of Melchizedek." Christ's priesthood in the order of Melchizedek will be explained in detail in chapter 7.

Having established this point, the author turns to the actual priestly work of Christ, which consists, shockingly, of his own sacrificial death. Verse 7 seems to be an **allusion** to the struggle of Jesus in the garden of Gethsemane (Mt 26:36–46), when Jesus was "overwhelmed with

exhortation

dience go together. And in Hebrews, at times it is difficult to distinguish between the two.

In verse 10 we are informed again that Jesus "was designated by God to be high *priest in the order of Melchizedek*," words drawn from Psalm 110:4, which was quoted in verse 6. The obedience of Jesus in dying on the cross in order to secure salvation was the work of a high priest. What qualifies Jesus for that office is his membership in the order of Melchizedek. This is something that our author intends to explain in some detail, but he cannot resist interrupting his argument here to issue an **exhortation** to his readers, and so the specific instruction concerning

Melchizedek is not continued until chapter 7.

An Exhortation to Maturity (5:11–6:3)

The author now pauses to indicate that he has much to teach his readers, a task made difficult because they are "dull of hearing" (RSV), meaning "slow to learn." This is virtually an admission that the argument to be presented in chapters 7–10 is for mature learners. The author's original readers, however, were ill prepared to understand this material.

In What Sense Was Jesus' Prayer Heard?

Hebrews 5:7 has caused considerable confusion. It seems to say that Jesus prayed to be delivered from death and that his prayer was heard. And yet, Jesus did die. In what sense, then, was his prayer heard? Perhaps in view here is being saved "from [or, 'out of'] death" through the resurrection. But the text does not actually say that the prayer of Jesus was to be delivered out of death by, for example, resurrection. This hardly seems to have been his prayer. Another suggestion, somewhat forced, is that Jesus prayed to be delivered from actually dying in the experience of agony in the garden of Gethsemane, such was the intensity of Jesus' suffering there. A variation on this is that he prayed to

be delivered from the fear of death (so Calvin). There has even been desperate speculation that a negative has been inadvertently dropped from the text, and so it should read "he was *not* heard" (so von Harnack, without any manuscript evidence). But if so, then the final words of the sentence, "because of his reverent submission," make little or no sense.

So, how was his prayer heard? Yes, Jesus prayed in the garden that he might avoid the cup of suffering (i.e., death). He also prayed, however, that not his will, but his Father's will, be done. This is the bottomline, fundamentally important prayer for Jesus. Most likely, our author has in mind here the tradition con-

cerning Jesus in the garden. There, Jesus' (ultimate) prayer of obedience to the will of the Father was what was heard, and that obedience led him to the cross. He thereby "learned obedience" and "became the source of eternal salvation" (vv. 8–9).

Further reading:

Attridge, H. W. "'Heard Because of His Reverence' (Heb 5:7)." *Journal of Biblical Literature* 98 (1979): 90–93.
Lightfoot, N. "The Saving of the Savior: Hebrews 5:7ff." *Restoration Quarterly* 16 (1973): 166–73.
Omark, R. E. "The Saving of the Savior: Exegesis and Christology in Hebrews 5:7–10." *Interpretation* 12 (1958): 39–51.

The Word "Eternal" in Hebrews

The author of Hebrews has a particular liking for the word "eternal" (*aiōnios*), since it points to the all-sufficient and finally effective atoning work of Jesus. At the same time, it indirectly points to the insufficient and temporary work of the priests in the Jerusalem temple.

While 6:2 refers to "eternal judgment" and 9:14 to the "eternal Spirit" through which Jesus offered himself, the remaining four references point in different ways to the new reality brought about by Christ:

eternal salvation	(5:9)
eternal redemption	(9:12)
eternal inheritance	(9:15)
eternal covenant	(13:20)

We begin now to discover more about those to whom our author writes.

Although the readers had been Christians long enough to be teachers of the faith, they needed once again to learn the ABCs, "the elementary

"The Elementary Doctrine of Christ"

This consists of teachings in the Christian faith also contained in Judaism. These are good in themselves, but they fall far short of the teachings that constitute a full Christianity, and will not equip the readers and enable them to attain maturity and faithfulness.

repentance from dead works
faith toward God
ablutions
laying on of hands
resurrection of the dead
eternal judgment

truths of God's oracles." In view here is a basic Christian interpretation of the Old Testament, in contrast to a more advanced understanding of the sort that our author is presenting. Like infants, the readers needed milk and could not cope with solid food (cf. 1 Cor 3:2; 1 Pt 2:2). Thus, they lacked an adequate understanding of "the word of righteousness," which is probably the equivalent of "the elementary truths of God's oracles" (v. 12). Had they been mature (the Greek word translated as "mature" is *teleios,* literally meaning "perfect," again in the sense of completeness or fulfillment) and able to eat solid food, they would have been able "to distinguish good from evil." Since this is the same language used by secular ethical teachers, these last words probably reflect the influence of Hellenistic ethical teaching upon our author.

The "elementary teachings about Christ" (literally, the "beginning of the word of Christ") in 6:1 appear to be the items that are mentioned in the remainder of the sentence. These are basic beliefs that Christianity shares with Judaism—not only, obviously, repentance and faith in God, two of the central features of Judaism, but also the laying on of hands, eternal judgment, and even "baptisms" (i.e., "washings" or "purifications") and the resurrection of the dead (as we know from the Pharisees). There is, in fact, nothing in the items mentioned in 6:1–2 to which a non-Christian Jew could not subscribe. Thus, the readers appear not to have moved much beyond beliefs that they probably already held before they became Christians. Quite probably, they were deliberately holding to a minimalist Christianity that also could pass as a form of Judaism (and thereby avoid persecution). These beliefs, however, composed a foundation that did not need to be laid again. Instead, the readers needed to press on to the more mature doctrines of Christianity, to the completeness and fulfillment brought by Christ. And our author hopes the best for his readers in his implicit prayer: "God permitting, we will do so." Behind these words is the conviction of the absolute sovereignty of God.

The readers need to press on to a mature Christianity rather than falling back to their earlier Jewish faith. If they did press on to maturity, they would become teachers of others and from solid food be able to pursue the good and persevere under testing. But now the author will turn to the danger head-on, and put the strongest possible warning before the readers.

Key Terms

allusion
perfect
exhortation

Study Questions

1. How does the author of Hebrews allude to similarities and differences between the roles of the high priest and Jesus?

2. Discuss how Jesus "learned obedience" and was "made perfect."

3. What does the author have in mind when he exhorts the readers to maturity?

Further Reading

Stewart, R. A. "The Sinless High-Priest." *New Testament Studies* 14 (1967–68): 126–35.
Williamson, R. "Hebrews 4:15 and the Sinlessness of Jesus." *Expository Times* 86 (1974–75): 4–8.

6 Apostasy and Divine Faithfulness

We now see whom he excluded from the hope of pardon, even the apostates who alienated themselves from the Gospel of Christ, which they had previously embraced, and from the grace of God; and this happens to no one but to him who sins against the Holy Spirit.

—John Calvin,
Commentary on Hebrews

Supplemental Reading

Isaiah 5; 2 Corinthians 13:5–10

Outline

- **The Danger of Apostasy (6:4–12)**
- **The Fixed Character of God's Purposes (6:13–20)**

Objectives

1. Describe the implications of apostasy.
2. Explain the significance of God's oath.
3. Identify the emphasis of chapter 6 over against what the chapter is popularly known for.

apostasy

To answer the frequently asked question: there is but one unforgivable sin, that of **apostasy**. Apostasy is like no other sin because by its very nature it cuts a person off from the gracious God who always stands ready to forgive. Apostasy has an absolute character because it is the denial of the very basis of grace. Our author presents to his readers the strongest warning possible. Nothing could be more serious than to deny the truth of God's work in Christ.

Without weakening the importance of what is said in the preceding paragraph, we must stress immediately that our author is not concerned to provide an objective statement that fairly outlines all the possible options. Rather than providing a cool, theoretical statement, he presents us with an impassioned plea rooted in the most pragmatic of concerns. The readers are tempted to return to their Judaism and thus to turn away from their Christian faith. This would be catastrophic for them, and for this reason only the sternest of warnings would suffice (see also 10:19–39). If the readers deny their Christian faith, they truly will be lost. Nor must they contemplate the possibility of an eventual future return to Christian faith. To fall into apostasy is to cut oneself off decisively and absolutely from the God who is the source of all grace. From that position there is no sure return.

The Danger of Apostasy (6:4–12)

The Christianity of the readers is not in doubt. They are described as "enlightened" (v. 4), meaning that they have been brought from darkness to light (cf. 10:32, "after you had received the light"). They also have "tasted" of "the heavenly gift" and "the goodness of the word of God" ("word" here is not *logos*, referring to Christ as the Word of God, but *rhēma*, referring to what God has spoken). The word "taste" does not mean that they only partook of Christianity partially and did not participate fully in Christian salvation. In a similar way, the word "taste" in 2:9 does not mean that Christ did not fully die. This word is an idiom for experiencing the reality of something. The readers had become "partakers of the Holy Spirit," the certain mark of genuine Christians. Furthermore, they had "tasted" (i.e., "experienced") "the goodness of the word of God and the powers of the age to come." These last words are a clear indicator of the author's perspective of realized eschatology.

These Jewish Christian readers, who had so clearly participated in the fruit of Christian salvation, now contemplated turning away from it all. Nothing could be more serious in our author's view. He insists that their apostasy would be a form of betrayal and the shocking equivalent of crucifying Jesus and subjecting him to public shame yet once again. In effect, their apostasy would be a mockery of the cross itself.

By its very nature, apostasy is a final act, not a temporary one. This is the point our author wants to make when he says that it is "impossible" to restore again those who have decisively turned away. In principle, the point is true. What would our author say to the fact that some apostates indeed have returned to faith? He would not deny that God *can* restore apostates to faith. Nevertheless, he hardly wants to present that option to his readers. They must not think that even if they "temporarily" apostatize, they of course may always come back later. By the very nature and seriousness of apostasy, no return can be guaranteed. That is the force of the word "impossible" here. The denial involved in apostasy amounts to a burning of bridges. That very fact cuts one off from the possibility of return. Apostasy therefore is a decisive and most dangerous act.

Apostasy and the Question of the Eternal Security of the Believer

The warnings contained in Hebrews 6:4–6 and 10:19–39 presuppose the possibility that true Christians can fall into apostasy. The readers confronted that actual temptation. Furthermore, the statements in 6:4–5 make it quite clear that the readers were genuinely Christian, not just Christian in appearance.

Paradoxically, the New Testament contains passages that indicate the security of the believer and passages, such as the present one, that warn about the danger of falling away and the need for faithful adherence to the gospel (cf. 3:14). The warnings given by Paul, who strongly believed in election and that salvation was God's act, not ours, can hardly be regarded as merely hypothetical (see, e.g., 1 Cor 15:2; 2 Cor 6:1; 13:5; Phil 2:16; 3:11).

In this matter, systems of theology, whether Calvinist or Arminian, need to exercise restraint. We do well to limit ourselves to the full scope of the specific statements of Scripture, the raw data of biblical theology, and to preserve the tensions we encounter therein. This also holds true for matters such as free will and the sovereignty of God, election/predestination and human responsibility, the deity and humanity of Christ, the problem of evil and the goodness of God. It is not a question of refusing to think through these matters clearly and consistently, or of throwing logic to the winds, but rather, of listening to all that Scripture has to say on an issue. We must not let our theological systems cancel out one side or the other of biblical teaching, even if presently the various materials appear to be incompatible.

Scripture provides us assurance of our security, and at the same time warns us. Either side can be focused on, depending on an individual's need. Thus, those who are worried about losing their salvation (which itself, by the way, guarantees that they have not committed apostasy) should dwell upon the passages teaching the security of the believer; those who have become complacent and overly comfortable in their faith need to consider the warning passages. The Scriptures truly offer us security, but exclude an unresponsive complacency.

Further reading:

deSilva, D. A. "Hebrews 6:4–8: A Socio-Rhetorical Investigation." *Tyndale Bulletin* 50 (1999): 33–57; 225–35.
Hughes, P. E. "Hebrews 6:4–6 and the Peril of Apostasy." *Westminster Theological Journal* 35 (1972–73): 137–55.
Marshall, I. H. "The Problem of Apostasy in New Testament Theology." *Perspectives in Religious Studies* 14 (1987): 65–80.
———. *Kept by the Power of God: A Study of Perseverance and Falling Away.* 3rd ed. London: Paternoster, 1995.
McCullough, J. C. "The Impossibility of a Second Repentance in Hebrews." *Biblical Theology* 20 (1974): 1–7.
McKnight, S. "The Warning Passages in Hebrews: A Formal Analysis and Theological Conclusions." *Trinity Journal* 13 (1992): 21–59.
Nicole, R. "Some Comments on Hebrews 6:4–6 and the Doctrine of the Perseverance of God with the Saints." In *Current Issues in Biblical and Patristic Interpretation*, ed. G. F. Hawthorne. Grand Rapids: Eerdmans, 1975. Pp. 355–64.
Trotter, A. H., Jr. *Interpreting the Epistle to the Hebrews.* Grand Rapids: Baker, 1997. Pp. 210–22.

91

Postbaptismal Sins

In the early church, Hebrews 6:4–6 frequently was interpreted as having to do with sins committed after baptism. Failing to see that the question was apostasy, some feared that it was impossible to receive forgiveness for postbaptismal sins. This led to the practice of postponing baptism until just before death. The belief in baptismal regeneration, along with texts such as 1 John 3:6, reinforced this practice. Hebrews, on the other hand, presupposes the ongoing availability of the forgiveness of sins to the believer through the atoning work of Christ, our high priest (see, e.g., 9:14; 10:22).

oath

In this passage the author does not address the question of the perseverance of the saints. We may safely say, however, that *perseverance is what finally demonstrates the reality of Christian faith* (see 3:14; 6:11). Most importantly, sufficient resources are available for the readers to sustain them in their difficult circumstances and to enable them to persevere. This has been made clear in 2:18 and 4:14–16, and will be emphasized again in 10:23.

The point about perseverance is reinforced by the parabolic and well-known imagery of verses 7–8. Land that is fruitful receives blessing from God, while land that produces thorns and thistles is cursed and subject to destruction. The analogy is reminiscent of the image in Isaiah of Israel as an unproductive vineyard. If the readers do not persevere in their faith, then they will be like unfruitful land, and subject to God's judgment.

In verses 9–12 our author turns to very specific application to the readers. Thus far, he has addressed the subject of the dangers of apostasy in a rather general fashion. Although the readers clearly are in danger, he now indicates that he has confidence that they will remain faithful. He is confi-

dent of "better things" regarding them, things that belong to salvation. His mind turns to the love and good work that they had exhibited, and continued exhibiting, in "serving the saints." In view may be their solidarity with suffering Christians, referred to in 10:32–34. Verses 11–12 are an exhortation to the readers to manifest the same kind of effort and persistence even "until the end." Those who have "faith and patience" and hence inherit the promises are put before the readers as people to be imitated. Again, this encouragement and exhortation have the specific need of the readers in mind. It is true, of course, that the same words can easily carry a meaning extended to Christians of any era.

The Fixed Character of God's Purposes (6:13–20)

The position of Christians is one of full confidence because it relies upon what God has said and done. Of course, God's word alone is fully reliable. But when God confirms his word with an **oath**, it is doubly fixed. In his reading of the Old Testament, our author noticed that in Genesis 22:16 God confirmed his promise to Abraham with an oath. The words just prior to those quoted here in 6:14 are as follows: "I swear by myself, declares the Lord, that because you have done this and have not withheld your son, your only son. . . ." (The story of Abraham, his faith and endurance, will be referred to in some detail in 11:8–12, 17–19.) As our author indicates, if God takes an oath, he must swear by himself, since there is no greater name that might be called upon. But the remarkable thing is that God would take an oath at all. God's word is fully trustwor-

anchor

thy without an oath. No further confirmation is needed. In this case God chose "to show more convincingly . . . the unchangeable character of his purpose" (v. 17).

Thus, it was "through two unchangeable things" (v. 18)—his word and his oath—that God confirmed his promise to Abraham. Furthermore, the wording of the promise in verse 14 is emphatic and perhaps best rendered this way: "Surely I will bless you and surely I will multiply you." Abraham, encouraged by this, "patiently endured" and "obtained the promise" (v. 15), meaning the offspring referred to in God's covenant (cf. Rom 4:17–21; Gal 3:16). But the words are meant for us too, so that "we who have fled for refuge might have strong encouragement to seize the hope set before us" (v. 18).

In verses 19–20, our author emphasizes the confidence and security that we have in Christ. He likens our "hope" to "a sure and steadfast anchor of the soul" (v. 19). In the New

The temple platform seen from the direction of the Mount of Olives

Testament, the word "hope" connotes a confident expectation. In a world filled with uncertainties and insecurities that seem constantly to threaten believers, we have a fixed point, an **anchor** for our souls (this is the only place in the New Testament where the word "anchor" is used metaphorically). Our confidence and security is such that it now can be spoken of in the unusual language of "a hope that enters into the inner shrine behind the curtain" (v. 19). The point is that through Christ we who have such a hope enter the very presence of God, symbolized in the vocabulary describing the Holy of Holies in the temple. Into that inner sanctuary we have been preceded by Jesus, "a forerunner on our behalf" (v. 20). This fact offers the readers the greatest possible security.

Only the high priest could enter the Holy of Holies and he could do so only on one special day of the year (see 9:7). So when our author states that Jesus has gone into the inner

A model of first-century Jerusalem, with the temple at the top of the picture

shrine before us, the role of Jesus as high priest again comes into the picture. We have already been introduced to Jesus as "a high priest after the order of Melchizedek" (5:10). Here, we again encounter this description of Jesus with the added word "forever." Our author has not yet explained this concept, and he turns to it next.

Chapter 6 of Hebrews begins with the gravest of warnings, but ends with a very strong emphasis on security. Unfortunately, the chapter is most known for its statement of the impossibility of repentance from apostasy, while the great affirmation in the remainder of the chapter concerning the believer's security is neglected. The author wants the read-

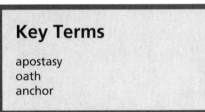

Key Terms

apostasy
oath
anchor

Study Questions

1. Why is the author's warning so stern?

2. Discuss how the author emphasizes the confidence and security of the Christian position.

Further Reading

Adams, J. C. "Exegesis of Hebrews VI.1f." *New Testament Studies* 13 (1966–67): 378–85.
Peterson, D. G. "The Situation of the 'Hebrews' (5:11–6:12)." *Reformed Theological Review* 35 (1976): 14–21.

ers to turn away from the weak faith that prompts them to apostasy and instead to count upon the certainty of God's faithfulness. God has provided us with "two unchangeable things," the promise and the oath, so that we might "take hold of the hope offered to us" and "be greatly encouraged" (v. 18). This provides us with "an anchor for the soul, firm and secure" (v. 19). Herein lies the emphasis of the chapter.

7 The Priesthood of Melchizedek

Those who have Christ as their high priest and mediator with God have in Him a Savior whose saving power is available without end, not liable to the mischances of mortal life. He lives eternally, eternally engaged to bless and protect those who have committed themselves to Him.

—F. F. Bruce, *The Epistle to the Hebrews*

Supplemental Reading

Genesis 14:17–20; Psalm 110

Outline

- **Abraham and Melchizedek (7:1–10)**
- **The High Priesthood of Jesus in the Line of Melchizedek (7:11–22)**
- **The Perfect and Permanent Priestly Work of Christ (7:23–28)**

Objectives

1. Identify Melchizedek.
2. Show the relationship between Melchizedek and Christ.
3. Explain the rationale for the argument concerning the priesthood of Christ.

The strange and mysterious Melchizedek has always fascinated and puzzled Bible readers, ancient and modern. Although he obviously is very important, we know very little about him. In the key passage, Genesis 14:18–20, Melchizedek seems to appear out of nowhere, and then almost as abruptly, to disappear again from the narrative, never to be heard of again. The Old Testament has but one further occurrence of his name, in Psalm 110:4, the verse so important to our author. In the New Testament only Hebrews refers to Melchizedek, and here, as we will see, not in a passing way, but to establish the legitimacy of the high priesthood of Christ.

Melchizedek also appears as a significant figure in the Jewish literature of the Second Temple period and later (see the sidebar "Melchizedek in Jewish Literature").

Abraham and Melchizedek (7:1–10)

We come now to one of the most important and creative arguments in the entire Book of Hebrews. The author had begun his discourse on Melchizedek in 5:10, but interrupted it with the digression of 5:11–6:19. He already has indicated that he had "much to say" about this subject, noting too that it would be "hard to explain" (5:11).

The application of the reference to Melchizedek in Psalm 110:4 to Christ is a brilliant insight, unique in the New Testament, and may well have been original to our author (see 5:5–6). His argument proceeds in logical succession, and he begins with a reminder to the readers of the story of Melchizedek as reported in Genesis 14:18–20. In the verses that follow, he uses the vocabulary of the Septuagint narrative in typically midrashic fashion as he explains the relevance of the story to his argument.

The words of verse 1 and the first part of verse 2 are drawn from the Septuagint version of the Genesis account. The essential elements of the story are given, in particular that Melchizedek blessed Abraham and that Abraham gave him a tithe of what he had captured in his recent victory over the kings. These are the points that our author will emphasize. The Genesis account provides the content of Melchizedek's blessing, not given by our author: "Blessed be Abram by God Most High, Creator of heaven and earth.

Melchizedek in Jewish Literature

Beyond the Old Testament references, the figure of Melchizedek is mentioned in the following:

Dead Sea Scrolls, *Melchizedek* (11QMelch), where Melchizedek, similarly to the archangel Michael, performs eschatological judgment upon the righteous and the wicked.
Philo, *Allegorical Interpretation* 3.25–26, where he is referred to as "worthy of God's own priesthood."
Josephus, *Jewish Antiquities* 179–182, where he is referred to as "priest of God."
Babylonian Talmud, *Sukkah* 52b, where he is linked with Elijah.

Melchizedek also appears in gnostic texts. In an apocalyptic text named *Melchizedek* from Nag Hammadi (Codex IX,1), Melchizedek is identified with Jesus. Mention of Melchizedek also is found in *Pistis Sophia*. An earlier Melchizedek is mentioned in *2 Enoch* 71–72, in this case a priest taken by the archangel Michael to paradise, where he remains eternally.

Further reading:

Fitzmyer, J. A. "Further Light on Melchizedek from Qumran Cave 11." *Journal of Biblical Literature* 86 (1967): 25–41.

Caves near Qumran in which some of the Dead Sea Scrolls were found

And blessed be God Most High, who delivered your enemies into your hand" (Gn 14:19–20).

The first concern of our author is the identity of Melchizedek. He translates the Hebrew name "Melchizedek," which means "king of righteousness," and also the designation "king of Salem," which means "king of peace." Undoubtedly, Salem also refers to an actual place, of which Melchizedek was king, possibly Jerusalem (although it is nowhere else referred to in this way). Of the greatest importance to our author is the Genesis description of Melchizedek as "a priest of God Most High [*El Elyon*]." The words spoken by Melchizedek according to Genesis 14:19 identify "God Most High," the chief of the Canaanite deities, with the one true God, the Creator, and hence the God of Israel (explicit identification with Yahweh is made in Genesis 14:22, "I have raised my hand to Yahweh, God Most High [*El*

Elyon], Creator of heaven and earth"). Melchizedek is the first priest mentioned in the Old Testament, and he precedes the priests of the line of Aaron established at Sinai by several centuries. The recognition of his priesthood, fully outside the stream of Old Testament salvation history (note the comment "This man, however, did not trace his descent from Levi" [Heb 7:6]), as valid is quite remarkable. (For a similar example in the Old Testament, note Jethro, the father-in-law of Moses, who was a Midianite priest in the service of God [Ex 2:16; cf. 18:17–23].)

The statement in verse 3 that Melchizedek was "without father or mother or genealogy, and has neither beginning of days nor end of life" sometimes has misled readers into assuming that Melchizedek was eternal and thus represented an appearance of the preincarnate Christ to Abraham. These words merely mean, however, that in contrast to typical kings,

99

Melchizedek in Hebrews

"a priest forever, after the order of Melchizedek"	5:6 (quotation of Ps 110:4)
"a high priest after the order of Melchizedek"	5:10
"a high priest forever after the order of Melchizedek"	6:20
"Melchizedek, king of Salem, priest of the Most High God"	7:1, 10
"another priest . . . after the order of Melchizedek"	7:11
"another priest . . . in the likeness of Melchizedek"	7:15
"a priest forever, after the order of Melchizedek"	7:17 (quotation of Ps 110:4)

type

for whom generally we possess careful documentation, in the case of Melchizedek, we have no record of his genealogy, birth, or death. It is important here to understand that in the Jewish interpretation of Scripture, much can be made of what Scripture *does not say* at any particular point. (Philo uses the same Greek word for "without mother" in referring to Sarah, whose mother was unknown [*On Drunkenness* 59–62].) The effect of all the information available about Melchizedek is to give the impression that he is without beginning or end, and thus to underline that his priesthood is without end.

In Hebrews, Melchizedek serves as a forerunner or **type** of Christ. Paradoxically, although we do have records of Jesus' lineage, birth, and death, as the Messiah and the Son of God, he truly is without beginning or end. Christ is similar to Melchizedek also in that he is supremely the king of righteousness and the king of peace. The points of comparison between Melchizedek and Christ are striking. For all the resemblances, however, Melchizedek should not be regarded as representing an early, preincarnate appearance of Christ.

Rather, as our author points out in verse 3, "resembling the Son of God, he remains a high priest forever" (cf. 7:15). Melchizedek resembles the Son of God, but is not himself the Son of God.

Also to be noted here is that no end of the Melchizedekian priesthood is recorded, and thus implicitly, that this priestly line may be understood as still valid. As our author will point out emphatically, it is of this ongoing line that Jesus Christ becomes our high priest (cf. v. 17).

In further explicating the significance of Melchizedek, our author exclaims, "See how great he is!" Two matters establish this point. To be in a position to appreciate the argument, however, one must be aware of the very important place that Abraham holds in the Jewish perspective, as the first of the patriarchs, to whom God first made the covenantal promises that eventually led to the uniqueness of Israel among the nations.

The first point in the argument is that the great Abraham paid a tithe of the spoils to Melchizedek (v. 4; cf. v. 2). Paying tithes to priests was a practice well known in later Israel. The descendants of Abraham were required to pay tithes to the Levitical priesthood. As a part of their priestly office, the descendants of Levi "have a commandment in the law to take tithes from the people" (v. 5). But when Abraham paid the tithe to Melchizedek, in effect what happened was that Levi himself, the one to whom tithes were later paid, was paying a tithe to Melchizedek, since Levi was a descendant of Abraham (his great-grandson), although then "still in the loins of his ancestor" (v. 10). In receiving the tithe, therefore, Melchizedek is superior to both Abraham and Levi.

The second point is that Melchizedek blessed Abraham, the one to whom the promises had been given (v. 6). Our author draws out the significance of this with all clarity: "It is beyond dispute that the inferior is blessed by the superior" (v. 7). Thus, Melchizedek is the superior of even the great Abraham. The clear impli-

cation is that the priesthood of Melchizedek also is superior to that of the Levitical priesthood.

Motifs of Discontinuity with the Old Testament in Hebrews

In a document that stresses fulfillment and therefore continuity with the Old Testament as much as Hebrews does, it is remarkable to find also such strong elements of discontinuity. Such is often the case in the New Testament writings. The discontinuity is necessitated by the undeniable and revolutionary newness brought by the fulfillment of the gospel. In this tension between continuity and discontinuity lies much of the challenge and richness of biblical theology.

These are the main motifs of discontinuity in Hebrews:

7:12 "For where there is a change in the priesthood, there is necessarily a change in the law as well."

7:18 "A former commandment is set aside because of its weakness and uselessness."

8:7 "For if that first covenant had been faultless, there would have been no occasion for a second."

8:13 "In speaking of a new covenant he treats the first as obsolete. And what is becoming obsolete and growing old is ready to vanish away."

9:9–10 "This is an illustration for the present time, indicating that the gifts and sacrifices being offered were not able to clear the conscience of the worshiper. They are only a matter of food and drink and various ceremonial washings—external regulations applying until the time of the new order."

9:23 "Thus it was necessary for the copies of the heavenly things to be purified with these rites, but the heavenly things themselves with better sacrifices than these."

10:1 "The law has but a shadow of the good things to come instead of the true form of these realities."

10:9 "He abolishes the first in order to establish the second."

The High Priesthood of Jesus in the Line of Melchizedek (7:11–22)

The author now asks why Jesus had to come as high priest, if in fact, as the readers were inclined to believe, the Levitical priesthood was adequate in itself and able to attain unto "perfection" or "completion" (v. 11). By this perfection/completion is meant the full realization of the goal of God's plan of salvation. Why, more specifically, was it said of Christ that he was made a priest after the order of Melchizedek, as Psalm 110:4 indicated (see v. 17; cf. 5:6)? The unmistakable implication in all of this is that the Levitical priesthood was inadequate (see v. 18). Such a revolutionary thought has implications that our author will not hesitate to draw out as his argument proceeds, as, for example, in 10:4, where he says, "It is impossible that the blood of bulls and goats should take away sins." Indeed, it is important to note that to attack the Levitical priesthood is in principle to attack the law. The vital link between the two is in view in the words "on the basis of it [the Levitical priesthood] the law was given to the people" (v. 11). The point is made very explicitly in the statement that follows: "For when there is a change in the priesthood, there is necessarily a change in the law as well" (v. 12). The change from the temporary Levitical priesthood to that of a permanent

101

Melchizedekian priesthood is of enormous consequence.

Such a radical conclusion of a change in the law was made necessary by the fact that Christ had come to do the work of atonement as a priest of the order of Melchizedek. The law of Moses knows of only one priesthood, that of the line of Aaron/ Levi. Jesus, however, was born of the line of Judah ("descended from" is literally "rose up from," probably in deliberate allusion to the messianic passage in Nm 24:17), and thus did not qualify to be a priest. "In connection with that tribe Moses said nothing about priests" (v. 14); that is, nothing in the Pentateuch legislates a priestly line other than that of Levi. Here we encounter the brilliance of our author's argument. By virtue of the words in Psalm 110:4, "You are a priest forever according to the order of Melchizedek," understood as spoken to the one who according to Psalm 110:1 is invited to sit at God's right hand, the priestly credentials of

Jesus are established. Thus, the one who accomplished atonement for sin on the cross and ascended to God's right hand fulfilled the words of verses 1 and 4 of Psalm 110.

Thus, it was not in the usual way, "not according to a legal requirement concerning bodily descent [literally, 'not according to a carnal commandment']" (v. 16), that Jesus qualified to be high priest. Rather, what qualified him was his personal identity as the one who was raised to sit at God's right hand. If Jesus is the Messiah, David's Lord, according to Psalm 110:1 (see Mt 22:41–46), who has ascended to the right hand of God, then he has been raised from the dead. He therefore has become the priest of Psalm 110:4, "by the power of an indestructible life" (v. 16).

Our author does not shy away from the implied conclusion; indeed, it will become important in the argument of the chapters that follow. The fact that Jesus comes as a priest *not* of the tribe of Levi means that "a former

Site of the Essene community of Qumran, with the Dead Sea in the background

The View of the Law in Hebrews Compared to Paul's View

The author of Hebrews is as strong as Paul is on the subject of the end of the authority of the law. A difference between the two writers is that Paul seems to address primarily the moral law, while the author of Hebrews has in mind primarily the ceremonial law. It is, however, a matter of emphasis only; Paul would agree that the ceremonial law has been outmoded, and the author of Hebrews would agree that the moral law has been displaced. The reason for this agreement is that for the Jews the law re-mained a unity, so that a change of one part of it had necessary implications for the totality.

The subject of the law is one that demands careful thought and articulation. Despite the strong statements concerning disconti-nuity, which cannot be minimized, all the writers of the New Testament were convinced that the law, which had a preparatory function, was fulfilled by Christ—that is, not so much brought to an end as brought to its intended goal and meaning—and thus, in a deeper sense, was upheld. Jewish Christians in particular, such as the readers of Matthew and Hebrews, but Paul himself too, were convinced that Jesus was the true interpreter of the law, and that to follow his teaching was in effect to fulfill the entirety of the law in its ultimate intention. In this way, all of the New Testament writers share a common and fundamentally important commitment to the righteousness of the law, and the gospel does not overturn the law.

commandment is set aside because of its weakness and uselessness" (v. 18): the commandment that only Levites could become priests. The Levitical system and the sacrifices of the temple had only a preparatory role to play, and now that the fulfillment has come, they are outmoded and use-less. The added parenthetical comment in verse 19, "for the law made nothing perfect" (or "brought nothing to completion") (cf. v. 11), indi-cates again that the atoning work of Jesus makes the law obsolete. The salvation that the law had promised and foreshadowed had now come, with the consequent annulment of the law.

The resultant new situation is that "a better hope is introduced, through which we draw near to God" (v. 19). The idea here is close to the mention of "a hope that enters into the inner shrine behind the curtain" (6:19). The work of Christ as high priest, in con-trast to that of the Levitical priest-hood, brings us to a better reality, de-scribed here as a "better hope." This hope involves a confidence that en-ables us to come directly into the presence of God. As will become clear, the sacrificial work of Christ is what brings about the atonement and makes possible this access to God.

Just as our author pointed out in 6:13–18 that the promise to Abraham was confirmed with an oath, so also he reminds his readers that the words of Psalm 110:4 include a refer-ence to God's oath: "The Lord has sworn and will not change his mind, 'You are a priest forever'" (v. 21). By contrast, no such oath was invoked in connection with the Levitical priest-hood. This again points to the inferi-ority of the latter. As our author puts it, "This makes Jesus the surety of a better covenant" (v. 22). This first ref-erence to "a better covenant" shortly will be paired with a reference to the "new covenant" and the quotation of Jeremiah 31:31–34 (in 8:8–12). Jesus is

guarantee

The Word "Covenant" in Hebrews

In 7:22 we encounter the first occurrence of the word "covenant," which will be used no less than fourteen times in the next three chapters of Hebrews. To capture the contrast between the old and the new, the following chart groups the various uses of the word.

"the first covenant" 8:7; 9:1, (4), 15, 18, (20)	"a new covenant" 8:8, (10), 13; 9:15; (10:16, 29); 12:24
the weakness of the first covenant 8:7, 9, 13	"a better covenant" 7:22; 8:6
	"the eternal covenant" 13:20

The Qualities of Jesus as High Priest

As high priest, Jesus exhibits many very impressive qualities. The following list is representative.

"merciful and faithful"	2:17
"able to help those who are tempted"	2:18
"great . . . passed through the heavens"	4:14
"not unable to sympathize with our weaknesses"	4:15
"tempted as we are, yet without sin"	4:15
"appointed by God"	5:5
"a forerunner on our behalf"	6:20
"holy, blameless, unstained, separated from sinners"	7:26
"exalted above the heavens"	7:26
"made perfect forever"	7:28
"seated at the right hand of the throne of the Majesty in heaven"	8:1
"a minister in the sanctuary and the true tent"	8:2
"a high priest of the good things that have come"	9:11
"entered once for all into the Holy Place, taking . . . his own blood"	9:12
"securing an eternal redemption"	9:12

the **guarantee** of a covenant that is better than the first covenant. The establishing of this point will be the main concern of chapters 8–10.

The Perfect and Permanent Priestly Work of Christ (7:23–28)

The risen Jesus holds a priesthood that is permanent. As we have already been told, his is "the power of an indestructible life" (v. 16). Under the previously valid system there had to be a succession of many priests simply because of their mortality. But because Christ "continues forever" (v. 24), his priesthood is permanent ("You are a priest forever" [Ps 110:4]).

Two benefits of Christ's eternal priesthood are now brought forward. First, "He is able for all time to save those who draw near to God through him" (v. 25). Thus, salvation is perpetually available. This is the only time our author uses the verb "to save" in reference to salvation, although he frequently uses the **cog-**

cognate **nate** noun "salvation" (e.g., 2:10; 5:9; 9:28). In 9:12 he refers to redemption (cf. 9:15); more often, he refers to forgiveness of sins or Christ as a sacrifice for sins (e.g., 2:17; 7:27; 9:26, 28; 10:12). It is in this latter sense that we are saved "through him." Second, "He always lives to make intercession for them" (v. 25). In view here is Christ's work as high priest, since a priest's task is to represent humanity to God. The same intercessory work of Christ is in view in Romans 8:34, while the intercessory work of the Spirit is mentioned in Romans 8:26–27. No more efficacious intercessor could be imagined than this high priest who now sits, as the risen Son of God, at the right hand of the Father. Thus, the full provision for, and

security of, believers is established beyond question (cf. 1 Jn 2:1).

The opening words of verse 26, "it was fitting," imply that it was the will of God, for it is God who has seen to it that these matters are as they are. The reference to Jesus being "exalted above the heavens" (cf. 4:14) alludes yet again to Psalm 110:1. The description of our high priest as "holy, blameless, unstained, separated from sinners" points not only to the sinlessness of Christ (cf. 4:15), but also to the pure qualities required of a perfect sacrifice. This is a unique high priest who alone could do what he did.

In verse 27 our author presents the central thesis of his argument, which he will elaborate at length in chapters 9 and 10. In contrast to the work of the high priests, who of necessity had to offer sacrifices repeatedly, beginning with a sacrifice for their own sins and only then making sacrifices for the people (see Lv 16:6–34), Jesus, the perfect high priest, did not need to offer sacrifice for his own sins, but accomplished the sacrifice for the people "once for all when he offered up himself." The shocking fact that in this case the high priest offers *himself* as a sacrifice should not be missed. Here, indeed, we encounter the mystery of the cross, for which no explanation is adequate. Our author will not ignore the fact that in this remarkable and unique instance the priest and the offering are one and the same (see 9:12).

Two important contrasts emerge in verse 28. The first is between the high priests in their "weakness" and the Son "who has been made perfect forever." The difference between the high priests and the high priest who is the Son has been made clear by the contrasting of their respective works. Here, the words "Son forever" are put together instead of "priest forever," thus combining allusions to Psalms 110:4 and 2:7 (cf. the quotation of both successively in 5:5–6).

"Once for All" in Hebrews

One of the most striking affirmations in Hebrews is the stress upon the "once for all" character of Christ's sacrifice in contrast to the necessity of the repeated sacrifices of the Levitical priesthood. This points to the weakness and provisional character of the Levitical priesthood and to the sufficiency and finality of Christ's sacrificial death on the cross.

Two words, almost exactly the same in form (*hapax* and *ephapax*), and with exactly the same meaning, are used.

hapax ("once for all"):

"he has appeared once for all at the end of the age to put away sin by the sacrifice of himself"	9:26
"Christ, having been offered once for all to bear the sins of many"	9:28

ephapax ("once for all"):

"this he did once for all" (offered up himself)	7:27
"he entered once for all into the Holy Place"	9:12
"through the offering of the body of Jesus Christ once for all"	10:10

Study Questions

1. Discuss the superiority of the Melchizedekian priesthood.

2. Discuss the consequence of a change from the Levitical priesthood.

3. Discuss Jesus' qualifications for high priesthood and the benefits brought forward by it.

The second contrast is between "the law" and "the word of the oath." The law is what establishes the Levitical priesthood, with its succession of high priests. As our author has already pointed out in his exposition of Psalm 110:4, the appointment of Christ as a priest according to the order of Melchizedek was with the word of an oath (7:20–21). That word "came later than the law," and thus supersedes the law. Everything points to the superiority of the Son and his work as high priest. The reference to the Son "made perfect forever" has in view the completion or fulfillment of God's purposes, as it typically does in Hebrews.

By its appeal to the mysterious priest Melchizedek, who was greater even than Abraham, the somewhat technical chapter 7 explains the high priesthood of Jesus Christ. Psalm 110:4 is what makes the argument possible. The one who has ascended to sit at God's right hand according to the first verse of that psalm is in the fourth verse declared by an oath of God to be a priest forever according to the order of Melchizedek. This has a number of ramifications that are worked out by our author. But the centerpiece is the work of Christ

Further Reading

Cockerill, G. L. "Melchizedek or 'King of Righteousness.'" *Evangelical Quarterly* 63 (1991): 305–12.

Culpepper, R. H. "The High Priesthood and Sacrifice of Christ in the Epistle to the Hebrews." *Theological Educator* 32 (1985): 46–62.

Demarest, B. *A History of the Interpretation of Hebrews 7,1–10 from the Reformation to the Present Day.* Tübingen: Mohr, 1976.

———. "Hebrews 7:3, A *Crux Interpretum* Historically Considered." *Evangelical Quarterly* 49 (1977): 141–62.

Ellingworth, P. "'Like the Son of God': Form and Content in Hebrews 7,1–10." *Biblica* 64 (1983): 255–62.

Fitzmyer, J. A. "Now This Melchizedek . . . (Heb. 7,1)." *Catholic Biblical Quarterly* 25 (1963): 305–21.

Horton, F. L., Jr., *The Melchizedek Tradition: A Critical Examination of the Sources to the Fifth Century* A.D. *and in the Epistle to the Hebrews.* Society for New Testament Studies Monograph Series 30. Cambridge: Cambridge University Press, 1976.

Longenecker, R. N. "The Melchizedek Argument of Hebrews." In *Unity and Diversity in New Testament Theology*, ed. R. A. Guelich. Grand Rapids: Eerdmans, 1978. Pp. 161–85.

Neyrey, J. H. "'Without Beginning of Days or End of Life' (Hebrews 7:3): Topos for a True Deity." *Catholic Biblical Quarterly* 53 (1991): 439–55.

Paul, M. J. "The Order of Melchizedek (Ps 110:4 and Heb 7:3)." *Westminster Journal of Theology* 49 (1987): 195–211.

Rooke, D. W. "Jesus as Royal Priest: Reflections on the Interpretation of the Melchizedek Tradition in Heb 7." *Biblica* 81 (2000): 81–94.

Thompson, J. W. "The Conceptual Background and Purpose of the Midrash in Hebrews VII." *Novum Testamentum* 19 (1977): 209–23.

Key Terms

type
guarantee
cognate

as high priest in the accomplishing of the atonement upon which our salvation depends. Our author, as we have come to expect, does not fail to draw out some practical significance: "Jesus has become the guarantee of a better covenant. . . . Therefore he is able to save forever those who come to God through him, because he always lives to intercede for them. Such a high priest meets our need" (vv. 22, 25–26). The foundation is now laid for chapters 8–10.

8 The New and Better Covenant

The New Covenant is not only better, and founded upon better promises than the Old; but, yet more, it supersedes the Old. The characteristics of the New Covenant, and the very name which it bears, point to the abrogation of that which has now become "the old."

—B. F. Westcott, *Commentary on the Epistle to the Hebrews*

Supplemental Reading

Exodus 25; Mark 13:1–2; 2 Corinthians 3

Outline

- **The High Priest of the True Tent (Tabernacle) (8:1–6)**
- **The Promise of a New Covenant and Its Implications for the Old (8:7–13)**

Objectives

1. Explain the dualism of the earthly and the heavenly temples.
2. Describe the content of the new covenant according to Jeremiah.
3. Elaborate on the implications of the new covenant for the old covenant.

New and better things have come to us in Christ—new compared to the old, better compared to inferior. This is one of the main themes of Hebrews, and we have already encountered it more than once. Now the theme is daringly expressed in the new language of earthly, shadowy copies of heavenly, eternal realities. Again we should remind ourselves of how radical this must have sounded to Jewish ears in the first century. It sounds no less radical and unacceptable to Jews today. Christianity is the fulfillment of Judaism, and thus brings the former realities to an end. But it does so—and this is exceptionally important—not by turning its back on the old, but by taking it up and bringing it to its divinely in-

tended purpose. The result is that it is the rightful perpetuation of the old. That can be said, however, only when one accepts the truth of the new—something that is a given for our author and for all Christians of the first generation.

The High Priest of the True Tent (Tabernacle) (8:1–6)

Our author now attempts to restate what he believes concerning Christ as high priest. He comes to the main point of what he has to say as he begins an exposition of the priestly work of Jesus that will continue through chapter 10. Jesus is an incomparable high priest (an allusion to Ps 110:4) who has ascended to heaven, where he sits at the right hand of God (an allusion to Ps 110:1; cf. 1:3, 13; 4:14), and there "serves in the sanctuary, the true tabernacle set up by the Lord, not by man" (v. 2). Here, the word "serves" indicates one who performs priestly duties, in particular a priest who works in "the holies" (the tabernacle, Israel's tent shrine). "True tabernacle" points to the "heavenly sanctuary," the archetype that will be alluded to in verse 5, according to which Moses constructed the tent shrine. In view here is not an actual sanctuary in heaven in which Jesus offers his own blood (cf. 9:11–12). The language is not to be taken literally. Rather, it is a way of speaking that affirms the ultimate importance, efficacy, and finality of Christ's sacrificial death on the cross as the fulfillment of the earthly sacrifices of the tabernacle/temple. It is the divine reality ("set up by the Lord, not by man") of which the

The western wall, original to the Herodian temple, known as the Wailing Wall, an especially holy site for Judaism

covenant

dualism

polemic

earthly sacrifices were but anticipations and foreshadowings.

It is practically a definition of the work of a high priest to say that he "offers both gifts and sacrifices" (v. 3), indeed, "gifts prescribed by the law" (v. 4). And so it is necessary that the priest Jesus also "have something to offer" (v. 3). Our author has already indicated that Jesus "offered up himself" (7:27), but soon he will elaborate this central point in considerable detail (chs. 9–10). But before he comes to that, he stresses how the sacrificial ritual of the old **covenant** was preparatory to the new covenant realities that have come in Christ. Thus, there is no longer a need for priests in the earthly sanctuary to offer their repeated, and hence ineffectual, sacrifices (7:27; 10:11). The work of Jesus as priest was not a part of the existing earthly sacrificial system. Therefore, our author can say that on earth, "he would not be a priest at all" (v. 4). His priestly work,

by startling contrast, was accomplished in the heavenly, or finally effective, realm, of which the earthly was but "a copy and shadow" (v. 5). The last point is established by the quotation of Exodus 25:40, where Moses is commanded to construct the tabernacle by carefully following the pattern that was shown to him on the mountain. Much debate has centered on this distinctive line of argument in Hebrews, with many scholars concluding that the author was influenced by the metaphysical **dualism** of Platonic philosophy. Despite the similarity of the language, however, our author more likely works in the framework not of metaphysical dualism, but of a temporal dualism that points from the preparatory to the finally perfect (see the sidebar "Dualism in Hebrews: Metaphysical or Temporal?").

At this point, our author cannot resist stressing the significance of what he has been saying for the

Why Does Hebrews Refer to the Tabernacle Rather Than the Temple?

Hebrews refers consistently to the "tent" ("tabernacle") rather than to the "temple," a word not used by our author. The word "tent" in this sense, though very common in the Pentateuch, occurs elsewhere in the New Testament only in Acts 7:44. The "tent" refers to the portable tent shrine that was the center of Israel's religious life from the Sinai experience until Solomon built the first permanent structure that we call the "temple." This tent shrine was the prototype of

the Jerusalem temple.

Our author refers to the tabernacle rather than the temple because the tabernacle was the original earthly manifestation of the sacrificial ritual of the old covenant (cf. 9:1–10). It was the tabernacle that was set up according to the command of God (8:5). But since the Jerusalem temple was the contemporary counterpart to the wilderness tabernacle, criticism of the latter was also implicit criticism of the former. This could not have been missed by any of the

original readers. The sacrificial ritual of the temple was no more effectual than that of the tent shrine.

It is worth noting that the work of the high priest and other priests is very often described using present tenses. This may suggest the contemporaneity of the author's **polemic**, but cannot be used to support a pre-70 date for Hebrews. The work of the priests often is described using present tenses long after the destruction of the Jerusalem temple (e.g., *1 Clement*).

Dualism in Hebrews: Metaphysical or Temporal?

The dualism that we encounter in the reference to the earthly sanctuary and sacrifices as "a copy and shadow" of the "true" or "heavenly" realities that exist in heaven (8:2–5; 9:23–25; 10:1) sounds very much like that of the Greek philosopher Plato, who argued that earthly objects are the particular manifestations of perfect and eternal "ideas" or "forms" that cannot be perceived by the senses but known only through the intellect. This dualism between matter and idea/form was widely influential in the Hellenistic world. It is found extensively in the writings of Philo, a first-century Hellenistic Jew of Alexandria. This is one important reason for associating the author of Hebrews with Alexandria (hence, the plausibility of Apollos as possibly the author), where this Greek dualism appears to have been very popular. It has also been popular to infer the influence of Philo upon the author.

Certainly, our author's language reflects this widespread Greek dualism. At issue is whether he means the same thing by this language as was meant by Greek philosophy. This seems unlikely. When, for example, he refers to Christ as "a minister in the sanctuary and the true tent" (8:2), or more specifically, as entering "once for all into the Holy Place, taking not the blood of goats and calves but his own blood" (9:12; cf. 9:24), this is probably not meant to be taken literally. Rather, this way of speaking intends to point to the perfection and finality of Christ's sacrifice.

Indeed, our author has a perspective quite different from that of Philo and Platonic dualism. He thinks primarily in terms of historical sequence, and of promise and fulfillment. The comparison he wishes to make is not between earthly and metaphysical realities, but rather, between earlier and later, between preliminary and finally effective, realities.

Thus, the dualism that our author employs is a temporal dualism, and not a metaphysical dualism. It is not a vertical dualism, but a timeline dualism that involves a contrast between prophecy and fulfillment, between preparation or anticipation and finality.

Interestingly, Paul says something very similar concerning the Sabbath and dietary laws: "These are only a shadow of what is to come; but the substance belongs to Christ" (Col 2:17).

Further reading:

Hurst, L. D. "How 'Platonic' Are Heb. viii.5 and ix.23f.?" *Journal of Theological Studies,* n.s. 34 (1983): 156–68.

Williamson, R. "Platonism and Hebrews." *Scottish Journal of Theology* 16 (1963): 415–24.

———. *Philo and the Epistle to the Hebrews.* Leiden: Brill, 1970.

"first" or "old" covenant. And here our author is at his most revolutionary. The contrast between the work of the earthly priests and that of Christ indicates that Christ has received a ministry that is "as superior to theirs as the covenant of which he is mediator is superior to the old one" (v. 6). In view is the excellence of the new compared to the old, and the necessary conclusion that the new is better, as it is "founded on better promises" (v. 6). The point has already been made that Jesus is "the guarantee of a better covenant" (7:22), and he will be described specifically as "the mediator of a new covenant" in 9:15 and 12:24 (see the sidebar "Christ as the Mediator of the New Covenant" in chapter 9). We have here, then, a threefold superiority of the new to the old: a more excellent ministry, a superior covenant, and better promises (v. 6).

discontinuity

continuity

The Promise of a New Covenant and Its Implications for the Old (8:7–13)

The very fact of a second covenant itself suggests the inadequacy of the first. For if the first had been adequate, then why would there have been any need for a second? The logic is clear. In our author's language, the first covenant was not "faultless" (v. 7). Again, the highly subversive nature of what is said is noteworthy.

As with Paul's criticism of the law (see Rom 7:11–12), however, our author finds the real fault not so much with the covenant as with the people's failure. Thus, the pronoun "them" (NIV specifies "the people") in verse 8 is very important. What is blameworthy is not "it," the covenant, but "them," the people: "he finds fault with them." Nevertheless, it remains true that the old covenant was unable to bring the in-

tended salvation to God's people. Only here in the entire New Testament do we find the language of "first" and "second" in relation to the old and new covenants.

Given the high importance of Jeremiah 31:31–34 as an anticipation of all that arrives with Jesus, it is remarkable that in the New Testament this text is quoted only in Hebrews (although it is alluded to in a few places, such as Rom 2:15; 11:27; Jn 6:45). Through this quotation the very **discontinuity** that is our author's focus is shown to have been anticipated in the old itself. We should also note, however, that at the same time we are able to conclude that the new is actually part of a larger **continuity** within God's constant purposes. Jeremiah 31:31–34 is an ideal text for the author's purpose.

Although this Jeremiah text is well known, its importance makes it worth quoting in its entirety here, in the form in which our author presents it.

Torah scroll, kept by Jews in this form to revere God's covenant with Israel

The time is coming, declares the
    Lord,
        when I will make a new cove-
            nant
    with the house of Israel
        and with the house of Judah.
It will not be like the covenant
    I made with their forefathers
when I took them by the hand
    to lead them out of Egypt,
because they did not remain faith-
    ful to my covenant,
        and I turned away from them,
            declares the Lord.
This is the covenant I will make
        with the house of Israel
    after that time, declares the
        Lord.
I will put my laws in their minds
    and write them on their hearts.
I will be their God,
    and they will be my people.
No longer will a man teach his
        neighbor,
    or a man his brother, saying,
        "Know the Lord,"
because they will all know me,

from the least of them to the greatest.
For I will forgive their wickedness and will remember their sins no more.

Astonishingly, our author does not comment on the meaning of these lines, as he does so frequently in other instances. He will, of course, have occasion to comment on portions of the text that he quotes again (see the sidebar "Jeremiah 31:31–34 in Hebrews"). Probably, this was an exceptionally well-known passage of great importance to Jewish Christians, who needed little help in understanding how what they had come to believe was the fulfillment of the Jeremiah text.

To begin with, they would have thought of themselves as "the house of Israel" and "the house of Judah" (vv. 8–10) who had become the recipients of the promised new covenant. Undoubtedly, they would have perceived themselves as the righteous remnant of Israel (cf. Rom 11:5). We should note that Jeremiah recorded this prophecy at the gloomiest time in the history of the nation. The southern kingdom, Judah and Jerusalem, recently had fallen to the Babylonians as the result of the disobedience of the people. This failure already implies the weakness of the old covenant; it was never able to have its intended effect. But again, we must observe that the real fault was in the people: although God had delivered them from Egypt, "they did not remain faithful to my covenant" (v. 9).

The new covenant would be different: "not like the covenant that I made with their forefathers" (v. 9). The difference is made specific in three new elements: (1) "I will put my laws in their minds and write them on their hearts" (v. 10); (2) "they will all know me, from the least of them to the greatest" (v. 11); (3) "I will forgive their wickedness and will remember their sins no more" (v. 12). Clearly, the last of these three is the most significant for our author's purpose, and explains why his quotation extends to include it. Mercy and forgiveness depend finally on the death of Jesus as the one effectual sacrifice toward which all previous sacrifices pointed. This leads the author directly into the main argument of chapters 9–10.

The author appends a brief but revealing concluding comment on the Jeremiah passage (v. 13). Picking up the word "*new*" from the quotation, he concludes that the first covenant has been made old; that is, it has become "obsolete." But whereas Jeremiah looked to the future for the coming of the new, for the author and readers of Hebrews, the new had already arrived. Thus, the obsolescence of the old was all the more evident, and its end was bound to be near. The words "will soon disappear" may well be an allusion to Jesus' prophecy concerning the de-

Jeremiah 31:31–34 in Hebrews

The full quotation of this passage in 8:8–12 is foundational to the argument of important sections of chapters 9 and 10. Some of the same material is quoted in 10:16–17 (cf. 8:10ab; 8:12).

9:15 (allusion):

new covenant	Jeremiah 31:31 (Heb 8:8)
redemption from transgressions under the first covenant	Jeremiah 31:34 (Heb 8:12)

10:16–17 (quotation):

this is the covenant I will make with them	Jeremiah 31:33 (Heb 8:10)
I will put my laws upon their hearts and write them upon their minds	Jeremiah 31:33 (Heb 8:10)
I will remember their sins no longer	Jeremiah 31:34 (Heb 8:12)

The New Covenant in the New Testament

The words "new testament" and "new covenant" are alternate translations of the Greek words *kainē diathēkē*.

In addition to their occurrence in the quotation of Jeremiah 31:31 in 8:8 (cf. 8:13) and in 9:15 (cf. 12:24, but with a *nea*, a different word for "new"), the words are found in Luke 22:20; 1 Corinthians 11:25; 2 Corinthians 3:6 (cf. Gal 4:24). Of course, the "new covenant" is often in view in the New Testament in the single word "covenant" without any adjective (or with a different adjective, as in "eternal covenant" in 13:20, with which compare Jer 32:40).

Without question, the most important Old Testament anticipation of the new covenant is the announcement in Jeremiah 31:31–34. A second important anticipation, although with the adjective "everlasting" rather than "new," is found in Ezekiel 11:19–20; 16:60–63; 36:26–29; 37:26–28.

Key Terms

covenant
dualism
polemic
discontinuity
continuity

struction of the temple, known to the author and readers from oral tradition underlying the Synoptic Gospels (see Mk 13:1–2 and parallels). The word "soon" clearly seems to indicate that Hebrews was written before the destruction of the temple in A.D. 70. Was the Roman invasion of Jeru- salem already on the horizon when the author wrote?

The strong emphasis on discontinuity at the end of chapter 8 constitutes a theological, not a racial, argument. That is, in no way does it support anti-Semitic attitudes or actions. The author and readers would not have rejoiced to see the temple destroyed; indeed, for them it would have typified the horrific prospect of apocalyptic judgment. Nevertheless, they would have been alive to the theological implications of the end of the temple, and ready to draw them out in expounding the truth of their Christian faith.

It should be the cause of gratitude and rejoicing on the part of Gentile Christians that they are the recipients of the new covenant promised to Jeremiah. The new covenant rests squarely on the finished work of

Further Reading

Attridge, H. W. "The Uses of Antithesis in Hebrews 8–10." *Harvard Theological Review* 79 (1986): 1–9.

Kaiser, W. C. "The Old Promise and the New Covenant: Jeremiah 31:31–34." *Journal of the Evangelical Theological Society* 15 (1972): 11–23.

Lehne, S. *The New Covenant in Hebrews*. Journal for the Study of the New Testament Supple- ment Series 44. Sheffield: JSOT Press, 1990.

Omanson, R. L. "A Superior Covenant: Hebrews 8:1–10:18." *Review and Expositor* 82 (1985): 361–73.

Peterson, D. G. "The Prophecy of the New Covenant in the Argument of Hebrews." *Reformed Theological Review* 38 (1979): 74–81.

Study Questions

1. How does the author of Hebrews contrast the earthly and the heavenly temples?

2. Discuss the superiority of the new covenant to the old.

3. What purpose does the discontinuity of the Jeremiah quotation have for the author of Hebrews?

Christ, who is the mediator of that covenant (v. 6). With the establishment of the new covenant through the death of Christ, the universal purposes of God—already expressed in the Abrahamic covenant (Gn 12:3)—and the election of Israel to be a light to the nations (Is 42:6) come to their realization. The church, consisting of Jews and Gentiles, depends for its existence upon the reality of the new covenant.

9 Christ the Definitive Sacrifice

The symbolism of the high priesthood and sacrifice of Jesus in the heavenly sanctuary is therefore designed to convey the truth that the relations of men with God are based finally upon Jesus Christ.

> —J. Moffatt, *A Critical and Exegetical Commentary on the Epistle to the Hebrews*

Supplemental Reading

Exodus 24:3–8; Leviticus 5:5–13; Romans 3:21–26

Outline

- The Sacrificial Ritual of the First Covenant (9:1–10)
- The Definitive Work of Christ the High Priest (9:11–14)
- Christ as Mediator of the New Covenant (9:15–22)
- The Single Sacrifice of Christ as the Final Answer to Sin (9:23–28)

Objectives

1. Discuss the sacrificial system of the Old Testament.
2. Show how the unique sacrifice of Christ is parallel to and the fulfillment of the former sacrifices.
3. Explore the idea of Christ as the mediator of the new covenant.

Only with great difficulty can we imagine what the fully functioning temple must have been like, with its elaborate rituals, its sizable corps of priests, the crowds, the continual sacrifice of large numbers of animals, the associated blood and gore. It was an enormous enterprise that dominated the city of Jerusalem, not only at the times of the great pilgrimage festivals, but also on ordinary days. Was there any ultimate meaning to it all? Was it of self-contained importance, or did it point beyond itself to something yet to come?

Our author now comes to the very heart of his exposition, in which he further draws out the parallels between the repeated sacrifices of the tabernacle and the single, efficacious sacrifice of Christ (cf. 7:23–27). He does so by depending on the descriptions provided in the Books of Exodus and Leviticus.

The Sacrificial Ritual of the First Covenant (9:1–10)

In order to set the sacrifice of Christ in context, our author presents an overview of the sacrificial ritual of

The Tabernacle, the Priesthood, and the Sacrifices: Lessons on God's Holiness

An amazing amount of space in Exodus and Leviticus is devoted to detailed instructions concerning precisely how the tabernacle was to be constructed, what it was to contain, and so forth. Everything was to be done in a particular way. A special class of priests was to be established, the type of vestments they were to wear was specified, the manner in which sacrifices were to be offered was stipulated, and particular instructions concerning ritual defilement and purification are listed. After the instructions are presented, the detailed account of their implementation is given, with repetition of the same language.

All of this concentration on detail may strike us as arbitrary and perhaps even in-significant. Why is it there in the Torah? From our perspective, there are at least two major lessons to learn from this material. The tabernacle/temple was built to symbolize the presence of God in the midst of Israel: "Have them make a sanctuary for me, and I will dwell among them" (Ex 25:8). The separation of the Holy of Holies from the Holy Place by a curtain, and the limited entry to the former by the high priest on one day in the year, point to the total otherness of God. Just as no one can see God and live, one cannot simply come into God's presence in the way one comes into the presence of any other person. This is the thrice-holy, sovereign and almighty God, Creator of all that exists, before whom no one can come and stand at will. Second, since human beings are sinners, they may not enter the presence of God with empty hands. Sacrifices of atonement carefully offered in the specified ways are required of sinful beings. Even these must be mediated by priests, not brought directly.

These are basic lessons to be learned from this kind of material. What is so striking about Hebrews, and other parts of the New Testament, is that the language used for these things becomes spiritualized and is readily applied to the Christian believer. Now that Christ has accomplished his definitive atoning work, we have bold access into God's very presence; we ourselves may now draw near and offer spiritual sacrifices.

The Mercy Seat of the Ark of the Covenant as the Place of Atonement

The centerpiece in the Holy of Holies was the ark of the covenant. The high priest entered the Holy of Holies once a year to sprinkle blood on the golden lid of the ark to make atonement for the sins of the people. The lid was called in Hebrew *kapporeth*, from the verb *kpr*, which may mean "to cover," as with a lid, and then metaphorically "to cover sin." More probably, however, the verb means "to make atonement." There also is a cognate noun, *koper*, which means "ransom." The same root is found in Yom Kippur, the Day of Atonement. The Septuagint regularly translates the noun with the word *hilastērion*, which comes into the New Testament at the two important passages of Romans 3:25 and Hebrews 9:5.

The translation of this word in the New Testament has been controversial. The KJV, following Tyndale, translates it as "mercy seat," and this in turn depends upon Luther's translation of the word as *Gnadenstuhl*, or "seat of grace." The idea of a seat, however, is an importation not related to the word. What is meant is "place of atonement."

In Romans 3:25 Christ is declared to be our *hilastērion*, and this prompts the NIV to translate the word as "sacrifice of atonement"— not the place of atonement, but the sacrifice itself. Considerable debate about the meaning of the word took place between C. H. Dodd, who argued that the word meant **expiation**, a removal of the guilt of sin, and Leon Morris, who argued that it meant **propitiation**, the appeasing of the anger of God. The KJV and NASB translate the word as "propitiation," and the RSV and NAB as "expiation." Since both ideas are probably correct, one can do no better than to translate the word "sacrifice of atonement," as do the NIV and NRSV. The word in Hebrews 9:5, on the other hand, is best translated as "place of atonement" (NAB: "place of expiation"), although surprisingly, some translations keep the traditional "mercy seat" of the KJV (NASB, RSV, NRSV). The current version of the NIV uses the strange combination "atonement cover," which replaces the original NIV translation, "the place of atonement."

What is important to notice is that for both Paul and the author of Hebrews, the death of Christ corresponds to the sprinkling of blood on the lid of the ark in the Holy of Holies by the high priest on one day in the year. The ideas have come together, the work of the high priest foreshadowing the work of Christ.

expiation

propitiation

the Old Testament. This brief review of the "regulations for worship" under the old covenant begins with a description of the physical setting of the tabernacle (the tent shrine that was later replaced by the temple structure). The tabernacle was built according to the instructions found in Exodus 25–26. One large tent was divided into two parts, an outer and an inner tent, the former called the "Holy Place" and the latter the "Holy of Holies," separated by a curtain. The Holy Place was the location of daily activity of the priests, while the Holy of Holies was entered but one day of the year (Yom Kippur, the Day of Atonement), and only by the high priest himself (Leviticus 16). The various furnishings mentioned would have been lost when the first temple was destroyed in 587 B.C. The "ark of the covenant" (vv. 4–5) in the Holy of Holies, the most important of its furnishings, contained items related to the foundational episodes in Israel's history, commemorating especially the exodus and the giving of the law

Shekinah

at Sinai. Of the greatest significance was the lid of the ark, traditionally called the "mercy seat," upon which the high priest sprinkled blood to make atonement for sins on the Day of Atonement (Leviticus 16). The NIV translates the Greek word *hilastērion* as "atonement cover." The word refers to the place of atonement and occurs again in the New Testament only in Romans 3:25 (for the cognate verb, see Heb 2:17; Lk 18:13), where Paul refers to Christ as a *hilastērion*, translated as "sacrifice of atonement" (NIV, NRSV). The mention of the "cherubim of glory" (v. 5) probably alludes to the **Shekinah** glory that symbolized the presence of God (hence, NIV: "cherubim of the Glory"; cf. Lv 16:2; Ex 40:34–35). The place of atonement can only be in the very presence of God.

The repetitive work of the priests (v. 6) as well as the requirement that the high priest offer blood for the forgiveness of his own sins (v. 7; cf. 5:3; 7:27) points to the intrinsic ineffectiveness of the arrangements of the old covenant. A further limitation of the old system is that it covered only unintentional sins, those "committed in ignorance" (v. 7; cf. Lv 4:2, 13, 22, 27; Nm 15:27–29), and thus by implication it was not as comprehensive as the forgiveness available through Christ.

The Holy Spirit (v. 8) has a lesson to teach the church in all of this. That lesson has to do with the ineffectiveness of the sacrificial system of the old covenant and the contrasting effectiveness of the sacrifice of Christ. The arrangements of the old system could not open the way into the sanctuary. Here, the Greek text refers literally to "the holies," i.e., "the holy place," but it is clear that the Holy of Holies is meant (hence, NIV: "Most Holy Place")—that is, the very presence of God. Nor could the old system accomplish a lasting atonement, as is indicated by the necessarily repetitious nature of the sacrifices. The irony is that the very constitution of the old system thus had built-in signs of its ineffectiveness; and the implication is that it was meant to point to something yet to come, something that would be powerfully effective. Our author regards this situation as an "illustration" (literally, "parable") of the present era (v. 9), by which he means his own day, when, presumably, the temple was still standing (cf. v. 8) and able to function. The sacrificial ritual of the temple, by its very nature—its inherent limitations—pointed beyond itself to something yet to come. And for our author and his first readers, that awaited reality had now come in the form of the Messiah, God's Son, whose death ac-

A diagram of the construction of the tabernacle/ temple, showing the degrees of access to the Holy of Holies

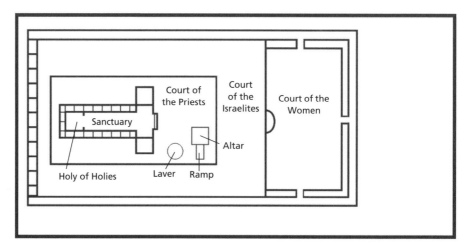

A model of the ark of the covenant with the cherubim overshadowing the mercy seat

complished the effectual atonement to which the temple sacrifices could only point.

But the heart of the failure of the old system to accomplish what was needed is its inability to cleanse the inner person, "the conscience of the worshiper" (v. 9). This may be regarded as an aspect of salvation, and nearly interchangeable with it. To "perfect the conscience" (RSV, NRSV) is, in keeping with the meaning of the verb "to perfect" in Hebrews, to bring it to fulfillment, or its intended goal: the full salvation of the person.

Our author most closely approaches a polemic concerning the law in verse 10. The laws concerning food, drink, and ritual washings are familiar from the Torah. These "ceremonial" laws, like the sacrifices, deal more with the outer than the inner, more with the external than the essential. Furthermore, these regulations were only temporary until the time when the new would come (cf. Col 2:16–17), "the time of the new order," or more literally, "until the time comes to set things right" (NRSV). This line of thought is not far from Paul's perspective on the law (cf. Gal 3:23–25; Rom 7:6; 10:4). The new

order is a "reformation" (NASB). As F. F. Bruce puts it, a "'reformation' in the sense of 'reconstruction'; the coming of Christ involved a complete reshaping of the structure of Israel's religion" (*Epistle to the Hebrews*, 211).

The Definitive Work of Christ the High Priest (9:11–14)

Our author now stresses the great differences between the work of the priests under the regimen of the old covenant and the priestly work of Christ. In this way the superiority of the latter becomes increasingly clear. All is related to the new era, the time referred to in verse 10, that has dawned with the coming of the Christ. Although some manuscripts refer in verse 11 to the good things "about to come," the oldest and best manuscripts have the past tense: the good things "that have come." This reference to the present experience of salvation is consonant with the emphasis in Hebrews on realized eschatology (as in 1:2, and especially 12:18–24).

Christ's work of atonement is definitive. This is the point of the language concerning the "greater and more perfect tent" that is not a part of the created order (v. 11) and the "Holy Place" referred to in verse 12. This is symbolic language, precisely as in 8:2 and 8:5, and again in 9:24, and does not indicate a literal temple in heaven. On the contrary, this is our author's way of referring to the ultimate and all-sufficient atonement accomplished by Christ. This definitive atonement could not be made by the blood of animals, but only by the blood of Christ. The result is the shocking

The Contrast between the New and the Old in Hebrews

New	Old
the good things already here (9:11, 23–24; 10:1)	shadows, copies (8:5; 9:23; 10:1)
the greater and more perfect tent (9:11, 24)	the earthly sanctuary made with hands (9:1, 11, 24)
Christ entered the Holy of Holies once for all (9:12, 25–28; 10:1–3, 10–14)	priests enter sanctuary every day; high priest once a year (7:27; 9:7; 10:1)
Christ's own blood (9:12; 10:4–10)	the blood of goats and bulls (9:12, 18–22)
eternal salvation obtained (9:12; 10:14)	temporary cleansing that cannot perfect (9:9; 10:2, 11)
purifies the conscience (9:14–15)	takes away ritual uncleanness (9:13)
the consummation of the ages (9:26)	until the time of the reformation (9:10)

The Emphasis on the Eternal in Hebrews

A major theme in Hebrews is the contrast between the transitory and temporary character of the old covenant sacrificial system and the permanent, eternal character of what Christ has accomplished. The eternal is of great importance in the argument of the book, as can be seen in the following references:

Christ a priest forever	5:6; 6:20; 7:17, 21, 24
Christ continues forever	7:24
Christ the same yesterday, today, and forever	13:8
a Son made perfect forever	7:28
the eternal Spirit	9:14
eternal salvation	5:9
eternal redemption	9:12
eternal inheritance	9:15
eternal covenant	13:20

irony that in this instance the high priest comes bringing "his own blood" (v. 12). This high priest is *simultaneously the one who offers and the offering itself.* For this reason, the death of Christ was able to obtain not merely a temporary redemption, but an "eternal redemption," accomplished "once for all" (v. 12). It is important to note that this atonement was made on Calvary's cross, not subsequently in some literal heavenly sanctuary after Christ had passed into the heavens (4:14; 7:26).

Our author draws a further contrast between the cleansing from ritual uncleanness and the cleansing of the conscience, meaning the inner person. While the blood of goats and bulls (Lv 16:15–16) and the ashes of a heifer (Nm 19:9, 17–19) could accomplish an external cleansing, only the blood of Christ can purify the sinful heart, which is, after all, the real problem of the human race. Only where there is such inner cleansing does it become possible to "serve the living God" (v. 14). Christ was em-

covenant

will

powered by "the eternal Spirit" (i.e., the Holy Spirit, the agency of God's saving will) to offer himself up as a sacrifice "without blemish" (the language of the animal sacrifices, but here referring to Christ's sinlessness; cf. 4:15).

Christ as Mediator of the New Covenant (9:15–22)

By his atoning death, Christ has become the mediator of the new and better covenant (see the sidebar "Christ as the Mediator of the New Covenant"): that which had been promised in Jeremiah 31:31–34 (cf. 8:8–12). One of the most prominent aspects of the prophecy of Jeremiah is the promise of the forgiveness of sins (quoted in 8:12). The death of Christ is what makes the forgiveness of sins possible, specified here as "the trans-

gressions under the first covenant" (v. 15), in order again to underline the success of this sacrifice compared to the failure of the sacrifices of the old covenant (cf. 10:17–18). (Of course, the death of Christ atones for the sins of every era, including that of the new covenant.) The new covenant makes possible the receiving of "the promised eternal inheritance" (v. 15), words filled with special significance to Jewish readers, but finding their fulfillment not in a national-political entity, but in the church, "those who are called" (cf. 3:1).

The argument of verses 16–17 is possible because the Greek word *diathēkē* can mean either **"covenant"** or **"will,"** depending on the context. Our author now takes the word to mean "will." Paul made use of the same double meaning of the word in Galatians 3:15–17. The *will* of a person takes effect only upon the death of the person. Likewise, a *covenant* can be established only by blood, that is, by death—in the case of the first covenant by the death of animals, in

Christ as the Mediator of the New Covenant

A mediator is one who serves as a bridge between two individuals or groups, and one who therefore must have credibility with both sides, ideally by participation in some sense with both. Two offices of the Old Testament, those of prophet and priest, have a mediatorial character: the prophet represents God to humanity, the priest humanity to God. Both must do so, however, only as human beings, albeit with divine commissioning. We have noted that in the open-

ing lines of Hebrews, Christ serves as both prophet and priest. His humanity and deity make him ideally qualified to function as both. The combination of his full deity and full humanity is what enables him to give himself as the all-sufficient sacrifice that constitutes the very basis of the new covenant. It is for this reason, offering his own blood, that he is the mediator of that covenant (note the reference to Christ as the pioneer of our salvation in 2:10; cf. 12:2). With

the death of this mediator we have entered a new time frame in salvation history.

In addition to 9:15, Christ is referred to as mediator in 8:6 ("of a better covenant") and 12:24 ("of a new covenant"). The only other occurrence of the word in the New Testament is in 1 Timothy 2:5: "there is also one mediator between God and humankind, Christ Jesus, himself human, who gave himself a ransom for all."

the case of the new covenant by the death of God's Son.

Thus, when Moses had recited the commandments to the people, he took the blood of calves and goats (together with water) and sprinkled both the book and the people (v. 19, alluding to, e.g., Ex 24:3–8; Nm 19:18–19; Lv 8:15, 19). The accompanying announcement "This is the blood of the covenant which God has commanded you to keep" (v. 20; cf. Ex 24:8) has an authenticating effect. Just as the first covenant was ratified by blood, so also does the new covenant depend upon blood, but the blood of Christ, not of animals. Thus, Jesus speaks of the cup at the Last Supper saying, "This is my blood of the covenant, which is poured out for many for the forgiveness of sins" (Mt 26:28). Our author notes that "without the shedding of blood there is no forgiveness" (v. 22). The importance of blood in this regard can be seen from Leviticus 17:11: "For the life of a creature is in the blood, and I have given it to you to make atonement for yourselves on the altar; it is the blood that makes atonement for one's life."

The tabernacle itself and the implements within it also were cleansed by blood (v. 21). Indeed, so central is blood to purification, according to the Scriptures, that this becomes a governing principle, and one could say that practically everything is cleansed by blood (v. 22). The only exceptions would be the offerings allowed for those too poor to present the usual sacrifice—for example, flour, pigeons, incense.

The Single Sacrifice of Christ as the Final Answer to Sin (9:23–28)

This summarizing section repeats the main points made in verses 11–14, the repetition indicating their importance to the author (v. 24 corresponds to v. 11, and vv. 25–26 to v. 12). The purification by the blood of animals spoken of in the immediately preceding verses was required of the earthly things that were but copies of the heavenly realities (a point already made in 8:5; cf. 10:1). But as for the heavenly realities themselves, something better was required: not more

The Meaning of "Many" as Those Benefiting from Christ's Work

The word "many" in 9:28 should not be taken literally as limiting the scope of Christ's atoning death, as though some were not meant to be included in its benefit. This is unmistakably clear from this statement in 2:9: "so that by the grace of God he might taste death for everyone [hyper pan-

tos]." The word "many" probably is to be explained by its occurrence in Isaiah 53:12, "he bore the sin of many," a passage understood in the early church as referring to Christ. Depending on the context, "many" is a Semitic expression that can mean "all." Thus, for example, "many" in Mark

10:45 very probably should be understood as meaning "all" (cf. 2 Cor 5:14–15; 1 Tm 2:6). The point is strikingly clear when the "many" of Romans 5:15 and 19 is compared with the parallel statement referring to "all" in Romans 5:18.

or different animal sacrifices, but, as the author will make clear in the following verses, the single, once-for-all sacrifice of Christ (despite the plural "sacrifices" in v. 23, which is the result of the formal parallel). As we have already seen, the original sacrificial system of the old covenant was temporary, and was designed to foreshadow the single sacrifice that alone could accomplish effective atonement.

Christ did not enter any earthly (literally, "handmade") temple to accomplish his priestly work. The earthly temple was a mere copy, an "antitype" (a different word than "copy" in 8:5, but with the same meaning) of the real one. He entered heaven itself, into the very presence of God (v. 24). This again is the author's way of pointing to the definitive and final character of Christ's atoning death on the cross. In God's presence Christ now continues his mediatorial work on our behalf ("for us"; cf. 7:25). As our author never tires of telling us, Christ's sacrifice

by its very nature was a one-time event, not a repeated sacrifice (contrast "again and again" in v. 25), not every day, not even every year, as in the case of the high priests. Verse 26 adds interesting time aspects, referring to the two termini of creation's history: the foundation of the world and the consummation of the ages. This is the argument: Since Christ brings his own blood to make atonement, his own death is a requirement. But that death (the meaning of "suffer" here) cannot be repeated, let alone repeated from the beginning, as would be necessary if salvation were dependent on *his repeated* sacrifice. Death, after all, comes to human beings only once (v. 27; cf. Gn 3:19). Instead, Christ came once

Key Terms

expiation	covenant
propitiation	will
Shekinah	

Further Reading

Campbell, K. M. "Covenant or Testament? Heb. 9:16, 17 Reconsidered." *Evangelical Quarterly* 44 (1972): 107–11.

Cody, A. *Heavenly Sanctuary and Liturgy in the Epistle to the Hebrews: The Achievement of Salvation in the Epistle's Perspective.* St. Meinrad, Ind.: Grail, 1960.

Graystone, K. "Salvation Proclaimed: III. Hebrews 9:11–14." *Expository Times* 93 (1982): 164–68.

Hughes, J. J. "Hebrews ix 15ff. and Galatians iii 15ff.: A Study in Covenant Practice and Procedure." *Novum Testamentum* 21 (1979): 27–96.

Selby, G. S. "The Meaning and Function of *Syneidesis* in Hebrews 9 and 10." *Restoration Quarterly* 28 (1985–86): 145–54.

Stanley, S. "Hebrews 9:6–10: The 'Parable' of the Tabernacle." *Novum Testamentum* 37 (1995): 385–99.

Swetnam, J. "A Suggested Interpretation of Hebrews 9,15–18." *Catholic Biblical Quarterly* 27 (1965): 373–90.

———. "'The Greater and More Perfect Tent': A Contribution to the Discussion of Hebrews 9,11." *Biblica* 47 (1966): 91–106.

———. "Hebrews 9,2 and the Uses of Consistency." *Catholic Biblical Quarterly* 32 (1970): 205–21.

Thompson, J. "Hebrews 9 and Hellenistic Concepts of Sacrifice." *Journal of Biblical Literature* 98 (1979): 567–78.

Young, N. H. "The Gospel According to Hebrews 9." *New Testament Studies* 27 (1981): 198–210.

Study Questions

1. Discuss some of the details of the sacrificial system of the Old Testament and how they are relevant to Hebrews.

2. Compare and contrast the work of the priests under the old covenant and the priestly work of Christ.

3. Compare and contrast the sacrifices of the old covenant and the single sacrifice of Christ.

for all to do away with sin permanently by his single sacrifice. This saving event accomplished by the coming of the Messiah, God's Son, brings us to the consummation of the ages, the dawning of the eschato-logical era we have now entered (cf. 1:2; 1 Cor 10:11).

The reference to the appointed death of humans brings with it the thought of judgment. The prospect of the judgment that awaits all in turn sharpens the universal need of salvation. The final verse of the chapter offers welcome comfort. It is precisely because Christ in his single sacrifice was able to bear the sins of "many" (a Semitic expression connoting "all") that he can appear bringing salvation. He no longer needs to bear sin. That has finally been accomplished for all time on the cross. But he will come "a second time" to bring salvation in its fullness and perfection to those who eagerly wait for him (cf. Phil 3:20; 2 Tm 4:8). That will be the time for the harvesting of the fruit already won by Christ. This thought reconfirms the finality and sufficiency of Christ's work on Calvary.

10A Moving from the Imperfect to the Perfect

10:1–18

In this one and (in this respect) unique passage of Scripture [10:5–7], the unsatisfactory nature of the legal sacrifices, and their impotence to effect any real reconciliation between God and man, is set in the clearest contrast with the personal self-oblation of Christ, in its infinite power to accomplish the divine will by effecting that reconciliation.

—F. J. Delitzsch,
The Epistle to the Hebrews

Supplemental Reading

Exodus 29:38–46; Leviticus 16:1–22; Matthew 9:10–13

Outline

- **What the Old Covenant Sacrifices Could Not Do (10:1–4)**
- **The Old Replaced by the New according to Psalm 40 (10:5–10)**
- **The Perfect Offering That Establishes and Fulfills the New Covenant (10:11–18)**

Objectives

1. Summarize the heart of the argument of Hebrews.
2. Explain the quotation and midrashic interpretation of Psalm 40:6–8.
3. Comment on the sacrifice of Christ as the fulfillment of Jeremiah's new covenant.

forgiveness

It is no accident that the cross became the chief symbol of Christianity. Christ's sacrificial death on the cross is the very essence of the new covenant and the Christian faith, and the decisive turning point between the old and the new. It is the fulfillment of all that preceded, and brings us to a new stage—indeed, a turning point—in salvation history. Stepping back from the complicated argument of the preceding chapters, can we put it all together in a bottom-line statement to say where we are? This our author now seems eager to do for us. The first part of chapter 10, up through verse 18, concludes the central discourse section and expresses the very heart of the Book of Hebrews. The section functions as a summarizing conclusion and repeats several of the main points made in the preceding sections. The only new material is found in verses 5–10, as we will see, but it too is used to make familiar points.

What the Old Covenant Sacrifices Could Not Do (10:1–4)

These verses repeat what is already familiar to us from previous passages such as 8:1–7 and 9:23–26. The point is reiterated that "the law"—that is, the old covenant's sacrificial system—was not of self-standing or independent importance, but only a "shadow" (so too 8:5; cf. Col 2:17) of "the good things that are coming" (and have now come—the future idea is from the perspective of the old, not that of our writer [cf. 9:11]). It did not have the reality or substance of that which it adumbrated. This is clear from the neces-

sity of the same sacrifices being offered repeatedly, year after year (cf. "day after day" in 7:27). That very repetition points to their incompleteness and inability to provide an effectual, lasting remedy to the problem of human sin. As our author loves to put it, those sacrifices could not "make perfect"—in the sense, as we have seen, of bringing to a full salvation, a full "cleansing"—those who would draw near to God's presence. On the contrary, the sacrifices of the old system actually served as painful reminders of the ongoing failure. Given the whole picture provided by our author, that failure should come as no surprise, however, since this old covenant system always had been intended as preparation, and never as an end in itself. Thus, the metaphor of shadow, in the sense of the shadow of something approaching, in a shape similar to the concrete, closely related to it yet vastly different, is especially suitable.

The author now comes to the most basic affirmation in light of his argument, a conclusion familiar and sensible to us, but new and shocking to the participants in the sacrificial system of the old covenant: "It is impossible for the blood of bulls and goats to take away sins" (v. 4). This impossibility is what explains the fundamental weakness and failure of the old covenant. The statement is set forth as a timeless principle. Animal sacrifices never did and never could provide the answer to sin: this means that the once-for-all sacrifice of Christ covers the entire time span from the fall to the eschaton. In other words, the **forgiveness** of sins in any era—past, present, or future—depends solely upon Christ's atoning death. Its effects reach back in time as well as forward into the future. Christ's death, and Christ's death alone, is the means of forgiveness for sinners and their reconciliation to God.

128

The Insufficiency of the Temple Sacrifices according to the Old Testament

It is interesting that long before the New Testament era there was a consciousness that the sacrifices were not the be-all and end-all of human relationship with God. A number of Old Testament passages seem to point this out.

"Sacrifice and offering you do not desire.... Burnt offering and sin offering you have not required" (Ps 40:6).

"For you have no delight in sacrifice; if I were to give a burnt offering, you would not be pleased" (Ps 51:16).

"What to me is the multitude of your sacrifices? says the LORD; I have had enough of burnt offerings of rams and the fat of fed beasts; I do not delight in the blood of bulls, or of lambs, or of goats" (Is 1:11).

"For I desire steadfast love and not sacrifice, the knowledge of God rather than burnt offerings" (Hos 6:6).

"I hate, I despise your festivals, and I take no delight in your solemn assemblies. Even though you offer me your burnt offerings and grain offerings, I will not accept them; and the offerings of well-being of your fatted animals I will not look upon" (Am 5:21–22).

"With what shall I come before the LORD . . . ? Shall I come before him with burnt offerings, with calves a year old? Will the LORD be pleased with thousands of rams, with ten thousands of rivers of oil? . . . What does the LORD require of you but to do justice, and to love kindness, and to walk humbly with your God?" (Mi 6:6–8).

The point of these passages is not that God is displeased with the sacrifices themselves, which, after all, he had commanded in the first place, but that the sacrifices alone, unaccompanied by lives lived in accordance with his will, were of no use; indeed, they were an insult to God. After the destruction of the temple in A.D. 70, when the Jews no longer could engage in animal sacrifices, Judaism took comfort in these passages, arguing that forgiveness was available by means of repentance and prayer alone. For the author of Hebrews, however, animal sacrifices were in principle ineffective, and now were no longer needed because the sacrifice of Christ replaced them.

But a lesson may be learned by Christians also from the above passages. No New Testament writer, including the author of Hebrews, would tolerate a dependence upon the sacrifice of Christ by persons whose lives in basic ways contradicted the will of God.

---

sacrifice

offering

The Old Replaced by the New according to Psalm 40 (10:5–10)

In an absolutely brilliant piece of christological interpretation, our author now finds in Psalm 40:6–8 the very point of his argument: the failure of the old and the corresponding successful achievement of Christ. Again the author offers a midrashic commentary (using the actual words of the passage) on the quoted passage to bring out its meaning for the readers (vv. 8–10).

Structurally, the quotation from the Septuagint version of Psalm 40:6–8 has an ABAB pattern:

A: **Sacrifice** and **offering** you did not desire,
B: but a body you prepared for me;
A: with burnt offerings and sin offerings you were not pleased.
B: Then I said, "Here I am—it is written about me in the scroll—I have come to do your will, O God."

As typically the case in the early Christian reading of the psalms, the

Depiction of the ark of the covenant during transport in the wilderness, from the synagogue ruin at Capernaum

passage is understood christologically; Christ is taken to be the speaker of these words ("when he [Christ] came into the world" [v. 5]), and he speaks to God. This understanding of Psalm 40:6–8 may be original to our author or it may have been one shared among other early Christians (although no other New Testament texts allude to the passage). Whether it was his own discovery or not, our author must have been thrilled to find that the basic contrast of his principal argument was to be seen in the A and B elements of the psalm passage.

The A elements indicate that the sacrifices were neither desired by nor pleasing to God. This indirectly confirms our author's argument that the sacrifices of the old system were ineffectual because they were unable to accomplish atonement and the forgiveness of sins.

The first B element, according to the Septuagint, "a body [sōma] you prepared for me," jumped out at our author as a reference to the incarnation of Christ. The full, physical humanity of Jesus is a particularly important point for Hebrews, since it enables him to be high priest; but more than that, it makes possible his death and hence our salvation, as we have already seen (cf. 2:9, 14, 17). Here, the Septuagint appears to be an interpretation of the Hebrew, which reads literally, "ears you have dug

for me." Most translations (including KJV, NASB, RSV) of this line of Hebrew in Psalm 40:6 take the words in the sense of the NRSV's "you have given me an open ear"—that is, able to hear and thus obey. The Septuagint translators, however, took the words as an allusion to the creation of Adam's body, which, being fashioned by God out of clay, would have required the digging out of the ears, as in the making of a sculpture. The words were highly appropriate when put into the mouth of the incarnate Christ: "a body you prepared for me." Christ could not have fulfilled the will of God—explicitly, he could not have died—without a body.

The second B element also contains material that fits Christ well. The words constitute a well-known formula of response to God's call. Christ is obedient to God's will, though that will lead him to the cross. What is "written about me in the scroll" probably was taken by our author as referring to what stood written in the Scriptures, as, for example, in Isaiah 53. At the least it implies the complete fulfillment of what God has ordained.

In verses 8–10 our author, as he so much likes to do, provides midrashic commentary, explaining his understanding of the passage. In verse 8 he combines the two A elements, using actual words of the citation in slightly different order. To these he adds the simple explanatory words "which are *offered* according to the law" (NASB). Against these he juxtaposes the second B element in abbreviated form (v. 9), and then sharpens the discontinuity by indicating that Christ "abolishes the first in order to establish the second" (cf. 7:18–19; 8:7, 13). This radical idea is already familiar to the readers, but is explained further in verse 10: "By this *will* we have been sanctified through the *offering* of the *body* of Jesus Christ once for all" (NASB, italicized words drawn from the quotation).

A four-horned altar of sacrifice from Beersheba

In Psalm 40, then, our author has found precisely the contrast he has been making in the preceding sections of the book. The one, all-sufficient sacrifice of the incarnate Christ has forever outmoded and replaced the animal sacrifices of the old covenant. Only this sacrifice can "sanctify" us (v. 10)—that is, cleanse us fully from sin, and thereby accomplish God's saving purpose.

The Perfect Offering That Establishes and Fulfills the New Covenant (10:11–18)

We now reach the end of the author's exposition of the contrast between the sacrifices of the old covenant and the atoning work of Christ. This concluding section provides both summary and emphasis. The definitive character and the finality of Christ's sacrifice are primarily in view. Thus, we encounter "a single sacrifice" (v. 12), a "single offering" (v. 14), and twice, the familiar "for all time" (vv. 12, 14). The passage also rounds out everything that has pre-

ceded by coming back to the citation of two of the basic Old Testament passages that are so important to the author's presentation: Psalm 110:1 and Jeremiah 31:31–34.

Again we have the two sides of the contrast presented. On the one side is the futility of the continually repeated sacrifices offered by the priests of the old system "day after day," which our author reiterates "can never take away sins" (v. 11). On the other side is the sacrifice of Christ, the "one sacrifice for sins for all time" (v. 12). This sacrifice *can* take away sins. Now the finality of that sacrifice is underlined by the citation of words from Psalm 110:1: Christ "sat down at the right hand of God." As our author said at the outset of his treatise, "When he had made purification for sins, he sat down at the right hand of the Majesty on high" (1:3; cf. 8:1; 12:2).

Verse 13 points to the odd interim period in which the church finds itself, sometimes described as being "between the times"—that is, between the first and second comings of Christ. Although Christ sits and, indeed, reigns at God's right hand (cf. 1 Cor 15:25), he is at the same time "waiting" for the time when his enemies will be made his footstool—yet a further allusion to Psalm 110:1. This was a point of some consequence in the interpretation of 2:8, where in reference to Psalm 8:6 our author noted, "But now we do not yet see all things put under him"—words very similar to the last line of Psalm 110:1, referring at once to humanity and also to Christ.

The work of Christ is summarized for the final time in verse 14: "For by a single offering he has perfected for all time those who are sanctified." Again for "perfected" we are to understand something like "brought to the fullness of salvation," and hence "for all time." The word "sanctified" often is used in the New Testament to refer simply to Christians. The sanctification refers to status more than experience, although it is always dangerous to separate the two. Exactly for this reason the central thrust of New Testament ethics is "to be what you are." Christians are not under the law, but, as our author is about to remind us, the law is written upon our hearts.

It is fitting that to bring this central exposition of Hebrews to an end, the author returns to one of his key texts, Jeremiah 31, which he quoted extensively in chapter 8. Again the message is for the church, as the introductory formula indicates: "The Holy Spirit bears witness to us." Now the author once again recalls the words of Jeremiah 31:33–34, slightly rearranging and telescoping them. He mentions "the covenant that I will make with them" as well as the law being written upon their hearts and minds, but seems especially interested in the final words, which use the Greek *ou mē*, expressing the strongest possible negative: "I will remember their sins and their lawless deeds no more" (v. 17). This points directly to the sufficiency of Christ's sacrifice and to the cessation of the sacrifices of the old system: "Where there is forgiveness of these, there is no longer any offering for sin" (v. 18).

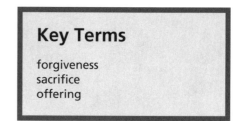

Key Terms

forgiveness
sacrifice
offering

On that powerful note our author concludes the main and, perhaps, most difficult of his discourse sections. Further discourse sections will come, but for the most part they will move along different lines. But now, in customary fashion—and one almost feels that he has gone on too long without application (the last previous application section was in 6:4–12)—in what follows he moves to apply this material to his readers.

Further Reading

Bruce, F. F. "A Shadow of Good Things to Come (Heb. 10:1)." In *The Time Is Fulfilled*, 77–94. Grand Rapids: Eerdmans, 1978.

Jobes, K. H. "The Function of Paranomasia in Hebrews 10:5–7." *Trinity Journal* 13 (1992): 181–91.

———. "Rhetorical Achievement in the Hebrews 10 'Misquote' of Psalm 40." *Biblica* 72 (1991): 387–96.

Kaiser, W. C. "The Abolition of the Old Order and the Establishment of the New: A Study of Psalm 40:6–8 and Hebrews 10:5–10." In *Tradition and Testament*, ed. J. S. and P. D. Feinberg. Chicago: Moody, 1981. Pp. 19–37.

Stylianopoulos, T. G. "Shadow and Reality: Reflections on Hebrews 10:1–18." *Greek Orthodox Theological Review* 17 (1972): 215–30.

Study Questions

1. What is the heart of the argument of Hebrews?

2. Discuss how the author of Hebrews interprets the contrasts found in Psalm 40.

3. Summarize the work of Christ as understood in the first ten chapters of Hebrews.

10B Faithfulness, Apostasy, and Endurance

10:19–39

Christians . . . have an entrance to the Divine Presence in virtue of Christ's Blood, a way made by the Incarnation, and an availing personal Advocate, a Priest over the house of God.

—B. F. Westcott, *Commentary on the Epistle to the Hebrews*

Supplemental Reading

Ezekiel 36:22–36; Mark 15:33–39; 1 Corinthians 13

Outline

- **Drawing Near to God: The Grounds for Faithfulness (10:19–25)**
- **The Danger of Apostasy and Judgment (10:26–31)**
- **Exhortation to Endurance (10:32–39)**

Objectives

1. Explain the grounds of faithfulness.
2. Expand on the danger of apostasy.
3. Discuss the importance of endurance.

No theology without application and no application without theology. Theology without application is abstract and merely an intellectual exercise; application without theology lacks a foundation that can motivate and energize. Such thoughts fit well our author's viewpoint. And now we reach a significant turning point in the book. Having presented the heart of his argument, the author turns in the remainder of chapter 10 to an extended application of the lengthy discourse that has occupied him in the preceding chapters. Despite the technical character of his arguments and the masterful exposition of the crucial differences between the old covenant and the new, the author is not ultimately interested in the argumentation for its own sake. Rather, as we have often seen earlier in Hebrews, he is concerned with the most practical matters—in particular, the dangerous tendency he has noted in his readers. The matter is one of extreme and urgent importance (as we have seen in 6:4–8, and are about to see again in 10:26–36). Only in the process of speaking to practical concerns does he work out the theology of the discourse sections of his sermon-treatise. In our author, as with the apostle Paul, we are dealing not with an "armchair theologian," but with a "task theologian." And now again he draws out the practical significance of what he has been expounding so eloquently.

Drawing Near to God: The Grounds for Faithfulness (10:19–25)

This exhortation section is based on three Greek hortatory subjunctive verbs, translated "let us draw near" (v. 22), "let us hold fast" (v. 23), and "let us consider" (v. 24). It is remarkably similar to the earlier exhortation of 4:14–16. Of special interest is that the familiar triad of faith, hope, and love (cf. 1 Cor 13:13) is found in the three exhortations respectively.

To begin with, our author provides as the premise of the exhortations a brief mention of what has been so carefully established thus far. The death of Christ opens up the way into God's presence. That death, indicated by "the blood of Jesus," is the instrument that enables us "to enter the sanctuary" (v. 19). Again, what is

The temple platform, viewed from the southeast, as it appears today, with its two mosques

Exhortations in Hebrews

One of the main and most obvious structural characteristics of the sermon-treatise we call Hebrews is its alternation of discourse and application. Hebrews is filled with exhortations. This is one of the main ways in which the author applies his material to the readers. We list here these imperatives and exhortations in the order in which they occur in the book. (Chapter 13 is filled with numerous imperatives not listed here.)

We must pay the closer attention to what we have heard (2:1).

Consider Jesus, the apostle and high priest of our confession (3:1).

Take care lest there be in any of you an evil, unbelieving heart (3:12).

Exhort one another every day, that none of you be hardened (3:13).

Let us fear lest any of you be judged to have failed to reach God's rest (4:1).

Let us strive to enter that rest (4:11).

Let us hold fast our confession (4:14).

Let us with confidence draw near to the throne of grace (4:16).

Let us leave the elementary doctrine of Christ and go on to maturity (6:1).

Show the same eagerness in realizing the full assurance of hope until the end (6:11).

Seize the hope set before us (6:18).

Let us draw near (10:22).

Let us hold fast the confession of our hope (10:23).

Let us consider how to stir up one another to love and good works (10:24).

Recall the former days (10:32).

Do not throw away your confidence (10:35).

Let us lay aside every weight and sin (12:1).

Let us run with perseverance the race that is set before us (12:1).

Consider him who endured from sinners such hostility (12:3).

Lift your drooping hands and strengthen your weak knees and make straight paths for your feet (12:12–13).

Strive for peace with all and holiness (12:14).

See to it that no one fails to obtain the grace of God (12:15).

See to it that you do not refuse him who is speaking (12:25).

Let us be grateful for receiving a kingdom that cannot be shaken (12:28).

Let us offer to God acceptable worship (12:28).

meant is the Holy of Holies, or as the NIV has it, "the Most Holy Place" (cf. the same usage in 9:8). No literal structure is meant by this; rather, it refers to the immediate presence of God. For that reason, the word "boldness" or "confidence" is in order. This new, bold access to God's presence is possible because of the sacrifice of Christ, described as "a new and living way" (v. 20). The newness of this way, we have seen, concerns both its means and its effects. When the author describes it as a "living way," he probably is referring to its enduring character in contrast to the old way, which has now come to an end.

In this new approach to God we must go "through the curtain"—that is, the curtain that hangs before the Holy of Holies (cf. 9:3). Again, no literal curtain is meant. In the remarkable paralleling of Christ's "flesh" (not "body," as in the NIV) with the curtain ("through the curtain, that is, through his flesh" [v. 20]) there is probably a deliberate allusion to the tearing of the curtain before the Holy of Holies at the time of the death of Jesus, symbolizing the end of the old regimen and the beginning of the new. This event is recorded in all three Synoptic Gospels: according to Mark 15:38 and Matthew 27:51, the curtain was torn from the top to the bottom, indicating that this event was an act of God (cf. Lk 23:45). Although our author does not mention any parallel tearing of the flesh of Jesus, the crucifixion readily implies it.

135

The Temptation of the Readers to Abandon Their Christian Faith

The following verses indicate the tendency in the readers to consider the abandonment of their Christianity.

2:1–3	lest we drift away from what we have heard; how shall we escape if we neglect so great a salvation?
3:12–14	take care lest there be in you an evil, unbelieving heart, leading you to fall away from the living God; that none may be hardened by the deceitfulness of sin; we share in Christ, if only we hold our first confidence firm to the end
4:1	let us fear lest any be judged as failing to reach God's rest
4:11	strive to enter that rest, that no one fall by the same sort of disobedience
6:4–6	impossible to restore them if they commit apostasy
10:26–31	if we sin deliberately; trampling under foot the Son of God, profaning the blood of the covenant, insulting the Spirit of grace
10:36	you have need of endurance
10:39	we are not of those who shrink back and are destroyed
12:3–11	that you may not grow weary or fainthearted; you have not yet resisted to the point of shedding blood; it is for discipline that you have to endure; at the moment all discipline seems painful
13:13	let us go forth outside the camp and bear the abuse he endured

confession

In these items that point to what Christ has done and that serve as the basis of the three exhortations, we come finally to the fact that we have a "great priest" (v. 21; cf. 4:14, "a great high priest"). The priesthood of Christ frequently has been mentioned in the preceding chapters. Representing us before God, he is the one who has gone before us with the one sufficient atoning sacrifice that has opened the way into God's presence. This is the one whom we have met earlier as the "pioneer of salvation" (2:10) and the "mediator of the new covenant" (9:15).

On the basis of these realities comes the threefold exhortation of verses 22–24. The initial exhortation, "let us draw near" (v. 22), may at first sound rather strange. No object is mentioned, and so we might reasonably ask, "Draw near to what?" From the context, it becomes clear that this is the language of the temple. What the author has in mind is the full and free access that Christians have to the very presence of God, in contrast to the highly restricted access entailed by the structure and regulations of the tabernacle/temple. Thus, we are to draw near to the presence of God, presumably to receive such things as courage, comfort, and strength (cf. 4:16). That is, we are to take full advantage of what Christ has accomplished on our behalf.

This drawing near to God requires of us no sacrifice but a true or sincere heart. Christ has done the rest. The "full assurance of faith" (v. 22) and the accompanying confidence or boldness that enable us to draw near are possible only because of our dependence upon the work that Christ has done on our behalf. Similarly, the condition of having our "hearts sprinkled clean from an evil conscience" (note again the language of the temple rites) is a benefit of what the new covenant alone could do (cf. 9:14; Ez 36:25–26). "Our bodies washed with pure water," on the other hand, refers not to temple-related ablutions, but probably to Christian baptism, the outward sign of the experienced reality of salvation.

The second exhortation is to "hold fast the confession of our hope" (v. 23). Here, as in 3:1 and 4:14, **confession** is used in the objective sense to refer to what is believed—our credo—and what is confessed at the time of baptism. The exhortation is to hold fast

paraenesis

the Day

to what we believe. Its relevance to the situation of the readers is immediately evident (cf. 2:1–3; 3:12–14; 4:1; 6:4–6; 10:26–29). We are enabled to hold fast in this way because of the faithfulness of God to his promises (cf. 11:11; for the importance of this idea elsewhere in the New Testament, see 1 Cor 1:9; 10:13; 2 Cor 1:18; 1 Thes 5:24; 2 Tm 2:13).

The third of the exhortations calls the readers to "spur one another on toward love" (the only other occurrence of the word "love" in Hebrews is in 6:10), the prime and comprehensive Christian virtue, and to "good works" (the only occurrence of this term in Hebrews). These items are fixed and standard elements in the **paraenesis** (ethical exhortation) of the epistles of the New Testament. Fellowship provides the ideal context in which this encouragement can happen, especially in difficult and dangerous circumstances. Some, however, probably even the readers, were neglecting such meeting together. The reason for this may well have been to avoid attracting attention and thus to lessen the likelihood of persecution. The thought of the approach of **the Day**, the time of eschatological judgment, brings with it an urgency (cf. the quotation of Heb 2:3 in v. 37) that should motivate the readers to be and to do their best. The felt urgency here may be the result of the belief that in fulfillment of the prophecy of Jesus (e.g., Mt 24:2), the fall of Jerusalem was imminent, and with it, the approach of the end of the age.

The Christian's Future Inheritance

10:34	knowing that you have a better and lasting possession
10:35	a great reward
10:36	you may receive what was promised
11:10	looking for the city that has foundations, whose architect and builder is God
11:14–16	a country of their own; a better country, a heavenly one
11:26	looking to the reward
11:35	a better resurrection
11:40	something better
13:14	here we have no lasting city; we are looking for the city to come

The Danger of Apostasy and Judgment (10:26–31)

This section is quite similar to 6:4–6, where the potential apostasy of the readers is also in view. The author returns to warning his readers of the consequences of turning away from their Christian faith. The willful sinning referred to in verse 26 is not ordinary sin of any kind, but rather, as in 6:6, specifically the sin of apostasy. This is evident from the immediate context (v. 29) with its reference to "trampling under foot the Son of God," "profaning the blood of the covenant," and "outraging the Spirit of grace." In view is the rejection of the central realities of the Christian faith "after receiving the knowledge of the truth" (v. 26; cf. 6:4). For the apostate person there can be no "sacrifice for sins," because apostasy entails the rejection of the sole means of salvation. By definition, apostates have cut themselves off from the single source of grace.

What awaits the apostate is only the prospect of a fiery judgment (the final clause of v. 27 may allude to the Septuagint of Is 26:11). Note that the apostates are not regarded as mere unbelievers, but now are called "adversaries" or "enemies." A comparison is made in verses 28–29 between the seriousness of unfaithful disobedience to the Mosaic law and to Christ, an argument used in 2:1–3 (and again in 12:25). So grievous was violation of the law of Moses that for certain offenses a person could be put to death on the testimony of "two or three witnesses" (cf. Dt 17:6; 19:15). The rejection of Christ's definitive atonement is, however, an even more serious matter, and deserves an even harsher punishment. The reason for this is found in the exceptionally strong language of the three clauses of verse 29. What the apostate has no regard for—"the Son of God," "the blood of the covenant," "the Spirit of grace"—is nothing other than God's final provision for salvation.

The two quotations in verse 30, drawn from Deuteronomy 32:35–36

(cf. Ps 135:14), underline the reality of the judgment to come. The judgment of "the living God" (cf. 3:12; 9:14; 12:22) is a terrifying prospect (cf. 12:29), especially for those who have turned away from the truth after once having received it (cf. 2 Pt 2:21). The readers need to keep this in mind when they contemplate turning away from their Christian faith.

Exhortation to Endurance (10:32–39)

What the readers desperately need is endurance (v. 36). They had exhibited endurance in the "former days," and now they need to do so again. Their past record should have been an encouragement to them. After they had been "enlightened"

Habakkuk 2:4 in Hebrews and in Paul

Habakkuk 2:4 is quoted in the New Testament in three places: Romans 1:17, Galatians 3:11, and Hebrews 10:37. The Pauline usage is familiar. Although the language of the Pauline quotations is itself ambiguous, it seems clear from the argument pursued in both Romans and Galatians that it should be translated taking "by faith" as modifying "righteous" rather than "will live"; hence, "the one who is righteous by faith will live," rather than "a righteous person will live by faith [i.e., faithfully]." (The Greek word pistis can mean either "faith"

or "faithfulness.") In the first instance, favored by Paul, righteousness comes by faith as the gift of God; in the second, righteous persons are characterized by faithful living. Of course, both of these statements are in themselves true and may be regarded as complementary. Paul's point, however, is made by the former understanding.

The use of the quotation by the author of Hebrews, on the other hand, focuses on the faithfulness of the righteous person. This is more in keeping with the meaning of the Hebrew text, which actually has "by his [the right-

teous person's] faith(fulness)." The Septuagint text (no pronoun, or in one important manuscript [A], "my faithfulness") lends itself better to the Pauline view. The author of Hebrews wants to emphasize the importance of remaining faithful, of enduring, even when under fire.

Further reading:

Fitzmyer, J. A. "Habakkuk 2:3–4 and the New Testament." In To Advance the Gospel. New York: Crossroad, 1981. Pp. 236–46.

Study Questions

1. Comment on the practical application of the threefold exhortation of verses 22–24.

2. According to Hebrews, why is the rejection of Christ a more serious offense than the rejection of the Mosaic law?

3. Why are the readers of Hebrews urged to endure?

Key Terms

confession
paraenesis
the Day
possession

possession

(cf. 6:4)—that is, come to Christian faith—they had experienced great "sufferings," "reproaches," "tribulations," and the "confiscation of . . . property." Not only did they endure these things, but also they extended themselves to others who were suffering, showing compassion (cf. 6:10)—for example, to those who were imprisoned for their faith. Probably in view here is the severe persecution under Claudius in 49, perhaps some fifteen years earlier, and not that of Nero in 65, which resulted in Christian martyrdoms (see 12:4).

The readers are told to remember the earlier record of their faithfulness and to be encouraged by it. They were motivated in their earlier endurance by their confidence in "a better and more lasting possession" (v. 34). This **possession**, this confidence in the future that would be theirs, enabled them to let go of all earthly security. Now the author exhorts the readers to take the same attitude and not to "throw away your confidence, which has a great reward" (v. 35). They did well in the past and their record was very positive. The faithful God who had sustained them in the past was ready to do so in the present. There is no reason why they could not persevere in the present circumstances, however grim they might be.

The bottom line is that the readers "have need of endurance" to do "the will of God" (v. 36). The quotation that the author now appends to his exhortation is perfectly suited to drive the point home. Habakkuk 2:3–4, rather freely quoted here from the Septuagint, begins with a promise of one who will come in the near future. "He who is coming" is virtually a messianic title and is understood by author and readers to refer to the second coming of Christ (cf. 9:28), which will bring to an end the persecution of the righteous. The second part of the quotation indicates that those who are righteous must live by faith—that is, live faithfully—and that anyone who "shrinks back" does not please God.

In typical fashion our author offers a very brief midrashic comment on the quotation, using two words drawn from it. Further encouraging his readers (in the same manner as in 6:9), he says that we do not identify with "those who *shrink back*," but with "those who have *faith* and so are saved" (v. 39). The readers have every reason to press on, to endure, and to be counted among those who remain steadfast in their faithfulness (cf. Lk 21:19). The alternative is the displeasure of God and the destruction that judgment will bring (cf. vv. 27–31).

In this major section of exhortation, the first readers, and readers of every era, are encouraged to take full advantage of the resources made available through the priestly work of Christ. By so doing they will be able to encourage their brothers and

139

Further Reading

Culpepper, R. A. "A Superior Faith: Hebrews 10:19–12:2." *Review and Expositor* 82 (1985): 375–90.

Dahl, N. A. "A New and Living Way: The Approach to God according to Hebrews 10:19–25." *Interpretation* 5 (1951): 401–12.

Leithart, P. J. "Womb of the World: Baptism and the Priesthood of the New Covenant in Hebrews 10.19–22." *Journal for the Study of the New Testament* 78 (2000): 49–65.

Lewis, T. W. "'. . . And if He Shrinks Back' (Heb X.38b)." *New Testament Studies* 22 (1975–76): 88–94.

Maasa, C. H. "The Fearful Results of Faith (Hebrews 10:19–39)." *Princeton Seminary Bulletin* 61 (1968): 55–59.

Richardson, A. "Whose Architect and Maker Is God: An Exegetical Contribution to Hebrews 10,19–25." *Theology Today* 8 (1951): 155–56.

sisters to produce the virtues of the Christian life (v. 24) and to remain faithful to their beliefs even under fire. Those who persevere in doing the will of God "will receive what he has promised" (v. 35).

11 Supreme Examples of Faith

Faith has this quality—that it can lift us into fellowship with the Unseen, that it can carry us within the veil. . . . Faith thus has a power of realisation, by which the invisible becomes visible and the future becomes present. While hope is the confident anticipation of a future regarded as future, faith appropriates that future as an experience of the present.

—A. S. Peake, *The Heroes and Martyrs of Faith*

Supplemental Reading

Genesis 4:2–16; 5:22–24; 6:9–22; 12:1–9; 21:1–7; 22:1–19; 27:27–40; 48:8–22; 50:22–26; Exodus 12:1–50; 14:19–31; Joshua 2; 6; Romans 4:16–22

Outline

- The Nature and Importance of Faith (11:1–3)
- The Faith of Abel, Enoch, and Noah (11:4–7)
- The First Example of Abraham's Faith (11:8–10)
- The Faith of Abraham and Sarah (11:11–12)
- A Parenthesis Concerning Hope for What Lies beyond the Present and the Earthly (11:13–16)
- The Supreme Example of Abraham's Faith (11:17–19)
- The Faith of Isaac, Jacob, and Joseph (11:20–22)
- The Faith of Moses (11:23–28)
- The Faith of the Israelites, Rahab, and Many Others (11:29–38)
- All the Saints Together Brought to the Goal (11:39–40)

Objectives

1. Explain the nature of faith.
2. List and elaborate on the key examples in which the dynamic of faith is at work.
3. Explore the faithfulness of God to those of faith.

faith

substance

The three words of the famous triad in 1 Corinthians 13:13 (also found in Heb 10:22–24) are among the most familiar, but also among the most poorly understood, words of the New Testament. "Love" has deteriorated practically into "what makes me feel good"; "hope" has become little more than "wishful thinking"; "faith" becomes "believing without evidence," or even "believing against the evidence," a kind of "leap into the dark." These words will not be understood correctly apart from listening to what the New Testament says about them. Certainly, one of the best-known chapters in the New Testament is chapter 11 of Hebrews, the chapter concerning **faith**. Here we are on solid ground, finding what we need to comprehend the nature of faith, and seeing concrete examples of what faith looks like in operation.

Again it is worth pointing out that our author does not provide us with an abstract discussion of faith. As always, he has an agenda, and that agenda drives him to write what he writes. He wants his readers to imitate the examples he provides. He wants to encourage his readers to face the future with confidence. The readers can take heart from his review of famous people from Israel's history who encountered the difficult and the unknown, and those who knew suffering, but whose faith sustained them and made it possible for them to endure.

The Nature and Importance of Faith (11:1–3)

Although the opening words of chapter 11 are often cited as a definition of faith, verse 1 does not so much define faith as provide us with a couple of faith's key attributes. The word

"faith" occurs in Hebrews far more often than in any other book of the New Testament, twenty-four times in this chapter alone. The sentence that begins verse 3 is the first of eighteen sentences in this chapter that begin with *pistei*, "by faith." The emphasis and cumulative effect are powerful. It is clear from chapter 11 that for our author faith involves an active obedience to God rather than a passive belief in the truth of God. Thus, belief and obedience are correlated in the same way that unbelief and disobedience are (cf. 3:18–19). The heroes of faith, it should be stressed, do not believe the incredible, nor do they believe blindly, without sufficient reason. On the contrary, they have reason to believe, and their acts of obedience are the result of their dependence upon the reliability of God's promises. Nevertheless, they often must move out courageously into the unknown.

Since in this chapter our author stresses repeatedly not the conviction or assurance of faith in the examples he reviews, but rather, the active expression of their faith, we should read the ambiguous nouns of verse 1 as pointing to the objective, rather than the subjective, aspects of faith. We should take our cue from the examples that compose the greater part of the chapter. Here we can find out what it is about faith that the author wants his readers to know.

From the examples of faith lifted up in this chapter it seems clear that what is *not* primarily in view is what we feel or possess—assurance, confidence—but rather, how faith substantiates, or gives **substance** to, what is promised, how it provides evidence of what is believed about unseen and hoped-for realities. Faith, indeed, has a way of making the future present and the unseen visible. Since faith is the cause of acts of obedience that are motivated by what is unseen and future, it calls attention to just those realities. Faith therefore

Faith according to Hebrews 11:1

The meaning of the words used to describe faith in Hebrews 11:1 is not entirely clear. The question concerns whether the words are meant to be understood as subjective or objective in orientation. Many translations take both words in the subjective sense. Thus, for example, RSV, NRSV, and NASB: "assurance" and "conviction"; NIV: "faith is being sure of what we hope for and certain of what we do not see." On the other hand, the KJV takes both words in the objective sense: "faith is the substance of things hoped for, the evidence of things not seen." Also emphasizing the objective sense of the first of the two words is the NEB (also REB): "gives substance to."

The first word, *hypostasis*, is used in two other places in Hebrews. In 1:3 it clearly is used in the objective sense of "substance," "being," or "nature." In 3:14 it usually is translated in the subjective sense of "confidence." Paul uses the word twice with the subjective meaning (2 Cor 9:4; 11:17). The second word, *elenchos*, occurs only here in the New Testament, but outside the New Testament it is used both subjectively and objectively. In the latter sense it means "a means of proof," or "evidence."

The resultant problem cannot be solved by counting occurrences or by consulting lexicons. What must remain finally determinative are the context and the flow of the argument. For this reason the objective sense is to be preferred for both words, and the KJV can hardly be improved upon.

The emphasis throughout chapter 11 is not on the subjective assurance of the individuals, but on the ways in which they gave expression to their faith, embodied it, gave substance to it. Above all, faith is active in obedience. For our author, faith acts in a way that points unmistakably to the reality of what is not seen. Faith gives substance to the things unseen. The Geneva Bible catches the exact idea of the chapter in its translation of the first verb: "faith is that which causeth those things to appear in deed which are hoped for."

We may paraphrase verse 1 this way: Faith through its active character gives substance to, that is, expresses the reality of, things hoped for; it demonstrates the truth of things not yet seen.

---

hope

brings them to expression. Faith makes concrete what is unavailable to our sight.

It is, of course, true that we may indeed have assurance and confidence. Such subjective conviction is possible because of the reliability and faithfulness of God. The word "hope" as used in the New Testament refers not to something we would like to have or see, a kind of personal wish, but rather, to something like "confident expectation." New Testament **hope** does not disappoint, because, like faith itself, it depends upon God's reliability and faithfulness, which will never fail us (cf. Rom 5:5; Heb 6:11).

Our faith is possible only because of God's faithfulness; indeed, our faith and God's faithfulness are like two sides of the same coin. Above all, however, our faith needs to be acted out. It requires a dynamic quality. And this is what we see in the list of examples provided by the author. It is by the dynamic, active quality of their faith that the great men and women of the Old Testament, the ancestors of the readers, gained a good reputation, or were "attested" (v. 2). The word "attested" is used again in verse 39 in the concluding remark concerning the men and women of faith. Above all, faith—an active faith marked by faithful obedience—is what characterized the famous figures of the Old Testament. In this regard they become models of faith for Christians. The faith that they exhib-

The Catalog of Supreme Examples of Faith in Hebrews 11

Chapter 11 of Hebrews is unique in the New Testament, though there are some earlier antecedents in the form of reviews of the high points in the history of Israel. We may note the following: Psalm 78; Wisdom of Solomon 10; Sirach 44–50; 1 Maccabees 2:51–64; Acts 7. None of these focuses on faith as does the present chapter. In each of the following instances, except the final two, the verse begins with the formulaic words "by faith" (*pistei*).

v. 4	Abel	offered a better sacrifice than did Cain (Gn 4:2–16)
v. 5	Enoch	was pleasing to God (Gn 5:22–24)
v. 7	Noah	prepared an ark (Gn 6:9–22)
vv. 8–10	Abraham	obeyed by going out to the promised land; lived as an alien in the land of promise (Gn 12:1–8; 23:4)
vv. 11–12	(Sarah)	was able to conceive (Gn 17:15–21; 18:9–15; 21:1–7)
vv. 17–19	Abraham	offered up Isaac (Gn 22:1–14)
v. 20	Isaac	blessed Jacob and Esau (Gn 27:27–29, 39–40)
v. 21	Jacob	blessed each of the sons of Joseph (Gn 48:15–20)
v. 22	Joseph	prophesied the exodus (Gn 50:24–25)
v. 23	(Moses)	was hidden for three months (Ex 2:1–2)
vv. 24–28	Moses	refused to be called the son of Pharaoh's daughter, left Egypt (Ex 2:11–15); kept the Passover (Ex 12:12–13, 21–30)
vv. 29–30	the Israelite people	passed through the Red Sea (Ex 14:21–29); caused the walls of Jericho to fall (Jos 6:12–21)
v. 31	Rahab	welcomed the spies in peace (Jos 2:1–24; 6:17, 23–25)

(For the remaining examples of faith in ch. 11, see the sidebar "The Examples of Faith in Hebrews 11:32–38.")

ited is the kind of faith that the readers desperately needed if they were to endure.

The first example of faith (v. 3), unlike those that follow, does not concern a specific person. Instead, it establishes a basic principle of faith: the material creation (literally, "the aeons"; cf. 1:2) gives substance to, and objective evidence of, the unseen. The creation came into existence by what cannot be seen, "the word of God" (here *rhēma*, not *logos* as in the prologue to John's Gospel). It was when God spoke, and not from anything that could be seen, that the creation came into existence (Gn 1:3; cf. Ps 33:6, 9). Only here in the whole of chapter 11 does the author use the "by faith" formula generally, applying it to himself and his readers. Only by faith—counting upon the reality of God and God's revelation—can we come to the understanding of all that exists as the creation of God. Our very knowledge of these things is the result of faith.

The Faith of Abel, Enoch, and Noah (11:4–7)

A list of heroes of faith begins here and lasts virtually until the end of the chapter. The author is less concerned with providing information than with motivating his readers, in effect calling upon them to imitate the examples he provides. As he had written earlier, he desires them to become "imitators of those who through faith and patience inherit the promises" (6:12). Because of their faith in relation to the unseen, these exemplars were obedient and thus are models for the readers.

The list begins with figures from the early chapters of Genesis. The first is Abel (v. 4), who "by faith" offered a "better sacrifice" than did his brother, Cain. The story is found in Genesis 4:1–16. While aspects of the story are not as clear as we might like, the main point seems to be that Abel's sacrifice was a sacrifice of the best he had and was the expression of a full and unreserved commitment. It was a genuine acting out of his faith in a way that Cain's offering somehow was not. The result was that Abel was "attested" as a "righteous" man (cf. Mt 23:35). The further fact that this was part of a larger pattern of deeds full of faith is indicated by our author in the mention of Abel being "attested" (second use of the word in the verse) by God "for his gifts," meaning other offerings made by Abel. The murdered Abel became the first martyr, and his innocent blood cried out from the ground (Gn 4:10; cf. Heb 12:24). But the way in which he continues to speak after his death is as an example of faith in action. Abel's offering reflected the orientation of his life toward the unseen realities of God and God's faithfulness.

We learn about the second example of faith, Enoch (v. 5), from Genesis 5:22–24, where twice it is said that "he walked with God." This Hebrew expression is interpreted by the Septuagint as "he pleased God." The quoted words "and he was not found because God took him up" are from the Septuagint of Genesis 5:24. The Greek root (drawn from the Septuagint of Gn 5:24) that underlies "to take up" occurs three times in verse 5, and means literally "to translate"—that is, to move from one realm to another. Enoch was translated from this life to the eternal realm without experiencing death. For this reason Enoch, together with Elijah (another who was taken to heaven without dying), becomes an important figure in the eschatological expectations of later Judaism, where he is expected to appear again as one of God's assistants. The point, however, is that all of this happened "by faith." That Enoch was a man of faith is clear from the fact that he pleased God (cf. v. 6). So when Enoch "walked with God," he did so by faith—that is, his life was controlled by the unseen reality of God.

Verse 6 articulates the basic and timeless principle that it is impossible to please God without faith. Faith requires first of all that one believes in the existence of the unseen God (literally, "that he is" [see Ex 3:14]; cf. Heb 11:27). Furthermore, one must believe that God will reward those who seek him, even though at times this may not appear to be the case (cf. vv. 35b–38). We know little about Enoch, but since he pleased God, we may conclude that he believed these things and that he ordered his life accordingly—that is, his faith produced a corresponding faithfulness.

The well-known story of Noah (Gn 6:9–22) provides our author with his third example of faith (v. 7). Noah provides a classic example of faith concerning the unseen and the future (cf. v. 1). In the whole of chapter 11, only here does what is unseen refer to the threat of judgment rather than eschatological blessing. With a reverent submission to God's command, Noah built the ark that would save his family. As Genesis 6:22 puts it, "Noah did this; he did all that God commanded him." Noah's faith indirectly was a condemnation of the world's lack of faith. The language at the end of the verse, concerning "the righteousness that comes by faith" (NIV; cf. KJV; NAB), sounds initially like Paul (but the Greek construction *kata pistin*, "by faith," is not Paul's *ek pisteōs*). Our author, however, has a view of faith rather more like that of James: the righteousness that comes by faith refers to a status that comes from obeying God (see Jas 2:24, 26). That is, faith is expressed in active obedience, of the kind that Noah exhibited. (These two views of faith should be regarded as complemen-

The Controlling Reality of the Unseen in Hebrews 11

A number of explicit references point to the great importance of things unseen as a factor in true faith, according to Hebrews 11. For this reason, the conduct of Christians can look foolish and unjustifiable.

v. 1	things hoped for, but not yet seen
v. 3	creation from what cannot be seen
v. 6	that God exists and rewards
v. 7	events yet unseen
v. 8	an unknown country
v. 10	the city with permanent foundations (cf. 13:14)
v. 13	seeing from a long way off (the things God promised)
v. 14	looking for a country
v. 16	the heavenly country
v. 26	keeping the future reward in view
v. 27	as though seeing the invisible God

metaphor

tary and not contradictory. In the final analysis, Paul too is concerned about practical righteousness and would agree that faith without resultant works of obedience is dead.)

The First Example of Abraham's Faith (11:8–10)

Our author has already referred to Abraham in 6:13–15, where he described him as one who "having patiently endured, obtained the promise." And it is no surprise that Abraham, that key person at the beginning of salvation history, figures as largely in chapter 11 as he does. More space is given to him than to anyone else; the "by faith" formula is applied to him no less than four times (vv. 8, 9, 11 [but see below], 17). It is the covenant with Abraham that initiates God's activity with the people who became Israel and that comes to fruition in the church. Paul also found Abraham to be a model of faith, but somewhat differently from our author. Paul cites Genesis 15:6, "Abraham believed God and it was reckoned to him as righteousness," and calls Abraham "the father of all who believe" (Rom 4:11; cf. Gal 3:9). The author of Hebrews thinks of Abraham more along the lines of James 2:21–22: "Was not Abraham our father justified by works, when he offered his son Isaac upon the altar? You see that faith was active along with his works, and faith was completed by works."

Abraham's faith is illustrated by two outstanding examples. The first (vv. 8–9) concerns his response to God's call to leave his Mesopotamian home to go to a land to which God would lead him, sojourning there "in tents," "as in a foreign land" (see Gn 12:1–4, 8; 13:3; 18:1; 23:4). Abraham demonstrates his faith in God's promises by his active obedience, "not knowing where he was going." The mention of Isaac and Jacob in verse 9 suggests that they too lived by faith in similar circumstances. All three were "heirs of the same promise." Verse 10 makes an important point. Although Abraham responds to a promise concerning the inheritance of the land, that promise is part of a much larger reality, so that ultimately Abraham's motivation concerns something beyond the temporal and earthly: "the city which has foundations, whose architect and builder is God" (cf. Philo, *Allegorical Interpretation* 3.83, which mentions in reference to the promise to Abraham "a city good, and large, and prosperous"). The city in this **metaphor** is necessarily eschatological and refers to what was called the "heavenly Jerusalem" (cf. the "city" of 11:16;

Monument over the cave of Machpelah in Hebron, the traditional burial place of the patriarchs and their wives: Abraham and Sarah, Isaac and Rebecca, Jacob and Leah

12:22; 13:14; Ps 87:1; Gal 4:26; Rv 21:2, 10, 14, 19). Already it was realized that the tangible things of this world are in effect anticipations or foreshadowings of eternal realities, and that the manner in which we live now therefore should be governed by the unseen and future (cf. v. 1). This is a point to which our author will return in verses 13–16.

The Faith of Abraham and Sarah (11:11–12)

One of the best-known examples of Abraham's faith is also familiar from the discussion of it in Romans 4:16–22. Abraham had been promised descendants as numerous as the sands of the seashore or the stars of the sky, and yet he and Sarah were unable to have children. Abraham is

described by both Paul and our author as being so old that he was "as good as dead" (v. 12; Rom 4:19). Nevertheless, as Paul puts it, Abraham "grew strong in his faith . . . fully convinced that God was able to do what he had promised" (Rom 4:20–21).

As the words appear in our text, "by faith" is followed immediately with the words "Sarah herself." Accordingly, this seems to point to Sarah as an example of the power of faith. Our author apparently wants to include Sarah alongside Abraham. Together they experienced the power of faith, even if in actuality it was by the faith of Abraham that the doubting Sarah (cf. Gn 18:12; 21:7) was able to conceive (see the sidebar "Sarah's or Abraham's Faith in Hebrews 11:11?"). Nevertheless, it was Sarah, with her baby boy Isaac (whose name means "laughter" or "he laughs"), who, though she had first laughed in unbelief, in the end rejoiced at God's faithfulness.

147

Sarah's or Abraham's Faith in Hebrews 11:11?

The grammatical subject of Hebrews 11:11 is not altogether clear. A major problem is that the initial verbal clause, translated literally, is "received power for the laying down of seed," language regularly used for the male act in procreation, not the female act of conception. A further problem is that according to the narrative in Genesis, Sarah is anything but a person of faith who believes what God promises (see especially Gn 18:11–15).

A further complicating factor is that "Sarah" appears to be in the nominative case and thus necessarily the subject of the verb. The textual committee that produced the commonly accepted Greek text, however, takes the nominative as a somewhat odd "Hebraic circumstantial clause" (translated as "even though Sarah was barren, he [Abraham] received power to beget"). On the other hand, "Sarah" (and the modifiers) also could be in the dative case, since the only difference would have been the Greek subscript iotas, which would not have been a part of the earliest Greek manuscripts (which were uncials, consisting of capital letters without spaces between words). In that case, it could be a dative of accompaniment (translated as "together with barren Sarah, he [Abraham] received power to beget").

Upon an initial reading of Hebrews 11, because of the form of verse 11 one fully expects Sarah to be the subject of the sentence, and thus the example of faith. At the very least, it seems that the author wanted to associate Sarah closely with Abraham's faith in a positive way. A few translations that keep Sarah as the subject rightly employ passive verbs. In effect, it was Abraham's faith that was instrumental, but Sarah still receives special attention, being named first, immediately after the words "by faith."

Translations focusing on Sarah:

KJV: "Through faith also Sarah herself received strength to conceive seed"

NASB: "By faith even Sarah herself received ability to conceive"

RSV: "By faith Sarah herself received power to conceive"

REB: "By faith even Sarah herself was enabled to conceive"

NJB: "It was equally by faith that Sarah, in spite of being past age, was made able to conceive"

Translations focusing on Abraham:

NIV: "By faith Abraham, even though he was past age—and Sarah herself was barren—was enabled to become a father"

NAB: "By faith he received power to generate, even though he was past the normal age—and Sarah herself was sterile"

NRSV: "By faith he received power of procreation, even though he was too old—and Sarah herself was barren"

Further reading:

Greenlee, J. H. "Hebrews 11:11: Sarah's Faith or Abraham's?" *Notes on Translation* 4 (1990): 37–42.

In verse 12 our author underlines God's faithfulness by indicating that God thus fulfilled the promise, quoting Genesis 22:17, that from Abraham would come descendants "as many as the stars of heaven and as the innumerable grains of sand by the seashore." Whereas in Romans 4 Paul takes this as referring to all those of faith, including Gentile believers ("the father of many nations" [Rom 4:16–18]), the author of Hebrews seems to have in mind simply Abraham's multitudinous Jewish descendants. The point is that always the faithfulness of God matches human faith.

A Parenthesis Concerning Hope for What Lies beyond the Present and the Earthly (11:13–16)

Our author breaks away from his catalog of the faithful to emphasize and extend a point already made in verses 8–10, with which we should compare verse 1. Again we hear of the importance of things unseen and things hoped for.

Although the people mentioned so far believed the promises and acted upon them in faith, they "died in faith" without having received the promises. So too did those yet to be mentioned in the remainder of chapter 11 (see v. 39). There was, to be sure, a degree of earthly fulfillment that had been experienced (cf. 6:15), but this only served as a reminder of greater realities. They welcomed those greater, transcendent realities, although they only saw them "from a distance" (v. 13; cf. Jn 8:56 for a similar, but not identical, thought). Participants in the new covenant see them, one might say, "from near." For those realities yet to come our author uses alternating metaphors. We have already seen the metaphor of the "city," used again here (v. 16; created by God, as in v. 10); now, however, he adds the metaphor of "a country of their own" (v. 14), which is not different from the "better" and "heavenly country" of verse 16. The metaphors are simply different ways of speaking about the same eschatological reality.

So in fact the earthly manifestations of God's faithfulness never were perceived as being of ultimate importance. They merely were pointers to far greater realities. Indeed, our models of faith never regarded themselves as being at home in this world (for the Christian counterpart, see 1 Pt 1:1; 2:11). On the contrary, they "confessed that they were strangers and exiles on the earth" (v. 13; cf. Gn 23:4; 1 Chr 29:15; Ps 39:12). If their goal had been an earthly inheritance, they could have returned to Mesopotamia (v. 15). But the point is that they did not. And the implication can hardly be missed that our author does not want his readers to return to their previous Judaism. What they need to do is let the incomparable, transcendent realities that await them motivate them to faithfulness in the present, in the same way that the exemplars of faith did (cf. 10:39).

The assertion that "God is not ashamed to be called their God" (v. 16) calls us back to an Old Testament verse like Exodus 3:6, quoted by Jesus in Matthew 22:32. When Jesus remarks that God "is not God of the dead, but of the living," the implication is that the patriarchs will, in connection with the resurrection, fully inherit the transcendent promises together with us (cf. v. 40).

The Supreme Example of Abraham's Faith (11:17–19)

The most impressive example of Abraham's faith is found, of course, in the offering of his son Isaac (Gn 22:1–14). The story of a father called to sacrifice his only son is poignant enough, but to this must be added, as our author reminds us, the fact that this son was intended to be instrumental in the fulfillment of the covenant God made with Abraham, "who had received the promises" (v. 17).

149

The Binding of Isaac (the Akedah) and Hebrews 11:17–19

Our author's dependence on the story of Genesis 22:1–14 reflects the popularity of the story for contemporary Judaism. The story known as "The Binding of Isaac" (the Akedah) was important especially in Jewish liturgies for the celebration of the Jewish New Year. Allusions to the story may be found in Wisdom of Solomon 10:5; Sirach 44:20; 4 Maccabees 13:12; 16:20. The New Testament story of God sending his own Son to die as a sacrifice obviously echoes the Akedah in striking ways. In-

stead of "only son" (*monogenēs* [Heb 11:17]), the Septuagint of Genesis 22:2 has "beloved" (*agapētos*) son. Both words are used of Christ in the New Testament (the first in John [e.g., 3:16, 18], the second in the Synoptics [e.g., Mk 1:11; 9:7; 12:6; and parallels]). The story is perhaps also echoed in Romans 8:32. The Akedah as a sign of Abraham's faith is pointed out in James 2:21–23 in a way quite similar to our passage. In the New Testament, only the author of Hebrews alludes to the

resurrection in the Akedah story.

Further reading:

Daly, R. J. "The Soteriological Significance of the Sacrifice of Isaac." *Catholic Biblical Quarterly* 39 (1977): 45–75.

Swetnam, J. *Jesus and Isaac: A Study of the Epistle to the Hebrews in the Light of the Aqedah.* Analecta Biblica 94. Rome: Biblical Institute Press, 1981.

Akedah

Thus, he adds that it was Abraham "to whom it was said, 'In Isaac your descendants shall be called'" (v. 18; quoting Gn 21:12).

This was a supreme "test" of Abraham's faith. Of course, God would not actually have required such a sacrifice, but Abraham could not have known that (but cf. Gn 22:5, 8), and nevertheless shows unquestioning obedience. He takes God at his word and displays a remarkable confidence, reasoning that if Isaac had to be killed, God also could raise him from the dead (v. 19; cf. Rom 4:17). Our author adds the intriguing words that "figuratively speaking [literally, 'in parable'], he did receive him back." This may mean that when God provided the ram for sacrifice, in effect Isaac was delivered from death. Nevertheless, it could be a deliberate attempt to parallel Isaac's deliverance with the resurrection of Christ. This in turn would complement the parallel often seen between the binding of Isaac (the **Akedah**) and the sacrifice of Jesus, God's only

Son. The story of the sacrifice of Isaac therefore becomes a foreshadowing of the sacrifice of Christ, including even the deliverance of both, granted in different ways. Thus, figuratively speaking, Isaac, like Christ, was received back from the dead.

The Faith of Isaac, Jacob, and Joseph (11:20–22)

Proceeding through the list, we next encounter three interconnected exemplars of faith, each of which points forward to the one that follows, and hence to the future. The first of these is Isaac, who was the subject of the immediately preceding verses. "By faith" Isaac was able to bless Jacob and Esau with regard to matters yet in the future, literally "things to come" (cf. Gn 27:27–29, 39–40). In verses 20–22, the verb

The Magen David, "Shield of David," from the synagogue ruin at Capernaum, now the symbol on the Israeli flag

"blessed" means to pass on the covenantal promises and the associated position of privilege. The line of promise in this case also was a line of faith, as Isaac emulated the faith of his father.

In succession, Jacob, on his deathbed, "by faith" blessed the two sons of Joseph (v. 21; cf. Gn 48:15–20). It is something of a surprise here to read not of Jacob blessing his twelve sons (see Genesis 49), but rather, of his blessing his two grandsons, in which he deliberately favored Ephraim, the younger of the two, over Manasseh (see Gn 48:14; 20). His insistence upon favoring Ephraim was based on his faith in the future that he foresaw for him. The strange inclusion of the last clause of the verse, drawn from the Septuagint of Genesis 47:31 (the Hebrew, by different pointing of the same consonants, has "bed" for "staff"), may point to the appropriateness of worship in the context.

Next, Joseph is set forth as a model of faith. From many possible examples, our author singles out that Joseph, as he was close to death, "by faith" spoke prophetically of the exodus from Egypt (v. 22; cf. Gn 50:24–25). Again we have the future affirmed by faith. The unusual note about his bones also is an indicator of Joseph's faith, and their deposition in the promised land (Ex 13:19; Jos 24:32) reminds us of God's faithfulness to his promises. The mention of

Joseph's prophecy leads our author in turn to the hero of the exodus, Moses.

The Faith of Moses (11:23–28)

It would be difficult to overestimate the significance of Moses to Judaism. One thinks immediately of the exodus and the giving of the law on Sinai—foundational events for Israel. Our author limits himself to only a few examples. The words "by faith" occur here four times. The faithfulness of Moses already has been mentioned in 3:5.

The initial words "by faith" in verse 23 are connected to Moses only by a passive verb, "was hidden." Thus, the faith of Moses' parents is what first comes into view. Their faith enabled them to preserve the life of their son (Ex 2:1–2) and kept them from being afraid to disobey Pharaoh's edict that every newborn Hebrew boy was to be thrown into the Nile. The note that the baby was beautiful (*asteios*) might imply that he was pleasing to God (note the same word in the phrase "beautiful before God," used in reference to Moses in Acts 7:20). If so, the parents may have understood that God had a special purpose for their son.

The second "by faith" has to do with Moses' turning away from the Egyptian court, from the special position of being Pharaoh's grandson, from "the passing pleasures of sin," and from the "treasures of Egypt" (vv. 24–26; cf. Ex 2:11–15). By faith he chose instead to identify with his people, the Hebrews, "the people of God." Most remarkable is the statement by our author that Moses considered "the reproach of Christ" as greater riches than those of Egypt (v. 26). The reference to Christ is an

anachronism

anachronism explained by the final clause of verse 26: "for he was looking to the reward." As we have repeatedly seen, an essential quality of having faith is being motivated by the future and the unseen. The basis for the anachronistic statement is located in the unity of salvation history and the unity of God's people. When Moses suffered reproach because he was loyal to God's people (v. 25), in effect he suffered reproach for being loyal to God's Messiah, who is so closely identified with God's people. The anachronism very deliberately has the readers in mind, since they are the ones called by their faithfulness to bear the reproach of Christ (see 13:13). The reward that Moses would enjoy in the future, and that he counted upon in his faith, was far greater than the treasures Egypt had to offer.

The third occurrence of the formula "by faith" in reference to Moses (v. 27) turns to his departure from Egypt without fear of Pharaoh. This probably is a reference to the exodus event itself (cf. the following verse, and Ex 12:51), since Moses *was* afraid when he first fled Egypt for Midian. And the complex events leading up to the exodus may well be suggested by the word "endurance." The added explanation of Moses' endurance provides further emphasis on one of the central themes of the chapter: "as though he saw him who is invisible" (cf. v. 1; 1 Tm 6:16). Thus, Moses was able to do what he did "by faith"; that is, he was motivated and controlled by the unseen. Faith is dependent on the conviction of the existence and faithfulness of God (cf. v. 6).

The fourth and final occurrence of "by faith" in reference to Moses (v. 28) takes up the particular event of the Passover (Ex 12:12–13, 21–30). Moses' faith expressed itself in obedience to God by "the sprinkling of the blood" upon the doorposts and lintels of the houses of the Hebrews, thereby causing "the destroyer" (a messenger from

God) to "pass over" them. In this way, they were delivered from the death of their firstborn. This event of deliverance made possible the exodus and was (and still is) celebrated annually by the Jews. Earlier in Hebrews we encountered the language of "sprinkling of blood" in connection with the work of the priests in the tent/temple, but only in this instance is it used to refer to the Passover (a different Greek word for "sprinkling" occurs here).

The Faith of the Israelites, Rahab, and Many Others (11:29–38)

As our author proceeds chronologically, the next two occurrences of the "by faith" formula (vv. 29–30) refer to the Israelites who exited from Egypt miraculously (Ex 14:21–29), and who then entered the promised land and conquered Jericho (Jos 6:12–21). Joshua's name could have been mentioned in the latter instance, just as Moses could have been mentioned in the former, but the author focuses instead on the faith of the people who followed their leadership. The exodus from Egypt and the entry into the promised land were possible only by faith. The people acted out their faith by an obedience that involved them in very strange activities indeed: crossing through parted waters and repeatedly marching around a city while blowing trumpets. By their actions they gave substance to their faith and evidence of their hope.

The same may be said of Rahab (v. 31), who is particularly striking for two reasons: she was a non-Israelite, and she was a prostitute. Rahab "by faith" was able to save herself and her family. By her reception and

The Examples of Faith in Hebrews 11:32–38

Facing the necessity of abbreviation, our author in these verses simply lists other names and types of sufferings that indicate the reality of faith in action.

Verse 32:

Gideon (Jgs 6:11–8:32)
Barak (Jgs 4:6–5:31)
Samson (Jgs 13:2–16:31)
Jephthah (Jgs 11:1–12:7)
David (1 Samuel 16–30; 2 Samuel)
Samuel (1 Samuel 1–12)
Prophets (e.g., Elijah, Elisha, Hosea, Amos, Isaiah, Jeremiah)

Verses 33–34:

"through faith" (*dia pisteōs*, not the usual *pistei*):

conquered kingdoms: Joshua, David
administered justice: David, Solomon
obtained promises
shut the mouths of lions: Samson (Jgs 14:6), David (1 Sm 17:34–35), Daniel (Dn 6:22)
quenched raging fire: Shadrach, Meshach, and Abednego (Dn 3:13–30)
escaped the edge of the sword: Elijah (1 Kgs 19:1–8), Jeremiah (Jer 26:23–24)
won strength out of weakness
became mighty in war
put foreign armies to flight

Verse 35:

women received back their dead by resurrection (1 Kgs 17:17–24; 2 Kgs 4:25–37)

Verses 35–38:

others (victorious in apparent defeat):

were tortured, refusing to accept release
suffered mocking and flogging: Jeremiah
suffered chains and imprisonment
were stoned to death: Zechariah (2 Chr 24:20–22)
were sawn in two: the tradition of the martyrdom of Isaiah (*Martyrdom and Ascension of Isaiah* 5:11–14)
were tested (textually doubtful, lacking in Papyrus 46 and other early witnesses)
were put to death by the sword: prophets (1 Kgs 19:10)
went about in sheepskins and goatskins: Judas Maccabeus and others (2 Maccabees 5:27)
were destitute
were persecuted
were mistreated
wandered in deserts, mountains, caves, and holes in the ground: Jews under Antiochus (2 Maccabees 6:11; 10:6)

protection of the spies (Jos 2:1–24; 6:17, 23–25) she provided evidence of her faith in the reality of the unseen, that the God of Israel is sovereign over all. Rahab became a popular figure in Jewish tradition as the first proselyte to the Jewish faith. She also is cited as an example in James 2:25, where the emphasis falls upon her works ("justified by works"), but in a context where works are the valid manifestation of faith. Again our author holds a perspective quite similar to that of James. Remarkably, Rahab's name appears in the Matthean genealogy of Jesus (Mt 1:5), where she is the mother of Boaz, who himself married the non-Israelite Ruth.

As though he were a preacher—and we *have* been hearing a sermon—who had just noticed that time was getting away from him, our author now indicates his frustration that he cannot continue speaking of specific examples of faith in this kind of detail (v. 32). He now must speak more generally, and he mentions a suggestive list of names, all well known to the readers, followed by a list of accomplishments of unidentified faithful people. (For the relevant Old Testament references for each name in v. 32, see the sidebar "The Examples of Faith in Hebrews 11:32–38.")

The various triumphs mentioned in verses 33–34 sometimes can be associated rather easily with specific Old Testament persons (again, see the sidebar "The Examples of Faith in Hebrews 11:32–38"), whereas in some cases they are so general that they would fit many individuals of the past. In all of these instances we see the power of exercised faith. Thus, the tone of this list is one of victory—not just the promised victory of the future, but also victory in the present. These are the ones who were blessed with a taste of triumph, who "obtained promises," as our author puts it. What they obtained, however, was not yet the final and perfect fulfillment, which comes only at the eschaton. This they will experience together with us, a point that will be emphasized in verses 39–40.

The most spectacular example of those who in this way experienced a taste of the future victory in the present is the women who "received back their dead by resurrection" (v. 35). In view are the famous cases of the widow of Zarephath, a non-Israelite (cf. Lk 4:25–26) whose son was raised by Elijah (1 Kgs 17:17–24); and the Shunammite woman whose son was raised by Elisha (2 Kgs 4:25–37). These resuscitations, like those performed by Jesus, anticipate the resurrection to a new order of life (the "better resurrection" mentioned at the end of v. 35) that will come only with the eschaton.

The remarkable verses 35b–38, beginning with the word "others," stand in strong contrast with the preceding material. Now we encounter a list of apparent defeats. How can our author put these forward as models for his readers? Although those who suffered in these ways (again, see the sidebar "The Examples of Faith in Hebrews 11:32–38") seem to have been defeated in the present, in fact they too are examples of the triumph of faith because of the future and certain reward that is theirs. Thus, we see the oddity of some who "refused to be released," welcoming death so that they might be the recipients of a "better resurrection" (v. 35). Our author points out the supreme irony of the situation,

since those who suffered in these ways were people "of whom the world was not worthy" (v. 38). The message could not be missed by the readers. No matter if they would have to suffer, even die, for their faith, still they would ultimately triumph in the same way that those before them had.

Here it is worth noting that clearly the Christian faith is not depicted as triumphalist in the sense that Christians are automatically protected from persecution, suffering, hardship—indeed, from any of the ills that characterize our present era, including disease and death. According to our author, we can be victorious in and through whatever may come our way, if by faith we keep our eyes on the glorious future that God has prepared for us (cf. 1 Cor 2:9). Nothing can take that future away from us (cf. Rom 8:37–39).

All the Saints Together Brought to the Goal (11:39–40)

Having concluded his list of examples, our author now repeats what he said in verse 2: all these models of faith were "well attested by their faith" (v. 39). And again with his mind on the future hope that awaits the saints, he concludes that they "did not receive what was promised." Whatever degree of partial fulfillments one may care to speak of in history and the present, ultimately the promise concerns a fulfillment that necessarily lies in the future. That is so because it must involve a transformation of the present order and, indeed, a transformation of us. Only in this way can the perfection that God promises be realized. In the

Study Questions

1. What is it about faith that the author of Hebrews wants his readers to understand, and how does he get his point across?

2. Discuss the motivation that the readers of Hebrews are to have for faithfulness in the present.

3. Discuss the faithfulness of God as seen in Hebrews' reflection on Abraham.

Key Terms

faith
substance
hope
metaphor
Akedah
anachronism

present the most we may experience are but relatively faint anticipations of the glorious future that will be ours (cf. Rom 8:18–25).

As wonderful as God's work was in the past, it pales in comparison with what God now has done in Christ. We have reached a new stage in the history of salvation. This is modestly expressed as "something better for us" (v. 40). We have repeatedly seen the word "better" in Hebrews used to describe the advan-

Further Reading

Barber, C. J. "Moses: A Study of Hebrews 11:23–29a." *Grace Journal* 14 (1973): 14–28.

Betz, O. "Firmness in Faith: Hebrews 11,1 and Isaiah 28,16." In *Scripture: Meaning and Method*, ed. B. P. Thompson. Hull: Hull University Press, 1987. Pp. 92–113.

Cockerill, G. L. "The Better Resurrection (Heb. 11:35): A Key to the Structure and Rhetorical Purpose of Hebrews 11." *Tyndale Bulletin* 51 (2000): 215–34.

Cosby, M. R. "The Rhetorical Composition of Hebrews 11." *Journal of Biblical Literature* 107 (1988): 257–73.

Eisenbaum, P. M. *The Jewish Heroes of Christian History: Hebrews 11 in Literary Context*. Atlanta: Scholars Press, 1997.

Hamm, D. "Faith in the Epistle to the Hebrews: The Jesus Factor." *Catholic Biblical Quarterly* 52 (1990): 270–91.

Hughes, P. E. "The Doctrine of Creation in Hebrews 11.3." *Biblical Theology Bulletin* 2 (1972): 64–77.

Johnsson, W. G. "The Pilgrimage Motif in the Book of Hebrews." *Journal of Biblical Literature* 97 (1978): 239–51.

Kendal, R. T. *Believing God: Studies on Faith in Hebrews 11*. Grand Rapids: Zondervan, 1981.

Laansma, J. *"I Will Give You Rest": The Rest Motif in the New Testament with Special Reference to Mt 11 and Heb 3–4*. Wissenschaftliche Untersuchungen zum Neuen Testament. Second series 98. Tübingen: Mohr Siebeck, 1997.

Longenecker, R. N. "The 'Faith of Abraham' Theme in Paul, James and Hebrews: A Study in the Circumstantial Nature of New Testament Teaching." *Journal of the Evangelical Theological Society* 20 (1977): 203–12.

Miller, M. R. "What Is the Literary Form of Hebrews 11?" *Journal of the Evangelical Theological Society* 29 (1986): 411–17.

Peake, A. S. *The Heroes and Martyrs of Faith: Studies in the Eleventh Chapter of the Epistle to the Hebrews*. London: Hodder & Stoughton, 1910.

Wilcox, M. "The Bones of Joseph: Hebrews 11:22." In *Scripture: Meaning and Method*, ed. B. P. Thompson. Hull: Hull University Press, 1987. Pp. 114–30.

tages of the new covenant over the old. But now our author insists that those of the past also will participate in these better things. Old covenant saints and new covenant saints have the same inheritance. The result is that those of the past cannot be brought to the ultimate goal ("be made perfect") apart from us. In the grand story of salvation, all will come together to enjoy one great final and perfect salvation perfectly realized. This will be the reward of those who believed and who expressed their faith, so giving faith substance and providing evidence of the unseen and of things yet to come.

12 A Call to Faithfulness

In actual fact all these things now spoken of [12:22–24] are invisible though worthy of our love, just as all the other things [12:18–21] were visible and deserving of fear. These must be approached in faith and in the spirit, just as the former were approached in actuality on the feet and in the flesh. And it is a great joy that by faith there is brought to pass for us, nay rather are actually ours, God, Christ, the Church, the angels, the saints and all else.

—Martin Luther, *Lectures on the Epistle to the Hebrews*

Supplemental Reading

Genesis 25:29–34; 27:30–40; Deuteronomy 29:16–18; Psalm 34:11–14; Isaiah 35:3–4; 2 Corinthians 4:16–18; 1 Peter 1:3–9; 4:12–19

Outline

- **Fix Your Gaze upon Jesus, the Peerless Example of Faith (12:1–3)**
- **The Role of God's Discipline in the Christian Life (12:4–11)**
- **A Call to Holiness and a Further Warning (12:12–17)**
- **The Glory of the Christian's Present Status (12:18–24)**
- **A Final Warning to Readers (12:25–29)**

Objectives

1. Highlight Jesus as the perfect model.
2. Explain the purpose of chastening from God.
3. Comment on the glory of the Christian's present status.

witness

No matter how exemplary they may be, human models always have their flaws, and so they are bound to disappoint sooner or later. None of the examples mentioned in chapter 11 was perfect. No Christian today is or can be perfect. In truth, there is only one who is worthy for us to fix our gaze upon, only one who will never disappoint, only one who is a perfect model. Thus, our author calls us finally to make Jesus our model. He proceeds to call his readers yet again to faithfulness, endurance, and holiness. Then, in characteristic fashion, he interrupts to present striking imagery in a discourse on the Christian's present glorious status before returning to a further warning.

Fix Your Gaze upon Jesus, the Peerless Example of Faith (12:1–3)

The examples given in chapter 11 provide a strong motivating impetus to faithfulness. The word "therefore" is particularly strong here as the author moves now to direct exhortation. On the basis of what preceded, this is what we (he includes himself with the readers) ought to do. Our author employs the picturesque language of being surrounded by a "great cloud of witnesses" (v. 1). This is not **witness** in the sense that they are observing us. Rather, the author is referring to those witnessed to or attested by their faith, mentioned in chapter 11 (cf. 11:2, 39). Their examples are meant to be an encouragement to the readers.

With the example of these faithful people of the past in mind, the readers are to run a comparable race, running it well and achieving the goal. The image of the race as a metaphor

for living the Christian life is not uncommon in the New Testament (see 1 Cor 9:24; Gal 2:2; 5:7; Phil 2:16; and especially 2 Tm 4:7). It gives rise to the accompanying metaphors of putting off "every encumbrance," running the course "marked out for us," and running it "with endurance," all as a runner must do. Appreciating these metaphors does not require much of the modern reader, since the running of races is done now in much the same way as in the first century. There is but one element that the author imports that is unfamiliar to racing itself: the idea that "sin" is something "that entangles us" and will keep us from running well. Sin is always an impediment to living the Christian life. Sin gets in the way of our fellowship with God, distorts our vision and our thinking, and makes us ineffective under even slight pressure. Sin provides us with a weight that will drag us down and lead to further stumbling. To run "with endurance" is precisely what the author has been urging his readers to do from the beginning (cf. 2:1–4). Endurance is one of the things most needed by them, especially given the circumstances they face.

In this race that is to be run, we are to "fix our eyes on Jesus, the author and perfecter of our faith" (v. 2). It is of the utmost importance here to note that Jesus is not merely our supreme example, but rather, as the titles "author" (or "pioneer" [cf. 2:10]) and "perfecter" indicate, the one who initiates faith and brings it to its intended completion (cf. 5:9). Jesus is there at the beginning and at the end of faith. As he goes to his death on the cross in obedience to his Father, what a supreme example of faith he is for the readers! When Jesus "endured the cross" and did so "for the joy set before him," he perfectly exemplified how the readers should behave in their present circumstances. They too must endure suffering and must have their mind set on the unseen re-

discipline

ward. They too must despise the shame of suffering, just as Jesus scorned the shame of the cross. An exhortation along this line will be given in 13:13: "Let us, then, go to him outside the camp, bearing the disgrace he bore." Having mentioned the cross, the fulfillment of the very heart of Jesus' mission, our author rounds out his statement by referring once more to the now familiar Psalm 110:1, saying that Jesus "sat down at the right hand of God" (v. 2).

The readers are urged to "consider" Jesus—that is, to set their minds firmly upon him who had to suffer such great hostility from sinners. Doing so will provide them with the strength and courage they need, so that they "will not grow weary and lose heart"(v. 3). In their sufferings they not only follow those examples of faith who suffered and triumphed in the past, but also they follow in the steps of their Lord, and as they consider this fact, they will find sustenance. Jesus is not only their example but also their empathic high priest, who will aid them (cf. 2:17–18; 4:15–16; 7:25).

The Role of God's Discipline in the Christian Life (12:4–11)

In verse 4 we find important information concerning the readers' past experience of persecution. They had struggled "against sin," which in this context means the resistance shown to their persecutors. This already had been indicated in 10:32–34. They had experienced intense suffering, but not yet to the point of "shedding blood," meaning martyrdom. The implication, however, is that matters could become that horrific in the

near future. As we have seen, this may well be the reason why these Jewish Christians were strongly tempted to leave their Christianity behind and to return to the protection afforded them within Judaism, as a legal religion (*religio licita*) in the Roman Empire.

But why must Christians suffer at all? This problem causes our author to present a brief defense of the positive role of suffering in the Christian life. He uses as his text in verses 5–6 a quotation from the Septuagint of Proverbs 3:11–12. Readers would have been familiar with this passage, and the same argument was used in Jewish circles (e.g., Philo, *On the Preliminary Studies* 175–177). It is an ideal passage for our author's purpose because it indicates that God's children are exactly those who may expect chastening from the God who loves them. As he likes so much to do, our author proceeds to comment on the quoted passage, drawing out its meaning in midrashic fashion (vv. 7–11), repeating more than once the words "sons" (note also the correlative "father") and "discipline." Thus, he says that it is for *discipline* that the readers are meant to endure, and that in the same way that a father *disciplines* a son, so God deals with us as *sons* (obviously, daughters are also included throughout) (v. 7). Accordingly, not to be under **discipline** raises the question about whether we are legitimate *sons* (v. 8). We readily accepted the *discipline* of our earthly fathers; we ought also to "be subject" to our heavenly Father, here called "the Father of spirits" (a deliberate contrast to "earthly fathers," literally, "the fathers of our flesh"). The goal of this is that we might "live" (v. 9). Our earthly fathers *disciplined* us for a short time and for limited purposes; God does so "for good," "that we may share his holiness" (v. 10). Finally, our author notes that all *discipline* is painful, but for those who understand its positive purpose, it ultimately leads

159

in his steps. We do not suffer because we have necessarily done something evil, but rather, because God, through our suffering, wants to make us holy. And for us, suffering is of limited duration and is the prelude to a wonderful future that awaits us. As the apostle Paul puts it so powerfully, "Our light and momentary troubles are achieving for us an eternal glory that far outweighs them all" (2 Cor 4:17; cf. 1 Pt 1:6–7; 4:12–14). This view is significant not only for the readers, but also for Christians in every era.

A Call to Holiness and a Further Warning (12:12–17)

Our author again turns to the rich resource of the Scriptures for imagery that he may apply to the readers. In this case, the picturesque language of verse 12 is drawn from Isaiah 35:3, and that of the first part of verse 13 from Proverbs 4:26, both according to the Septuagint. The readers are figuratively portrayed here as being in a state of discouragement and weakness. They need "level paths" to walk on so that they can be healed rather than further disabled. This metaphor provides an appeal for the readers to live in a way that is obedient and thus pleasing to God. Only so can their weakness and lameness be healed. Only faithful living will bring them successfully through the present circumstances.

There are two calls in verse 14, one to "peace" (an allusion to Ps 34:14), and the other to "holiness." Both themes occur frequently in the New Testament, and the idea of *shalom* (ultimate well-being in every respect) would have been an important concept for the readers. For the former, see especially Romans 14:19; 1 Peter

to "the peaceful fruit of righteousness" (v. 11). In this last verse, the word "trained" (*gymnazō*) is drawn from the imagery of the athletic games, where the experience of pain also has a positive goal.

This attitude toward present suffering turns the common view of other religions on its head. Almost universally, the religions of the world regard suffering as a mark of the disfavor of the deity. Indeed, the goal of these religions is somehow to get on the right side of the deity and thereby avoid suffering. The attitude of the Old Testament and the New Testament alike is quite revolutionary in this regard. Here, it is unhesitatingly affirmed that the righteous—that is, those who belong to God—may well suffer in the present, and that this is *not* necessarily a sign that God is angry with us or is punishing us for something we have done. On the contrary, there is an overarching paradigm that sanctifies suffering for the Christian: our Lord, who had himself done no wrong, suffered (cf. 5:8). We are called to walk

Mount Zion

realized eschatology

3:11; but also, Romans 12:18; 2 Corinthians 13:11; 2 Timothy 2:22. For the latter, see especially 1 Peter 1:15, but also Romans 6:19, 22; 1 Corinthians 1:30; 1 Thessalonians 4:3. These two characteristics are fundamental to the Christian life. In a striking parallel, the Matthean version of the Beatitudes juxtaposes peace and purity. Thus, in Matthew 5:9 we read, "Blessed are the peacemakers, for they will be called children of God," while in Matthew 5:8 we read, "Blessed are the pure in heart, for they will see God." In the latter, holiness is related to seeing God, in much the same way as in our passage. Note that holiness, or sanctification, is not an option but a requirement. Without it, one will not "see the Lord." These words are a reference to the eschatological vision of God (cf. Rv 22:4).

Verses 15–17 return more directly to the plight of the readers and the concern of the author. This renewed warning begins with an exhortation for the readers to care for one another (cf. 10:24–25) by looking out for others so that no one "fails to obtain the grace of God." This refers to apostasy, as the following verses make clear. The metaphor of a "root of bitterness" that can be a source of defilement to others alludes to Deuteronomy 29:18, where it refers to one "whose heart is already turning away from the LORD our God." Thus, whenever someone falls away, that has a negative effect upon others in the community.

To reinforce the warning, our author brings forward the illustration of Esau (vv. 16–17), which has direct relevance to the temptation facing the readers. Esau, described as "immoral or godless," "sold his birthright for a single meal" (Gn 25:33–34). In so doing, Esau is the very antithesis of the examples of faith in chapter 11. Esau traded off his rights of inheritance as the firstborn, something unseen and that lay in the in-determinate future, for the immediate gratification of the here and now: a meal of bread and stew (contrast the attitude of Moses referred to in 11:25–26). In the Esau story our author finds a further point that is exactly in line with what he wants to say to his readers. When Esau desired to repent of his rashness, he could not change what had been done (Gn 27:30–40). In a very similar way, if the readers turn away from their Christian faith, there will be no way back for them (cf. 6:4–6; 10:26–27). Again, then, we have a reminder of the grave seriousness of apostasy. The readers must not contemplate any course of action in the belief that there will always be the possibility of a way back. On the contrary, our author calls them to steadfast faithfulness even in the face of great adversity.

The Glory of the Christian's Present Status (12:18–24)

In what is one of the most vivid passages of the entire New Testament, our author draws out the contrast between the old and new covenants. In so doing, he is able to highlight the incomparable superiority of the new to the old. Similar contrastive passages may be found from Paul's letters (e.g., 2 Cor 3:6–18; Gal 4:24–31), but none is as powerful as the present one. Most significant is the description of **Mount Zion** as the present reality to which Christians have come. This provides a glorious picture of **realized eschatology** as the present reality of the Christian. The purpose of the contrast is to indicate what the readers already enjoy, and what they necessarily return to if they abandon their Christian faith. The contrast is particularly telling.

A Contrast of the Old and New Covenants: Mount Sinai and Mount Zion

The amazing contrast drawn between Sinai and Zion, as a way of comparing the two covenant realities, contains the following elements, which can be numbered in seven components on each side. Immediately obvious is the brevity of the first list compared to the fullness of language in the second.

Sinai	Zion
a mountain that may not be touched	the city of the living God, the heavenly Jerusalem
blazing fire	myriads of angels in festal gathering
darkness	the assembly of the first-born enrolled in heaven
gloom	God, judge of all
whirlwind	the spirits of the righteous made perfect
blast of a trumpet	Jesus, the mediator of a new covenant
fearful sound of words	the sprinkled blood, better than that of Abel
(Moses: full of fear and trembling)	

How could those who had come to Zion possibly want to go back to Sinai?

To begin with, our author presents a description of Mount Sinai as symbolic of Judaism and the religion of the law. The graphic imagery is drawn from various passages of the Pentateuch: Exodus 19:12–19; 20:18–21; Deuteronomy 4:11; 5:22–25. The revelation at Sinai revealed something of the power and authority of God, and it was a terrifying experience, as the mention of blazing fire, darkness, gloom, and whirlwind indicates (v. 18). The mountain was a tangible reality, but because of the absolute otherness (holiness) of God, no one was allowed to touch it (Ex 19:12). Death was the penalty for doing so, even for an animal, as the quotation of Exodus 19:13 in verse 20 indicates. According to verse 19, the Israelites could not bear the sound of the voice that spoke from the mountain, nor, according to verse 20, could they bear the commands that were given (the specific one mentioned may be taken as indicative of a wider unbearableness of the commandments). Those who heard "begged that no further words be spoken to them" (v. 19). In summarizing the terrifying character of Sinai, our author cites the great Moses himself as saying, "I am trembling with fear" (v. 21, based on Dt 9:19). Thus, Sinai is deliberately set forth in an unappealing way in order to sharpen the contrast with what our author calls Zion.

Turning to the new covenant, our author repeats the verb that was negated in verse 18, "you have not come," now using the positive, "you have come" (v. 22). The perfect tense of the Greek verb here is very important because it refers to something accomplished in the past with results lasting into the present. The emphasis is on present reality. What follows, therefore, is the description of the present enjoyment of an exalted, glorious status (cf. Eph 2:6, and its aorist tenses). But what is it that we have come to? More specifically, what constitutes the Mount Zion of the new covenant that is contrasted with the Mount Sinai of the old covenant?

In one of the New Testament's most astonishing expressions of realized eschatology, the author describes the reality of the new covenant by means of seven successive phrases. First, Zion, itself another name for Jerusalem in the Old Testament, is identified as "the city of the living God, the heavenly Jerusalem" (v. 22). This is a symbol for ultimate salvation and the experience of what

A view of the mountains of Sinai, taken from the summit of Mount Sinai

The City in Hebrews

There are more references to "the city," that is, the heavenly Jerusalem, in Hebrews than in any other New Testament book. For references to the same reality, we may compare texts such as Galatians 4:26; Revelation 21:2, 10; *2 Baruch* 4.

the city which has foundations, whose architect and builder is God (11:10)
God has prepared a city for them (11:16)
the city of the living God, the heavenly Jerusalem (12:22)
here we have no lasting city, but are looking for the one to come (13:14)

might be called an eschatological *shalom*. Just as Sinai stands for the old covenant, so Zion stands for the new covenant and all of its blessings. F. F. Bruce captures the point in these words: "As the earthly Zion was the meeting point for the tribes of old Israel, so the heavenly Zion is the meeting point for the new Israel" (*Epistle to the Hebrews*, 356).

Second, Christians have come to "innumerable angels in joyful assembly" (v. 22). These are the angels commonly associated with God's presence. They accompanied him at Sinai (Dt 33:2); they attend him in the heavenly court (Dn 7:10). Most im-

portant for our passage are the angels of Revelation 5:11, 7:11, and (probably) 19:6. These are angels in festive assembly, rejoicing and praising God for the salvation he has accomplished by the Lamb. That salvation is achieved now, is rejoiced in now, and only remains to be consummated.

Third, as Christians, the readers have come to "the assembly [literally, 'church'] of the firstborn," further defined as those "who are enrolled in heaven" (v. 23). The identity of these firstborn is difficult to establish. It is highly unlikely that angels are meant. Possibly the firstborn are Old Testament saints, but more likely the author has Christians (perhaps Christian martyrs) in mind (cf. "enrolled in heaven" in Lk 10:20). Christians may be regarded as the firstborn in the sense that they are the ones destined to inherit—that is, the heirs of the promise (see Rom 8:17). The readers not only have come to this assembly, the church, but also have become a part of it.

heavenly Jerusalem

Fourth, they have come "to God, the judge of all" (v. 23). They fearlessly (contrast Sinai) have come to God as judge (cf. v. 29; 9:27; 10:31), and can do so because Christ has gone before them as their high priest. This freedom is akin to the boldness of access into the presence of God through the sacrifice of Christ, of which we have repeatedly read in Hebrews (cf. 4:16; 6:19; 7:25; 10:19–21).

Fifth, the readers have come to "the spirits of the righteous made perfect" (v. 23). This probably is a reference to the saints of the Old Testament awaiting the resurrection—hence "spirits" (indistinguishable from "souls," i.e., the immaterial aspect of human beings). The designation is familiar from Jewish apocalyptic literature. The description of these saints as "made perfect" means, as always in Hebrews, that they have arrived at the goal, here envisioned as Mount Zion, the **heavenly Jerusalem**, and the fulfillment associated with it. It is important for our author that they arrive at this goal only together with us, and not apart from us (cf. 11:40). Thus, Zion is the possession of the entire family of faith, spanning both testaments.

Sixth, the readers have come to "Jesus, the mediator of a new covenant" (v. 24). This language we have already encountered in 8:6 and 9:15. The covenant mediated by Jesus is what makes Mount Zion a reality. The new covenant already anticipated in the old covenant now has come into existence, thereby bringing the old to its goal and fulfillment.

Seventh, and climactically, they have come to "the sprinkled blood," the atoning blood of Jesus (v. 24; cf. 10:22; 1 Pt 1:2). Again, we come to the heart of Hebrews: the death of Jesus as the fulfillment of the sacrificial ritual of the old covenant that was its foreshadowing and preparation. The new covenant depends totally upon

Realized Eschatology in Hebrews

Hebrews contains an unusually large amount of material that can be understood as realized eschatology. This idea of things strictly future that nevertheless have entered the present is introduced to the New Testament reader in the Synoptic Gospels. The gospel preached by Jesus concerns the present coming of the kingdom of God in and through his own ministry and death/resurrection. Although a future coming of the kingdom will transform the world that we know, the kingdom, in some real sense,

already has come. This state of affairs has been expressed as fulfillment of the promises, but a fulfillment short of the consummation of the promises. Thus, the future already has entered the present in advance of its full coming in the future. This perspective is a central feature of Paul's theology. We may assume that it is common throughout all of early Christianity. Hebrews has a number of passages in addition to 12:22–24 that could be said to contain realized eschatology. These passages stand in some tension with

those that speak of a definitely future eschatology (e.g., 2:8; 6:11; 9:28; 10:13, 25, 27, 30, 37).

in these last days (1:2)
we who have believed enter that rest (4:3)
those who have tasted the goodness of the age to come (6:5)
the good things that have come (9:11)
a shadow of the good things that are coming (10:1)
grateful for receiving a kingdom that cannot be shaken (12:28)

The New Covenant in Hebrews

The new covenant is of enormous importance in Hebrews, finding, as it does, its roots in the promise of Jeremiah 31:31–34, and its fulfillment in the work of Christ as its mediator.

The new covenant is in view in the following passages:

Jesus the guarantee of a better covenant (7:22)
the covenant that Jesus mediates is better (8:6–12; quotation of Jer 31:31–34)
the mediator of a new covenant (9:15)
the Holy Spirit testifying to the new covenant (10:16–17; requotation of Jer 31:33–34)
the blood of the covenant (10:29)
the mediator of a new covenant (12:24)
the blood of the eternal covenant (13:20)

speaks out of the ground for revenge (Gn 4:10; cf. "the blood of the righteous Abel" [Mt 23:35]), the blood of Christ speaks for forgiveness. This is in full accord with the promise of Jeremiah that in the new covenant God promises, "I will be merciful toward their iniquities, and I will remember their sins no more" (Jer 31:34, quoted in 8:12; 10:17). The blood of Jesus, and it alone, has brought us to the glorious fulfillment of Zion and to the wonderful catalog of blessings associated with it.

A Final Warning to Readers (12:25–29)

For a final time, our author warns the readers, as he has done throughout his sermon-treatise. This warning, with its form of argument from the lesser to the greater, is quite similar to that with which he began in 2:1–3 and that in 10:28–29. If in the lesser case, those of the past experienced judgment for unfaithfulness to the old and inferior, how much more, in the greater case, we may expect judgment for unfaithfulness to the

the death of Jesus, the shedding of his blood on the cross. The notion of "sprinkling" is used deliberately to draw out the parallel to the work of the Levitical priesthood (cf. 9:13–14, 19, 21). Our author adds that this blood "speaks a better word than the blood of Abel." Apparently, in view here is that whereas the blood of Abel

St. Catherine's Monastery, built at the beginning of the fourth century at the foot of Mount Sinai

Study Questions

1. In what ways is Jesus the perfect exemplar for those who are "running the race"?

2. Explain the reasoning that the author of Hebrews gives for why Christians must suffer.

3. Discuss how the author of Hebrews contrasts the old and new covenants, and what this means for the present status of Christians.

new and better. As we have repeatedly seen, this is far from a theoretical warning. It has in view the very real temptation of the readers to abandon their Christian faith. The one who "speaks" and "warns from heaven" is, of course, God (v. 25). In the former situation, God spoke from Sinai and "his voice shook the earth" (v. 26; see Ex 19:18; Ps 68:8).

But another shaking of the earth, and indeed of heaven, is promised in Scripture, as our author points out in his quotation of Haggai 2:6 (cf. Hg 2:21) in verse 26. As we have come to expect, the author provides a midrashic comment on the passage. The "yet *once more*," he asserts in verse 27, must have application to the things that "can be shaken" (not the same Greek word as in the quotation, but a synonym)—that is, things that have been created. The shaking in view here is that of future apocalyptic judgment, what we refer to as the end of the world (cf. Mt 24:29). Our author has already quoted a passage along these same lines, Psalm 102:25–27, in 1:10–12. After the apocalyptic shaking, only what has been established by God will remain.

The final shaking constitutes no threat to Christians, however, since they are receiving a kingdom "that cannot be shaken" (v. 28), a kingdom that will endure forever. The present tense of the participle "receiving" occupies middle ground between the past and future tenses we have encountered, and thus balances realized and future eschatology. The kingdom inaugurated by Christ provides security to the believer in all circumstances. It is the fruit of the new covenant. This security should motivate us to gratitude or thankful-

Further Reading

Black, D. A. "A Note on the Structure of Hebrews 12:1–2." *Biblica* 68 (1987): 543–51.

Caird, G. B. "Just Men Made Perfect." *London Quarterly and Holborn Review* 35 (1966): 47–73.

Croy, N. C. *Endurance in Suffering: Hebrews 12:1–13 in Its Rhetorical, Religious, and Philosophical Contexts.* Society for New Testament Studies Monograph Series 98. Cambridge: Cambridge University Press, 1998.

Dumbrell, W. J. "The Spirits of Just Men Made Perfect." *Evangelical Quarterly* 48 (1976): 154–59.

Ellingworth, P. "New Testament Text and Old Testament Context in Heb. 12:3." In *Studia Biblica 3,* ed. E. A. Livingston. Sheffield: JSOT Press, 1980. Pp. 89–96.

Jones, P. R. "A Superior Life: Hebrews 12:3–13:25." *Review and Expositor* 82 (1985): 391–405.

Thompson, J. W. "'That Which Cannot Be Shaken': Some Metaphysical Assumptions in Hebrews 12:27." *Journal of Biblical Literature* 94 (1975): 580–87.

Key Terms

witness
discipline
Mount Zion
realized eschatology
heavenly Jerusalem

ness, which in turn will enable an "acceptable worship with reverence and awe." Here, the particular word for "worship" (*latreuō*) is the technical word used for the priestly service of the old covenant (e.g., 8:5; 9:9; 10:2; 13:10; and the cognate noun in 9:1, 6), suggesting that Christian worship is the spiritual fulfillment of the Levitical temple service (see also this spiritualized sense of the word in 9:14). "Reverence and awe" are still appropriate for Christians, even though they have an unrestricted and bold access into the presence of God through the new covenant. Since God's character does not change, it remains true even for Christians that our "God is a consuming fire" (a quotation from Dt 4:24; cf. Dt 9:3), a point made frequently in the Old Testament (e.g., Is 26:11; 33:14; Zep 1:18; 3:8) and alluded to already in 10:27 (cf. 10:30–31). This somber note concerning the reality of God's fiery judgment is stressed by the author with the danger of the readers in mind. It is meant to remove any thought of apostasy and to call the readers to a continued faithfulness. On this point the argument proper concludes, although our author will touch on several of the themes again in his concluding comments.

13 Concluding Exhortations and Benediction

They had been accustomed to think of the "camp" and all that was inside it as sacred, while everything outside it was profane and unclean. Were they to leave its sacred precincts and venture on to unhallowed ground? Yes, because in Jesus the old values had been reversed. What was formerly sacred was now unhallowed, because Jesus had been expelled from it; what was formerly unhallowed was now sacred, because Jesus was there.

—F. F. Bruce, *The Epistle to the Hebrews*

Supplemental Reading

Jeremiah 32:36–41; Matthew 22:37–40; Mark 12:29–31; John 19:17–22; Philippians 2:12–13

Outline

- **Various Ethical Exhortations (13:1–9)**
- **The True Sacrifices (13:10–16)**
- **Obedience to Church Leaders (13:17)**
- **A Prayer Request and a Personal Note (13:18–19)**
- **Concluding Prayer and Doxology (13:20–21)**
- **Postscript with Personal Information (13:22–23)**
- **Greetings and Final Benediction (13:24–25)**

Objectives

1. List the recurring main themes of Hebrews.
2. Explore the content of the concluding prayer and doxology.
3. Interpret the significance of the specific concluding information.

Our author has concluded his main presentation. He has made his argument as persuasively as he can. But just as any person writing to loved ones thinks of more things to say at the end of a letter, the author now turns to a variety of practical matters concerning which he wants to exhort his readers before he brings the treatise-sermon-letter to a full conclusion. The matters that he turns to are similar to the practical exhortations found in almost any New Testament letter, except that he intersperses material that bears his distinctive stamp and concerns. The structure of this final chapter can be divided into four parts: the exhortations (vv. 1–19), the concluding prayer and doxology (vv. 20–21), a postscript with personal information (vv. 22–24), and a final benediction (v. 25). The character of this chapter, especially the postscript, is what qualifies Hebrews to be called a letter. From this material we are in a position to learn more about the readers.

Exhortations in Hebrews 13

The concluding chapter of Hebrews is filled with final exhortations directed to the readers. Most of these are specifically relevant to the first readers and their circumstances, but a number of them also are of a general or formulaic nature, comparable with what we typically find at the end of other New Testament letters.

continue in brotherly love
show hospitality to strangers
remember those in prison and ill-treated
hold marriage in high honor
let the marriage bed be pure
keep free from love of money
be content with what you have

remember your leaders
consider their way of life
imitate their faith

do not be misled by false teaching
go forth to Jesus outside the camp
bear the abuse Jesus suffered
offer continual sacrifice of praise
do not neglect to do good
share what you have

obey and submit to your leaders
pray for us

bear with my word of exhortation
greet all your leaders and all the saints

Various Ethical Exhortations (13:1–9)

The first exhortation comes directly to the heart of all Christian ethics, love—in this case spelled out specifically as "brotherly love" (*philadelphia*). The word "brotherly," of course, includes women as well as men in the church. Here, one thinks immediately of Jesus' brilliant summary of the law in the twofold love commandment: love God and your neighbor as yourself (Mt 22:37–40; Mk 12:29–31; cf. Rom 13:9–10). This exhortation is common in the epistles (see Rom 12:10; 1 Thes 4:9; 1 Pt 1:22). Our author has already exhorted his readers concerning love in 10:24. The form of the exhortation implies that they have been doing well, and need only to continue in the same manner (cf. 6:10; 10:34).

The second exhortation (v. 2) concerns hospitality—again, an important virtue in the New Testament (see Rom 12:13; 1 Tm 3:2; 5:10; Ti 1:8; 1 Pt 4:9; cf. the teaching of Jesus in Mt 25:35, 38, 44). It was important to provide food and lodging to traveling Christians who were passing through one's region, especially those working for the church, as 3 John 5–8 indicates. The idea of unknowingly entertaining angels alludes back to famous stories known to our Jewish readers (see Gn 18:1–8; 19:1–3 [Abraham]; Jgs 6:11–22 [Gideon]; 13:3–21 [Manoah and the mother of Samson]; Tobit 5:4–9 [Tobit]). Chapters 11–12 of the early Christian *Didache* (*Teaching of the Twelve Apostles*) affirm the provision of hospitality to Christian evangelists, who are to be received "as the Lord," but also set forth restrictions against the abuse of hospitality (two or three days maximum stay).

As for the third exhortation (v. 3), to remember those in prison, our author has already complimented the readers on their past performance (10:33–34; cf. 6:10). The last clause of verse 3 is somewhat obscure: literally, "since you yourselves are also in a body." Probably, this simply is a reminder of the frailty of the readers and the fact that they too could soon find themselves in prison and in need of such kindness. Part of the calling of Christians is to suffer with those who suffer (see Rom 12:15; 1 Cor 12:26).

The fourth exhortation (v. 4) at first may seem strange to us. Who would not honor marriage? The author's concern to defend the propriety of marriage suggests that the readers may have been tempted into an extreme form of asceticism (see also the matter of food in v. 9). It might well be that the readers were under some gnostic influence. The gnostic dualism between matter and spirit so exalted the latter that the physical body was regarded either as an actual obstacle to the life of the spirit or as merely inconsequential. This meant that one might be inclined to deny bodily pleasures altogether (such as sexual relationships, even within marriage), or, in just the opposite manner, to let the flesh indulge freely in everything because, after all, only the spirit was important. In keeping with the Jewish affirmation of the goodness of the material creation, our author affirms the propriety of marriage and at the same time cautions against sexual immorality of any kind. Like Paul, he warns that God will judge the sexually immoral (cf. 1 Cor 6:9; Eph 5:5; Col 3:5).

In the fifth exhortation (v. 5) the author turns to the perennial problem of "the love of money." In every culture and time the love of money has had a powerful effect over people, their priorities, and the ways in which they live. Jesus warned about the effect of loving money (Mt 6:24–34; Lk 12:15—written as though addressed to the materialism of our own era). For a New Testament passage along the same line, see 1 Timothy 6:6–10, where we read that "the love of money is the root of all evils; it is through this craving that some have wandered away from the faith."

Christians are to be content with what they have, knowing that they can rely upon the Lord to sustain them in all circumstances. In God as our helper we have a security that neither possessions nor money ever can provide (cf. 10:34). The point is supported by the quotation of two Old Testament texts. The first is from Deuteronomy 31:6, 8, but altered to the first person, "I will" (cf. Jos 1:5). What God said to the people of Israel he says now to Christian readers: "I will never fail you nor forsake you." In verse 6 the author extends the application of this thought to the situation of threat that was facing the readers, using a second quotation, this one from Psalm 118:6 (agreeing exactly with the Septuagint form): "The Lord is my helper, I will not be afraid; what can man do to me?" The security available to Christians transcends the concerns of their earthly existence. Their security is indeed of an ultimate kind that cannot be threatened by persecution or even by martyrdom. Accordingly, whatever the pressure they come under, the readers can and must remain true to their Christian confession.

the camp

Next, the readers are exhorted to remember their leaders and to "imitate their faith" (v. 7). These leaders were probably those who founded the community, as seems clear from their identification as "those who spoke to you the word of God." The call to imitate their faith reminds us of the lengthy presentation on faith in chapter 11. Obviously, these leaders had exhibited the same kind of active faith that counts upon and reveals the reality of the unseen. They therefore are examples worthy of emulation. In verse 17 the readers are told to obey their (present) leaders and in verse 24 to greet them.

The weighty statement of verse 8 has, in the Greek, the following literal word order: "Jesus Christ yesterday and today the same and forever." Although not directly connected with the immediately preceding or following sentences, this statement, in keeping with the main purpose of Hebrews, serves to provide both concrete assurance and motivation to the readers. It is not meant as an abstract or theoretical statement about the eternal existence of the Son. Rather, it begins by pointing to matters already dealt with in the epistle—such things as derive from Christ's unique high priesthood: the atoning work of Christ ("yesterday"; e.g., chs. 9–10), the intercessory work of Christ ("today"; 4:14–16; 7:25), and added to these the fact that Jesus Christ will remain unchangeable in his faithfulness ("forever"). On the last point, see 1:12 (applying Ps 102:27 to Christ) and 7:24: "he holds his priesthood permanently, because he continues forever." The bottom line is that Jesus Christ, the source of all that the epistle has expounded, may be counted upon unfailingly in the unrestricted future (cf. Rv 1:17–18).

Although the author does not spell out the content of the "diverse and strange teachings," clearly they had to do with prohibited foods. But because they are described as "strange," they were not the traditional teachings of Judaism concerning clean and unclean foods. They seem instead to have been derived from gnostic asceticism, such as we have already encountered in verse 4 (note the very same two issues mentioned in 1 Tm 4:3). Our author shares the apostle Paul's perspective on the matter of foods: what matters is the grace of God, not the eating or banning of certain foods (Rom 14:17; 1 Cor 8:8; cf. Col 2:16, 21–23).

The True Sacrifices (13:10–16)

This turns our author's mind yet once again to the contrast between the old and the new. The altar mentioned in verse 10 is the altar that has brought to us the grace mentioned in verse 9 and has made food laws inconsequential. That unique altar, with its unique sacrifice, stands in stark contrast to the altar of the tabernacle and temple. Since the framework of the old system was only preparatory and anticipatory, the priests, even the high priest, have no access to this altar and this sacrifice. It is available only to Christian faith. Indeed, the priests were not even allowed to eat the sacrifices of the Day of Atonement and other sin offerings, for in those instances the carcasses were burned outside the city.

This last point brings to the author's mind the fact that Christ was crucified outside the city walls (Jn 19:20; cf. Mt 21:39), and he will not miss the opportunity once again to call attention to Christ's blood and its sanctifying power (v. 12; cf. 9:12; 10:10). There is deliberate typological correspondence between the burning of the carcasses of the animal sacrifices outside **the camp** of Israel and the death of Jesus outside the walls of

Jerusalem, but the author does not pursue this point. Instead, he draws a parallel between the suffering of Jesus "outside the camp" and the suffering of his readers, whose Christian faith has put them outside the camp of Israel and subjected them to abuse. Thus, he exhorts them, "Let us go forth to him outside the camp and bear the abuse he endured" (v. 13). As our author has repeated again and again, the readers must hold true to their faith even in the face of bitter persecution (cf. 2:1; 3:12; 4:11; 6:4–6; 10:35; 12:3). "Outside the camp" means outside the city, and this enables the author to reiterate another earlier emphasis: "here we have no lasting city, but we seek the city which is to come" (v. 14; cf. 11:10, 14–16). Thus, by means of associated words in different passages our author moves from one point to another, drawing the applications he desires.

There are sacrifices to be offered in the era of the new covenant—not sacrifices of animals, since those no longer have any place after the definitive sacrifice of Christ, but what could be called "spiritual" sacrifices. The language is similar to that of the temple's sacrificial ritual, but the content is entirely different (for a striking example of this transposition of terminology, see 1 Pt 2:5). The spiritual sacrifices mentioned here are praising the name of God (to be "continually" offered; cf. 12:28), doing good to others, and sharing with others (vv. 15–16). Such sacrifices are designated as "pleasing to God" (cf. v. 21).

Obedience to Church Leaders (13:17)

The leaders of the church already have been mentioned as models of

faith a little earlier in this concluding chapter (v. 7). Quite probably, they are leaders of the past, the founders of the church. Now our author encourages obedience to the present leaders. It is for their own good that the readers submit to them, since the leaders have the responsibility to "watch over" them—that is, be vigilant for their spiritual welfare (here, "souls" refers to persons). Because this is their designated responsibility, they "will have to give account" of their performance. If they can give a joyful account when that time comes, that will mean that the readers have persevered in their faith.

A Prayer Request and a Personal Note (13:18–19)

These tantalizing verses, offering direct and specific information about the author, unfortunately are obscure. The readers know much more than we do. Certainly, the readers knew the author and his circumstances well. We, on the other hand, are left only with puzzling statements. The request for prayer in the same sentence with the mention of a "clear conscience" and acting "honorably in all things" strongly suggests that the author has been involved in some serious controversy, the nature of which is unclear to us. Equally unclear is how we are to understand the reference to the author's being "restored." In light of the author's confidence in being able to visit the readers expressed in verse 23, we probably can rule out imprisonment, unless he is about to be released. In any case, something still hinders him from coming to the readers, and so he urges them "the more earnestly" to pray for him.

173

Ruins of the Forum in Rome, the heart of the Roman Empire

Concluding Prayer and Doxology (13:20–21)

In some of the most beautiful lines of the entire Bible, our author now commits his readers to the care and provision of God. In this magnificent prayer he touches upon some of the key motifs of the entire treatise-letter. The description of God as "the God of peace" is a common formula in the New Testament, especially in Paul (see Rom 15:33; 16:20; Phil 4:9; 1 Thes 5:23; cf. 1 Cor 14:33; 2 Cor 13:11). The idea of peace (*shalom*) reminds us of the discussion of the present availability of Sabbath rest in 3:7–4:13.

The opening words further describe God as the one "who brought again from the dead our Lord Jesus." This is the only direct reference in the whole of Hebrews to the resurrection of Jesus, but obviously the author's

frequent reference to the ascension of Jesus to God's right hand presupposes the reality of the resurrection. Reference to Jesus as "the great shepherd of the sheep" finds parallels in "the chief shepherd" of 1 Peter 5:4 and in "the good shepherd" in John 10:11 (cf. Mk 14:27).

The phrase "by the blood of the eternal covenant" touches upon several key motifs in Hebrews. We have seen at the heart of our homily-treatise (chs. 9–10) an emphasis upon the significance of Christ's sacrificial death in fulfillment of the Old Testament sacrifices. There, the blood of Christ frequently was mentioned (e.g., 9:12–14; 10:19; cf. 13:12). Furthermore, just as here, the blood of Jesus is linked with covenant in 9:20 and the new covenant in 10:29 (from the context) and 12:24. The reference to "the eternal covenant" recalls references to the "better covenant" mediated by Jesus (7:22; 8:6; 9:15; 12:24) and the "new covenant" promised in Jeremiah 31:31 (quoted

doxology

in 8:8–12). Striking in this connection is the subsequent reference in Jeremiah 32:40 to the covenant as "eternal" (see also Is 55:3; Ez 37:26). The eternal character of the new covenant is implied in the reference to Christ as one who "holds his priesthood permanently, because he continues forever" (7:24; cf. "eternal redemption" [9:12]).

The actual content of the petition is that the readers be equipped "with everything good" for the purpose of doing God's will (v. 21). The request is general enough to include all that the author has concerned himself with in what he has written. Particularly interesting is the remark that in the doing of God's will it is God himself who is "working in you that which is pleasing in his sight" (cf. the same point exactly in Phil 2:12–13). The doing of God's will is the supreme work of the Christian.

Central to the accomplishment of God's will and purposes for the world and the individual is the work of Christ. What makes it all possible is the agency of Jesus Christ: "through Jesus Christ" (v. 21). Despite the pivotal role of the work of Christ for our author, this is, surprisingly, the only occurrence of the phrase "through Jesus Christ" (or with either name singly), so characteristic of Paul.

In the **doxology**, the words "glory for ever and ever" are directed to Jesus Christ. This is in contrast to the majority of New Testament doxologies, which are directed to God, but fully in keeping with the high Christology of our author. Indeed, it can be seen to form an inclusio with chapter 1, as it offers a reference to Christ as God at the end of the treatise corresponding to that at the beginning. Among the very few other doxologies to Christ in the New Testament, we may compare 1 Peter 4:11 (although this might be directed to God), 2 Peter 3:18, and Revelation 1:6. Inasmuch as the entire weight of Hebrews depends upon what Christ our high priest has done, this doxology strikes one as particularly appropriate.

The Arch of Septimius Severus in the Roman Forum

Postscript with Personal Information (13:22–23)

If the Pauline pattern applies here, quite possibly our author in this postscript writes a few words by his own hand. In verse 22 we have the author's own description of what he has written. He refers to it as a "word of exhortation" (*logos tēs paraklēseōs*). From the content of the epistle, with its regular and repeated exhortations interspersed between sections of discourse, we now can see how fitting this description is. Any final estimate of the document we call "Hebrews" must use three words: homily (for the exhortation), treatise (for the discourse), and letter (for the epistolary ending), with the emphasis on the first of the three. Whether the author actually has written "briefly" is, of course, debatable. He, at any rate, felt that he did so, and we should remember the comment at 9:5b, "Of these things we cannot now speak in detail," and the frustration expressed at 11:32, "I do not have time." Given the momentous subject matter and the scope of redemptive history covered in He-

brews, we may well agree that our author has indeed written briefly.

The Timothy spoken of in verse 23 almost certainly is the disciple and collaborator of the apostle Paul. Obviously, he was known to the readers, and this puts our anonymous author solidly within the Pauline circle. Timothy probably had been released from prison recently, although from the New Testament we know of no such imprisonment. It is not intrinsically improbable, however. We can draw one indirect conclusion from the reference to Timothy: he was not the author of Hebrews. Given how little we know, this plain fact is not uninteresting. The author hopes to visit the readers in the company of Timothy.

Greetings and Final Benediction (13:24–25)

Greetings are sent to the leaders as well as to "all the saints," meaning all the members of this Christian community. One further added note provides a small piece of historical information. But what does the reference to "those who come from Italy send you greetings" mean? It could mean that the author was writing *from* Italy to some other place and sending greetings from the Italians to the Christians there; or, that he was writing *to* Italy from somewhere else, and Italian Christians there wanted to send greetings to their homeland.

Study Questions

1. Where and how are the main themes of Hebrews found in this last chapter?

2. What does the last chapter tell us about the audience and author of Hebrews?

3. Write your own brief summary of the content of Hebrews.

benediction

Further Reading

Attridge, H. W. "Paraenesis in a Homily (*logos parakleseos*): The Possible Location of, and Socialization in, the 'Epistle to the Hebrews.'" *Semeia* 50 (1990): 211–26.

Cranfield, C. E. B. "Hebrews 13:20–21." *Scottish Journal of Theology* 20 (1967): 437–41.

Filson, F. V. "'Yesterday': A Study of Hebrews in the Light of Chapter 13." London: SCM, 1967.

Koester, H. "'Outside the Camp': Hebrews 13:9–14." *Harvard Theological Review* 55 (1963): 299–315.

Lane, W. L. "Unexpected Light on Hebrews 13:1–6 from a Second Century Source." *Perspectives in Religious Studies* 9 (1982): 267–74.

Robinson, W. C. "Jesus Christ the Same Yesterday, and Today, and Forever (Heb. 13:8)." *Evangelical Quarterly* 16 (1944): 228–35.

Sanders, J. A. "Outside the Camp." *Union Seminary Quarterly* 24 (1969): 239–46.

Saunders, L. "'Outside the Camp': Hebrews 13." *Restoration Quarterly* 22 (1979): 19–24.

Smith, T. C. "An Exegesis of Hebrews 13:1–17." *Faith and Mission* 7 (1989): 70–78.

Snell, A. "We Have an Altar." *Reformed Theological Review* 23 (1964): 16–23.

Thompson, J. W. "Outside the Camp: A Study of Heb 13:9–14." *Catholic Biblical Quarterly* 40 (1978): 53–63.

Walker, P. "Jerusalem in Hebrews 13:9–14 and the Dating of the Epistle." *Tyndale Bulletin* 45 (1994): 39–72.

The latter possibility seems much more plausible, though it cannot be proved. The majority opinion among scholars is that our author writes to a Jewish Christian community very probably located in Rome.

Most New Testament letters end with a **benediction** such as our author provides. The benediction confers grace on the readers. The ending is a convention, but also it makes use of the single word that beyond any other encapsulates the Christian message. Grace, the unmerited favor of God, is at the heart of the New Testament story, and it is the very basis of the new covenant established upon the sacrificial death of God's Son for the salvation of the world.

Conclusion

The Place of Hebrews in the New Testament and Its Contribution to Theology, the Church, and the Christian

Now may the God of peace, who brought back from the dead our Lord Jesus, the great shepherd of the sheep, by the blood of the eternal covenant, make you complete in everything good so that you may do his will, working among us that which is pleasing in his sight, through Jesus Christ, to whom be the glory forever and ever. Amen.

—Hebrews 13:20–21

Outline

- **What Are the Special Theological Emphases of Hebrews?**
- **What Does Hebrews Offer to New Testament Theology?**
- **What Does Hebrews Offer to the Church?**
- **What Does Hebrews Offer to the Individual Christian?**

Objectives

1. List the main theological distinctives of Hebrews.
2. Highlight the unique and enriching contribution of Hebrews to the theology of the New Testament.
3. Explore how the theology of Hebrews can affect the practical living of Christians in the world today.

Hebrews stands like an island in the New Testament. In many respects it is quite independent theologically, unparalleled by any other New Testament writing. The other writings of the New Testament have "relatives" to keep them company: the Gospels (and Acts), the Pauline letters, and the catholic, or general, letters (James is a possible exception) are groups of related writings. Only Revelation, the single apocalyptic book of the New Testament, is, like Hebrews, by itself in the New Testament canon, and even it has some interesting familial resemblances to the Johannine literature. Certainly, some similarities do exist between Hebrews and the Pauline letters, but these are relatively insubstantial compared to the fresh, new path expounded by our author.

In emphasizing the insularity of Hebrews we must not ignore the fact that Hebrews shares basic theological convictions in common with all the early Christian writings—for example, a high Christology, Christ's death as an atoning sacrifice, the fulfillment of the Old Testament in Christ's work, salvation through Christ, the enthronement of Christ at the right hand of God, and the dawning of the present era of realized eschatology. It must be admitted, however, that even some of these can take on a particular twist in Hebrews. The fact is that our author and the Christians whom he addresses are of one accord with the basic affirmations of Christianity. They are solidly orthodox and have their undisputed place in the first-century Christian church. Although unique in character, the Book of Hebrews contains nothing heterodox.

In concluding our study of Hebrews we now take stock of the contribution of Hebrews to the New Testament, New Testament theology, the church, and the individual Christian. This should enable us to assess the significance of this remarkable book and its importance in the New Testament canon and to the Christian faith. Inevitably, there will be some overlap in the conclusions that we draw concerning these matters.

What Are the Special Theological Emphases of Hebrews?

The central and unique theological emphasis in Hebrews is the presentation of *Christ as high priest*. Much of the theological argument of Hebrews derives from this single, basic affirmation. The author presents the qualification of Christ to be a priest by means of the famous argument concerning Melchizedek, based on Psalm 110:4. From that verse, because of the connection with Psalm 110:1, he is able to draw the conclusion that Christ's priesthood is eternal and is backed up by God's oath.

Having established that Christ is a priest according to the order of Melchizedek, our author depicts *the atoning work of Christ* in terms of the work of the high priest on the Day of Atonement. In so doing, he draws out both the parallels and the contrasts between the typical high priest of Israel and the unique high priest, Jesus. The high priests of Israel had to offer sacrifice for their own sins; Christ had no need to do so. And much emphasized by our author is that the work of Israel's priests had to be performed continually, day after day, and for the high priest in the Holy of Holies, year after year. Christ's sacrifice, on the other hand, was in itself sufficient for all time. It was, as our author repeatedly delights to note, a "once for all" sacrifice. This in itself points to the defini-

ritual

Menorah on an arch of the ancient synagogue of Ostia, the seaport of Rome

tive and final character of the death of Jesus as the means of salvation.

No other New Testament writer draws out the parallels between the sacrificial **ritual** of the tabernacle/ temple and the death of Christ in such detail as does the author of Hebrews. The language of the heavenly sanctuary as the paradigm for the earthly sanctuary, and the place in

181

which Christ performs his priestly duty, is unique to Hebrews. This use of dualistic language, reminiscent of the language of Plato, is, as we have argued, our author's way of referring to what is of *final and eternal significance*—that to which the ritual of the earthly sanctuary pointed and what it foreshadowed. It is this sense of arriving at the goal of God's saving purpose that the author has in mind when he uses the word "perfection."

Perhaps the most dramatic contrast between the work of the high priests and the high priestly work of Christ, however, is that *what Christ offers as priest is his own blood*. Here, priest and sacrificial victim are one and the same. The finished work of Christ takes place on Calvary's cross, but to bring out its significance and its fulfillment of the earthly sacrifices—its perfection—it is portrayed as occurring in the ideal, heavenly sanctuary.

The doctrine of salvation in Hebrews depends on the high Christology of the opening chapters. Only the person of Christ, the unique Son of God, now sitting at God's right hand, is able to accomplish the definitive salvation that has now been made available. He alone is the "author" or "pioneer" of salvation (2:10) and faith (12:2). Only in the early chapters of Acts—in the earliest Jerusalem church—is the same title used of Jesus (Acts 3:15, "the author of life"; Acts 5:31, "God exalted him at his right hand as pioneer and savior"). Jesus has gone ahead of us, preparing the way to God's very presence by his sacrificial death as a "forerunner" (6:20).

Two other subjects must be mentioned as special to Hebrews: the emphases on the new covenant and on faith. The new covenant language is found elsewhere in the New Testament, but no one develops the idea and its consequences as thoroughly as does our author. As we have seen, it is of the greatest importance for him that the new is announced already in the old, as he indicates in the

quotation from Jeremiah 31:31–34 in chapter 8. The new covenant may be thought of correctly as growing out of the old and as the fruition of it. This theme too is intimately connected with the idea of Christ as high priest. Where the **Levitical priesthood** is displaced by another, by the emergence of a priest according to the line of Melchizedek, a new situation comes into being, one that has distinct consequences for the law. Here the old covenant gives way to the new; Sinai gives way to Zion (see 12:18–24).

Another important emphasis in Hebrews is the nature and importance of faith. No other treatment of this subject in the New Testament compares with chapter 11 of Hebrews. Here the issue is not simply theological, however, but practical. Clearly, our author's discussion of faith evolves out of his concern for the readers to remain constant in their Christian commitment.

As always, our author is interested in the practical implications of what he discusses in his theological discourses. He draws practical significance especially from the understanding of Christ as high priest, but from other theological emphases too, as we will see.

What Does Hebrews Offer to New Testament Theology?

Hebrews represents an independent strand within the New Testament. The unique emphases just reviewed make an important—indeed, indispensable—contribution to the discipline of New Testament theology. The depiction of Christ's atoning work on the cross under the **ru-**

bric of Jesus as high priest of the order of Melchizedek is again the most fundamental point here. The establishment of the legitimacy of Christ's priesthood via the connection of Psalm 110:1 and Psalm 110:4 is a brilliant and apparently original point of our author. With Christ's priesthood comes the drawing out of the detailed parallels and contrasts with the work of the high priests in the sacrificial ritual of the Old Testament. In particular, our author shows how the death of Jesus corresponds to the sacrificial ritual of the tabernacle that foreshadowed it. The language of Jesus offering his blood in the Holy of Holies in the heavenly sanctuary as a way of indicating its final and definitive character also provides a new framework in which to understand Jesus as the source of eternal salvation. This, above all, is what New Testament theology owes to the Book of Hebrews.

But other wonderful contributions must be mentioned. By the way our author works out the relationship between the old and new covenants, the salvation-history perspective of New Testament theology is deepened. From the very opening words of Hebrews we see that *the story of Israel and the story of Jesus are one story*. The new has dramatically entered history, but at the same time it stands in continuity with what preceded because it is the fulfillment of the old, as our author's brilliant use of Jeremiah 31:31–34 shows. That this at the same time necessitates, in some sense, *the end of the old* is courageously affirmed by the author. This view is held by other New Testament writers, but our author greatly enriches it. Closely related to this is our author's presentation of *Christ as the mediator of the new covenant*, a point made only in Hebrews (8:6; 9:15; 12:24).

It cannot be doubted that our author's use of the Old Testament constitutes a significant contribution to New Testament theology. It is not that christological **exegesis**, *sensus plenior*, and midrashic interpretation are unique to him; these are used abundantly by most of the other New Testament writers. What we have in Hebrews is an enrichment of, rather than an addition to, New Testament theology. In particular, we have the application of these methods to new constellations of Old Testament passages in Hebrews. These open a wider window into how daring the Christian appropriation of the Old Testament was. The Jewish Christians of the early church unhesitatingly regarded the Bible (what we call the Old Testament) as *their* book—*the book that pointed to and validated what they as Christians had come to believe.*

A further contribution, though hardly new to New Testament theology, is the high Christology of Hebrews. The first two chapters of Hebrews are significant here, since they juxtapose *a balanced stress on the deity and the humanity of Jesus*. Our author is happy to conclude that the Old Testament addresses Jesus as God, and he is happy to affirm the temporary full humanity of Jesus. This, as we noted, reflects the same three-stage Christology found in Philippians 2:6–11: preexistence, incarnation, and glorification at God's right hand. The enormous emphasis that our author puts upon Jesus sitting at God's right hand (derived from Ps 110:1) is crucial. We also saw that he regards Jesus not only as the unique Son of God and Messiah, but also as prophet, priest, and king. For New Testament theology, no one more effectively articulates the logical necessity of *the incarnation as a precondition for the death of God's Son* (2:9, 14; 10:5–9).

Yet another enrichment of New Testament theology comes from our author's emphasis on realized eschatology. The view that *eschatological fulfillment has already come* is, of course, widely shared by New Testament writers. Our author indicates

The sixth-century Medaba map of Jerusalem, a mosaic floor in a church in the Transjordan

his perspective right from the start, referring to "these last days" in his opening lines. Even in the middle of his treatise-sermon he refers to Christ as appearing "at the end of the age." The assertion that "we who have believed enter that rest" (4:3) seems also to have a dimension of realized eschatology in mind. Most striking of all, however, is the remarkable description of Mount Zion to which the readers have already come (12:22–24). Here we encounter a number of distinctly eschatological images together with the claim that "we have [already] come" to this reality. It is something we have begun to experience in advance of its full manifestation in the future. Our author keeps the typical New Testament balance between realized, or present, eschatological experience and the confident expectation of a future consummation that will resolve the present ambiguity caused by the overlap of the ages (where the new has begun, but without bringing the old to an end).

What Does Hebrews Offer to the Church?

It would be a distinct delight to the author of Hebrews that at the end of our study we turn to two practical questions. He knew better than most that theology is not meant to remain abstract or theoretical, but to have a down-to-earth impact on believers. As we have seen, one of the most conspicuous features of the sermon-treatise that we call "the Book of Hebrews" is the way in which the author alternates between discourse and application/exhortation. What can we draw from Hebrews for the life of the church and of the Christian? Of course, these questions are hardly distinct, and so we may expect overlap in the answers given. But they can be asked separately, and there seems to be some benefit in considering them individually.

We turn first to the church. In our world of constant change, in which the church's theological affirmations are challenged repeatedly, Hebrews offers theological stability in *the conviction of the absolute truth of Christianity* compared to all other voices, however good. This view is comforting, if perhaps also difficult, in our day of the generous acceptance of all religions as equally true. If the church were to heed the Book of Hebrews, it would be steadfast in its basic convictions.

Closely related to this view—indeed, the cause of it—is *the incomparable superiority of Christ* to all else. This is a favorite theme of our author. Christ is superior to the angels and he is superior to Moses. As the unique Son of God, the Anointed One of the promise, he is God's matchless eschatological Word, spoken in this present era of fulfillment. Again, this is a conclusion that the church must not compromise. The inflated claims of contemporary scholars who would make Jesus into merely one teacher among others must be firmly resisted.

A further conclusion that follows from the preceding points is also stressed by the author of Hebrews: *the finality of Christ's atoning work.* The

triumphalism

cross of Christ is the one single, final, and fully effective answer to the sin of the human race. Here, and here alone, salvation is to be found. What the detailed sacrificial ritual of the Old Testament, with its holy shrine and special priesthood, prepared for and pointed to has been fulfilled definitively in the sacrifice of Jesus. Here, too, is something that today's church must champion.

Through these points of cardinal significance to our author, the Book of Hebrews offers the church a statement of what constitutes *its true identity*. The church is the recipient, confessor, and proclaimer of God's saving activity in history. It is imperative for the church to recover and maintain that sense of its identity, regardless of the pressures of our relativistic age. This is not a call to **triumphalism**, but a call to faithful commitment to, and resistance against dilution of, our Christian faith. If Christ is truly who and what Hebrews says he is, then the church must continue to proclaim that he is sovereign Lord and that salvation is available only through him. This is the glory, privilege, and responsibility of the church.

It is because of the absolute truth of Christianity that the call to commitment is an absolute one, and that all Christians, like the first readers of Hebrews, are called to faithfulness. The urgency of the appeal to faithfulness in Hebrews is no accident, of course. As we have repeatedly noted, the original readers were in a particular danger. But using only a little imagination, we can see how the application can be made to the church today. No alternate paths should lure us away from our foundations. We must resist the new and the faddish. We must hold fast to our confession.

At the same time, however, this call to faithfulness to the past is balanced by the call to the readers to move out courageously into the unknown, as the models of faith in He-

brews 11 did. The readers are to go "outside the camp," as the well-known phrase puts it (13:13). It therefore can be said rightly that they are called to be a pilgrim people. And this certainly is true also of the church. F. F. Bruce makes this observation at the end of his commentary: "The faith once for all delivered to the saints is not something that can be caught and tamed; it continually leads the saints forth to new ventures in the cause of Christ, as God calls afresh" (*Epistle to the Hebrews*, 416). What is true of the first readers of Hebrews is true of the wider church: "Only attachment to the *unchanging and onward-moving* Christ could carry them forward and enable them to face a new order with confidence and power" (*Epistle to the Hebrews*, 417, my italics). The church can and must move forward into the future with all confidence. With a sense of its identity, the church can safely maintain an openness to the future and God's leading. Like the supreme models of faith in Hebrews 11, the church must give substance to its faith in this way. It is true that faith involves risk, but it is also true that the church has received a kingdom that cannot be shaken (12:28). If the church remains the church, it has nothing to fear from the challenges of the future.

Finally, Hebrews offers the church *a vision of realized eschatology* that ought to excite the church's understanding of its present existence. To the body of the redeemed it is said, "But you have come to Mount Zion and to the city of the living God, the heavenly Jerusalem, and to innumerable angels in festal gathering, and to the assembly of the firstborn who are enrolled in heaven, and to a judge who is God of all, and to the spirits of just men and women made perfect, and to Jesus, the mediator of a new covenant, and to the sprinkled blood that speaks more graciously than the blood of Abel" (12:22–24). As we have seen, this is a highly metaphorical and poetic portrait of the glorious nature of the present, and not merely the future, salvation of Christians. This Mount Zion is supremely a place of rejoicing. The church ought to be marked above all by rejoicing and the celebration of the great salvation that God has graced it with. To be sure, the hope of the Christian is inseparable from a final consummation and transformation of the present fallen order, but in advance of that complex of events yet to occur, God has brought the church to the experience of a foretaste of the eschaton. The church would do well to take up this point and do much more with it than it has. This perspective ought to inform its thinking and the form of its corporate life. The dimension of realized eschatology is greatly underestimated, its potential for the church having gone almost unnoticed.

What Does Hebrews Offer to the Individual Christian?

It is abundantly clear that the author of Hebrews wants his readers to tap the resources that his theology offers. The discourse material is there always to support the exhortation. All that we have spoken of so far in this chapter is, ultimately, for the sake of individual Christians. The points mentioned under the preceding headings, of course, have relevance for the experience of the Christian, especially those concerning the church. Obviously, it is of great consequence to the living of the individual Christian life to count upon the absolute truth of the Christian faith, the incomparable superiority of Christ, and the finality of Christ's atoning work. So, too, the

concept of the Christian life as that of a pilgrim who acts courageously in faith, the urgent call to faithfulness under adversity, and the joyful imagery of presently fulfilled eschatology are significant for the individual Christian.

But so much more that applies to the actual living of the Christian life has been left unexplored thus far. And it is to these matters that we now turn. A good way to begin is to draw some of the practical consequences from the theological emphases of Hebrews that we touched upon in the first section.

We start with Christ as high priest. What does that mean for the individual Christian? The fact that we have in Christ a high priest who is both fully human and fully divine impels the author to call attention to the following resources. Christ's humanity means that the Christian has a "merciful and faithful high priest" who "because he himself has suffered and been tested, is able to help those who are tested" (2:17–18). Our high priest knows the human condition from the inside, so to speak. The point is made again in 4:15: "We have not a high priest who is unable to sympathize with our weaknesses, but one who in every respect has been tested as we are, yet without sin." The meaning of this is drawn out in the following verse: we may now "draw near to the throne of grace, that we may receive mercy and find grace to help in time of need." In short, *we have as our own high priest one who understands us and is able to help us in our weakness.* Whatever our situation of need, Christ our high priest is ready and able to provide help.

The deity of Christ as the unique Son of God, on the other hand, means that he has become a priest "not according to a legal requirement concerning bodily descent but by the power of an indestructible life" (7:16). He is a priest forever, "because he continues forever," and "consequently he is able for all time to save those who draw near to God through him, since he always lives to make intercession for them" (7:24–25). We have a priest whose existence will never come to an end and *who intercedes in unending prayer to his Father on our behalf*. Our high priest represents us before God in unceasing petition. The implications for the individual Christian are tremendous.

Turning to the atoning work of our high priest on the cross and its effective and finally decisive character, we see how our author finds practical significance here too for the life of the individual Christian. This theme is of great significance in Hebrews. Christ's atoning work provides forgiveness of sins (2:17; 9:14) and thus enables us to "draw near" to the very presence of God, there to receive "mercy and grace" (4:16). At the end of the central section of Hebrews, chapters 9–10, our author explores the significance of his presentation of Christ's sacrifice as the one efficacious sacrifice that fulfills what the Old Testament sacrifices foreshadowed. The initial "therefore" of 10:19 leads to the threefold exhortation, called forth by the preceding lengthy argument: "let us draw near" (v. 22), "let us hold fast our confession" (v. 23), and "let us consider how to stir up one another to love and good works" (v. 24). This is the very heart of the author's practical concern for his Christian readers. The first exhortation is of the greatest importance: *Christ's atoning work gives the Christian unhindered access to the presence of God*, enabling us to draw near in worship and prayer.

But our author extracts more from this theme. The most conspicuous application throughout Hebrews is found in the resources provided through the atoning work of Christ that will enable the readers to persevere in their Christian profession. *On the basis of what Christ has accomplished*

on the cross, we are able to "hold fast" to what we believe, even under the most adverse circumstances. Faithfulness becomes a possibility for us because of the security that is ours through the work of Christ. This same point is made in the unique imagery of 6:18–19. When forced to seek refuge from what assails us, we are able to be strongly encouraged by seizing "the hope set before us," which is the "sure and steadfast anchor of the soul," described as "a hope that enters into the inner shrine behind the curtain," where our high priest has preceded us "on our behalf." *The individual Christian has an anchor that provides the utmost security* through whatever storms may come. Because of the work of Christ on our behalf, our future is secure.

Furthermore, this fully accomplished atoning work of Christ truly has cleansed the conscience of the Christian, enabling her or him truly to serve God (9:14). The unshakable kingdom that we have received should cause us to "give thanks, by which we offer to God an acceptable worship with reverence and awe" (12:28).

Hebrews provides an account of the work of Christ that brings with it the resources necessary to "run with perseverance the race marked out for us" (12:1). Despite the "great cloud of witnesses" mentioned in chapter 11, we are not called to look to them, but rather, to "fix our eyes on Jesus, the author and perfecter of our faith" (12:2). *Jesus, by his work, not only provides the possibility and means for Christian living, but also is himself the perfect example and model of living the life of faith and obedience.*

The challenge to sanctification in Hebrews can hardly be missed. Alongside the many exhortations to perseverance are many exhortations that concern purely ethical matters (see the sidebars "Exhortations in Hebrews" in ch. 10B and "Exhortations in Hebrews 13" in ch. 13). This

The Quintessence of Hebrews

In fulfillment of his promises in the Scriptures of the Old Testament, God has sent his unique Son—the very manifestation of God and of perfect humanity and one who is greater than even angels—to be high priest of the order of Melchizedek and to offer the definitive, once-for-all sacrifice for sins—one foreshadowed by the sacrificial ritual of the temple and one requiring no repetition—by the sacrifice of himself and the offering of his own blood, not that of animals; thereby (1) inaugurating the new covenant prophesied by Jeremiah, (2) providing a forgiveness of sins that thoroughly cleanses, (3) offering to those who believe a Sabbath rest of joy, peace, and fulfillment, the confident expectation of an eschatological inheritance, and a joyous reality that has already begun to be experienced in advance of its full coming, and (4) calling us to a life of faith that counts on the yet unseen and that motivates us to boldness and bravery in the face of every difficulty and obstacle; wherein we may count on the faithful ministrations of our high priest who is now seated at God's right hand, the one who remains constant, that great shepherd of the sheep who remains the same yesterday and today and forever.

emphasis is found in virtually all the New Testament writers. Our author's language is strong: "Pursue peace with everyone, and the holiness without which no one will see the Lord" (12:14). Quite moving is his reference in the final great doxology, where his prayer is that God may "make you complete in everything good so that you may do his will, working among us that which is pleasing in his sight" (13:21). *Above all, the Christian is called to do the will of God.* As in Philippians 2:13, the point is made here that all of our efforts at sanctification are at the same time the work of God within us.

We conclude our discussion with an emphasis on three points for which Hebrews is particularly well known: faith, discipline, and rest. All three carry high significance for the individual Christian. The examples of faith in chapter 11 are not there merely to be examined; they are to be imitated. *Christians are called to give their faith substance by acting boldly in the face of the unknown, counting upon the reality of the unseen.* In a real sense, Christians are people of another world, motivated by the unseen heavenly and better country—indeed, the city of God. The specific call to the Jewish Christian readers to "go outside the camp" contains a message for all Christians: go forth fearlessly into the unknown.

The call to regard one's trials as God's discipline is a revolutionary thought. It is not original to our author. Indeed, he quotes Proverbs 3:11–12, and his argument flows from that passage. It must have had a powerful effect on the readers, given their difficult circumstances. But its application need not be restricted to them, since it is relevant to Christian experience of any era. It is a remarkable perspective that can turn our distinctly negative experiences into positive ones. *God wants to use our sufferings for our own benefit and to make us better children of his as a result of them.* Of course, this teaching is for the mature. Not all will be able to regard suffering as the discipline of their heavenly Father. But those who do so have the wonderful promise with which our author ends this section: despite the pain of present suffering, "later it yields the peaceful fruit of righteousness to those who have been trained by it" (12:11).

Finally, we turn to the unique emphasis in Hebrews upon the rest that is ours to enter now. As we have seen, this rest refers to a state of well-being that is all encompassing. It is the experience of salvation, or more exactly, the existential fruit of salvation already in the present. It is akin to *shalom*, and it is also like the Jewish Sabbath in that it is both a joyful anticipation and a taste of eschatological blessing. *This state of rest is the right of the Christian who understands what it is that Christ has brought to us.* Since our modern world is in an age of frenetic activity, deep insecurity, and gnawing anxiety, this rest must be appropriated by Christians. The Pauline equivalent might be the notion of "the peace that passes all understanding" (Phil 4:7). The rest that is ours, and ready to be appropriated,

Key Terms

ritual
Levitical priesthood
rubric
exegesis
triumphalism

is possible only because of the work of Christ, upon which it depends. Our author appeals to us, saying, "Today, as long as it is called 'today,' let us enter that rest." Indeed, strive to enter that rest.

The Book of Hebrews has much to offer the individual Christian. It is full of challenges and specific exhortations that we do well to heed. At the same time, it offers an accompanying emphasis on the abundant provision that is ours through the high priestly work of Christ. Above all stands the reality of forgiveness and a cleansed conscience. Our ultimate perseverance and faithfulness are possible only because we possess "an anchor of the soul" that depends upon God's prior grace. And there is the wonderful promise of rest here and now, of an exciting realized eschatology that is the anticipation and guarantee of our hope. And all—all that we have spoken of, and all that the Book of Hebrews has presented to us—is possible only because of Jesus, "the great shepherd of the sheep, by the blood of the eternal covenant." To him be glory for ever and ever.

Study Questions

1. What are the central ideas around which the theology of Hebrews is formulated?

2. In what ways is Hebrews able to enrich New Testament theology?

3. What things from the teaching of Hebrews are most important for today's church?

4. What is the most important benefit from Hebrews for your own Christian life?

Excursus

The Entry of Hebrews into the New Testament Canon

corpus

papyrus

codex

uncial

Although it cannot be proved, many scholars have concluded that Hebrews was written to a Jewish Christian community, or perhaps more than one such community, in the city of Rome. What is known with certainty is that our earliest knowledge of Hebrews comes from the quotation of Hebrews in an epistle from the Roman church to the Corinthian church in 96, a document found in the **corpus** of writings known as the Apostolic Fathers. This letter commonly is associated with the name Clement of Rome, and called *1 Clement*. A clear dependence on Hebrews is found in *1 Clement* 36.2–5; 21.9; 27.2, and in the use of Hebrews 11 in chapters 9–12. Although it is obvious that Clement revered Hebrews, he provides no information concerning the identity of its author, which almost certainly was known to him. The date of *1 Clement* is too early for us to draw any conclusion from it concerning the entrance of Hebrews into the New Testament canon. But that epistle's high esteem of Hebrews cannot be doubted, and is all the more interesting given the fact that the Western church was so uncertain concerning Hebrews until well into the fourth century, despite its acceptance as Pauline from a very early date in the Eastern church. In the second-century Roman church we also see very high regard for Hebrews from the author of the *Shepherd of Hermas*, and from Justin Martyr.

Papyrus 46, the earliest **papyrus codex** of the Pauline letters known to us (ca. 200, Egypt), includes Hebrews in the midst of the Pauline letters, where it is placed between Romans and 1 Corinthians. Obviously, this indicates that it was accepted as Pauline by those responsible for the production of the codex. By comparison, the major **uncial** manuscripts (Sinaiticus and Vaticanus [fourth century] and Alexandrinus [fifth century]) all include Hebrews among the Pauline epistles, but placing it after the letters to the churches and before the letters to individuals (i.e., the Pastoral Epistles and Philemon).

In the Muratorian Canon, on the other hand, Hebrews is conspicuous by its absence. Since this canon comes from Rome very probably around 180, the absence of Hebrews points to rejection of, or at least considerable uncertainty about, the document. A little further on toward the end of the second century, Irenaeus, bishop of Lyon in Gaul, quotes Hebrews, but he too seems to have denied its Pauline authorship (according to Stephen Gobarus [sixth century]).

Very early in the third century, Tertullian of Carthage in North Africa quotes Hebrews 6:4–8, introducing it as material from "one particular comrade of the Apostles . . . Barnabas—a man sufficiently accredited by God, as being one whom Paul has stationed next to himself in the uninterrupted observance of abstinence" (*On Modesty* 20). After the quotation, he adds that the author "learned this *from* apostles, and taught it *with* apostles."

At about the same time, Clement of Alexandria included Hebrews in the Pauline corpus, concluding that Paul wrote to the Hebrews in their own language and that his traveling companion, Luke, then translated it into Greek. (Much later, this view would be accepted by Thomas Aquinas [thirteenth century].) Eusebius, our source for this information, adds,

> Hence in the Greek version of this epistle we find the same stylistic color as in the Acts. The usual opening—"Paul, an apostle"—was omitted, with good reason. As Clement says: "In writing to Hebrews already prejudiced against him and suspicious of him, he was far too sensible to put them off at the start by naming himself.... Now, as the blessed presbyter [probably Clement's teacher, Pantaenus] used to say, the Lord, the apostle of the Almighty was sent to the Hebrews; so through modesty Paul, knowing that he had been sent to the Gentiles, does not describe himself as an apostle to the Hebrews, first because he so reverenced the Lord, and secondly because he was going outside his province in writing to the Hebrews too, when he was an ambassador and apostle of the Gentiles." (*Church History* 6.14)

Another third-century Alexandrian, Origen, struggled with the authorship of Hebrews. Again we depend upon Eusebius for the following information:

> In the epistle entitled *To the Hebrews* the diction does not exhibit the characteristic roughness of speech or phraseology admitted by the Apostle himself, the construction of the sentences is closer to Greek usage, as anyone capable of recognizing differences of style would agree. On the other hand the matter of the epistle is wonderful, and quite equal to the Apostle's acknowledged writings: the truth of this would be admitted by anyone who has read the Apostle carefully.... If I were asked my personal opinion, I would say that the matter is the Apostle's but the phraseology and construction are those of someone who remembered the Apostle's teaching and wrote his own interpretation of what his master had said. So if any

church regards this epistle as Paul's, it should be commended for so doing, for the primitive Church had every justification for handing it down as his. Who wrote the epistle is known to God alone: the accounts that have reached us suggest that it was either Clement, who became bishop of Rome, or Luke, who wrote the gospel and the Acts. (*Church History* 6.25)

In about the middle of the third century, the North African bishop Cyprian alludes to Hebrews, but never quotes from it. Probably, he denied its Pauline authorship, and may not have accepted it as authoritative.

A list of New Testament writings that probably derives from the beginning of the fourth century is found in the sixth-century Codex Claromontanus. This codex contains the Pauline letters and Hebrews in Greek and Latin, with Hebrews placed at the end. The Latin list of the writings of the New Testament that appears just before Hebrews seems inadvertently to have omitted the Thessalonian letters and Hebrews. In another fourth-century Latin list deriving from North Africa (the Cheltenham or Mommsen list), however, the Pauline letters are listed as thirteen, and there is no separate mention of Hebrews as canonical.

Eusebius, bishop of Caesarea, in the first part of the fourth century, to whom we are indebted so much for his *Church History*, and whom we have quoted for valuable information concerning the early Christian Fathers, provides his own assessment of the state of the canon at about 325. He divides books into three categories: recognized, disputed, and spurious (*Church History* 3.25). The Pauline Epistles are, of course, put in the category of recognized books. The fact that he earlier mentions fourteen letters of Paul indicates that he includes Hebrews in the Pauline corpus, but he still finds it necessary to add a caveat: "Paul on the other hand was obviously and unmistakably the author of fourteen epistles, but we must not shut our eyes to the fact that some authorities have rejected the Epistle to the Hebrews, pointing out that the Roman Church denies that it is the work of Paul" (*Church History* 3.3; cf. 6.41, where he makes use of material from Hebrews, attributing it to Paul).

In contrast to the situation in the East, only in the fourth century did Hebrews gain acceptance in the Western church. F. F. Bruce summarizes how it happened:

> In 340 Athanasius [bishop of Alexandria], exiled (for the second time) from his see in Alexandria, made his way to Rome and spent a few years in the fellowship of the church there. He established good relations with the bishop of Rome (Julius I) and other church leaders, and the Roman church profited in various ways from the presence within it of such a distinguished theologian from the east. It is probable that he persuaded the Roman Christians to fall into line with their eastern brethren in admitting the canonicity, if not the Pauline authorship, of Hebrews. From that time on the right of Hebrews to be accepted as a New Testament book was not seriously questioned at Rome, or in those western churches which fell within Rome's sphere of influence. (*The Canon of Scripture* [Downers Grove, Ill.: InterVarsity, 1988], 221)

The fourth-century Latin commentators Ambrosiaster and Pelagius both seem to have known Hebrews, but continued to refer to the Pauline corpus as consisting of thirteen letters, thus not accepting Hebrews as Pauline. They wrote commentaries on all the Pauline letters, but not on Hebrews. Late in the fourth century, Philaster, bishop of Brescia, accepted Hebrews as Pauline, while Ambrose, bishop of Milan, accepted the canon-icity of Hebrews without committing himself to Pauline authorship.

Writing about the New Testament canon at about the same time, Jerome said this: "The apostle Paul writes to seven churches (for the eighth such letter, that to the Hebrews, is placed outside the number by most)" (*Epistle* 53.9). Some years later, when Jerome makes use of Hebrews, he adds the following:

> This must be said to our people, that the epistle which is entitled "To the Hebrews" is accepted as the apostle Paul's not only by the churches of the east but by all church writers in the Greek language of earlier times, although many judge it to be by Barnabas or by Clement. It is of no great moment who the author is, since it is the work of a churchman and receives recognition day by day in the churches' public reading. If the custom of the Latins does not receive it among the canonical scriptures, neither, by the same liberty, do the churches of the Greeks accept John's Apocalypse. Yet we accept them both, not following the custom of the present time but the precedent of early writers, who generally make free use of testimonies from both works. And this they do, not as they are wont on occasion to quote from apocryphal writings, as indeed they use examples from pagan literature, but treating them as canonical and ecclesiastical works. (*Epistle* 129.3)

Augustine seems to have vacillated concerning the authorship of Hebrews. In his early writings he refers to Hebrews as being by Paul. Then for some years he seemed also to entertain the idea that Hebrews was written anonymously. In his later writings (ca. 409–30), however, he consistently refers to Hebrews as being anonymous, albeit without ever casting doubt upon its authority or canonicity.

The New Testament list authorized by the Third Council of Carthage (397) includes "the thirteen epistles of the apostle Paul, the one [epistle] to the Hebrews, by the same." Although the Pauline authorship of the epistle is affirmed, it nevertheless is listed separately from the thirteen. This reflects a matter that seems to have had at least some influence on the thinking of the early Roman church: if one counts the letters accepted universally as Pauline (at that time), and not Hebrews, then Paul wrote to *seven* named churches. This point is noted specifically in the Muratorian Canon and by Cyprian, the latter even saying that Paul "was mindful of this proper and definite number" and thus "wrote to *seven* churches" (*To Fortunatus: Exhortation to Martyrdom* 11). There seemed to be an appropriateness to the number of perfection and fullness, with the number seven much preferred over the number eight!

Leaping ahead to the early sixteenth century, we find that the Catholic scholars Cardinal Cajetan and Erasmus both denied the Pauline authorship of Hebrews. In his 1516 edition of the Greek New Testament, Erasmus wrote the following about Hebrews:

> I would wish you, good reader, not to consider this Epistle of less value because many have doubted whether it is the work of Paul or some other writer. Whoever wrote it is worthy of being read by Christians on many accounts. And though in expression it is very widely different from the style of Paul, it is most closely akin to the spirit and soul of Paul. But while it cannot be shown conclusively who wrote it, we may gather from very many arguments that it was written by some other than Paul.

Likewise, Martin Luther was unable to accept that Paul was the author of Hebrews, concluding that the author was "an excellent man of learning, who had been a disciple of the apostles and had learned from them, and who was very well versed in scripture" (*Preface to Hebrews*). Later, he made the plausible conjecture that Apollos was the author. But from our perspective it seems very surprising that Luther would relegate Hebrews, along with James, Jude, and Revelation, to an appendix to the New Testament, as an inferior writing that did not possess the same value as the other New Testament books. In Luther's view, Hebrews did not express the gospel with sufficient clarity because it did not contain the Pauline doctrine of justification by faith. He does appreciate and admire the way Hebrews uses the Old Testament. When all is said and done, Luther's final assessment is a mixed one: the author "does not lay the foundation of faith, but yet he builds upon it gold, silver, precious stones. Therefore even if we find perhaps wood, straw, or hay mingled with it, that shall not prevent us from receiving such instruction with all honor; though we do not place it absolutely on the same footing as the 'Apostolic Epistles'" (*Preface to Hebrews*).

Luther's fellow reformer, John Calvin, also rejected the Pauline authorship of Hebrews, although apparently he had not the slightest qualms about its canonicity, and happily wrote a commentary on it. About Hebrews he writes,

> I embrace it without doubt among the Apostolic Epistles; nor do I doubt but that it was through a device of Satan that some have questioned its authority. . . . Wherefore let us not allow the Church of God and ourselves to be bereft of so great a blessing; but let us vindicate for ourselves the possession of it with firmness. We need however feel little anxiety as to who wrote it. . . . I cannot myself be brought to believe that Paul was the author. . . . The method of instruction and style

sufficiently show that the writer was not Paul, and he professes himself to be one of the disciples of the Apostles, which is wholly alien from Paul's custom. (*Commentary on Hebrews*)

Another sixteenth-century reformer, Beza, writing in his 1565 edition of the Greek New Testament, is more positively inclined toward the Pauline authorship of Hebrews:

Let us however allow liberty of judgment of this point, provided only we all agree in this, that this Epistle was truly dictated by the Holy Spirit . . . while it is written in so excellent and so exact a method, that (unless we can suppose Apollos wrote it, whose learning and eloquence combined with the greatest piety are highly praised in Acts) scarcely any one except St. Paul could have been the writer.

Finally, we turn to the remarks of William Tyndale, who, in the 1534 edition of his English translation of the New Testament, had this to say about Hebrews:

About this epistle hath ever been much doubting and that among great learned men who should be the author thereof. . . . Now whether it were Paul's or no I say not, but permit it to other men's judgments, neither think I it to be an article of any man's faith, but that a man may doubt of the author. Moreover, many there hath been which not only have denied this epistle to have been written by any of the apostles, but have also refused it altogether as no catholic or godly epistle, because of certain texts written therein. . . . Of this ye see that this epistle ought no more to be refused for holy, godly and catholic than the other authentic scriptures. . . . It is easy to see that [the author] was a faithful servant of Christ's and of the same doctrine that Timothy

---

Key Terms

corpus
papyrus
codex
uncial

---

was of, yea and Paul himself was, and that he was an apostle or in the apostles' time or near thereunto. And seeing the epistle agreeth to all the rest of the scripture, if it be indifferently looked on, how should it not be of authority and taken for holy scripture?

To summarize: virtually from the beginning, Hebrews was accepted as canonical by the Eastern church, including Alexandria. This usually, but not in every instance, entailed the opinion that it was written by Paul. It was not until the fourth century that the same view prevailed in Rome and the Western church. Here too, however, the Pauline authorship of Hebrews remained less than certain. What all of this suggests is that the direct apostolic authorship, in this case by Paul, was not an absolute requirement for the acceptance of Hebrews as authoritative and canonical. What seems to have been required as a minimum was apostolic association—that is, that the author had been a member of the larger apostolic circle.

If it remains true that we cannot presently know the author of Hebrews, it also remains true that Hebrews is one of the great books of the New Testament, Luther's view of it notwithstanding. Its canonical standing and authority are secure by the providence of God and the leading of the Holy Spirit in the deliberations of the church down through the centuries.

Select Bibliography

Commentaries on Hebrews

After decades of relative neglect, Hebrews is now well furnished with excellent, major commentaries. Indeed, in recent years no less than five important technical commentaries on Hebrews appeared. Each of these is excellent and exhibits well the distinctive emphases of the respective series in which it appears:

Attridge, H. W. *The Epistle to the Hebrews*. Hermeneia. Philadelphia: Fortress, 1989.

deSilva, D. A. *Perseverance in Gratitude: A Socio-Rhetorical Commentary on the Epistle "to the Hebrews."* Grand Rapids: Eerdmans, 2000. More specialized in its approach, with valuable insights drawn from social and cultural phenomena such as patron-client scripts, kinship language, honor discourse, purity codes, and rituals.

Ellingworth, P. *The Epistle to the Hebrews*. New International Greek Testament Commentary. Grand Rapids: Eerdmans, 1993.

Koester, C. R. *Hebrews*. Anchor Bible 36. New York: Doubleday, 2001.

Lane, W. L. *Hebrews*. 2 vols. Word Biblical Commentary 47A, 47B. Waco, Tex.: Word, 1991.

Still useful are several of the older commentaries, among which the following deserve special mention:

Bruce, F. F. *The Epistle to the Hebrews*. New International Commentary on the New Testament. Rev. ed. Grand Rapids: Eerdmans, 1990. Still the most generally useful and best all-around moderately sized commentary on Hebrews.

Delitzsch, F. J. *The Epistle to the Hebrews*. 2 vols. ET, 1868. Reprint, Minneapolis: Klock & Klock, 1978. A classic that consistently repays close study.

Hughes, P. E. *A Commentary on the Epistle to the Hebrews*. Grand Rapids: Eerdmans, 1977. Rich theologically, with helpful references to patristic study of Hebrews.

Westcott, B. F. *Commentary on the Epistle to the Hebrews*. 1892. Reprint, Grand Rapids: Eerdmans, 1952. Masterful.

For shorter, less technical treatments, the following are useful:

Gordon, R. P. *Hebrews*. Readings: A New Biblical Commentary. Sheffield: Sheffield Academic Press, 2000.

Hagner, D. A. *Hebrews*. New International Biblical Commentary. Peabody, Mass.: Hendrickson, 1990.

Pfitzner, V. C. *Hebrews*. Abingdon New Testament Commentaries. Nashville: Abingdon, 1997.

Other Books and Articles

Anderson, C. P. "Hebrews among the Letters of Paul." *Studies in Religion/Sciences Religieuses* 5 (1975–76): 258–66.

Barrett, C. K. "The Eschatology in the Epistle to the Hebrews." In *The Background of the New Testament and Its Eschatology*, ed. W. D. Davies and D. Daube. Cambridge: Cambridge University Press, 1954. Pp. 363–93.

———. "The Christology of Hebrews." In *Who Do You Say I Am? Essays on Christology*, ed. M. A. Powell and D. R. Bauer. Louisville: Westminster John Knox, 1999. Pp. 110–27.

Bockmuehl, M. N. A. "The Church in Hebrews." In *A Vision for the Church:*

Studies in Early Christian Ecclesiology in Honour of J. P. M. Sweet, ed. M. N. A. Bockmuehl and M. B. Thompson. Edinburgh: Clark, 1997. Pp. 133–51.

Brooks, W. E. "The Perpetuity of Christ's Sacrifice in the Epistle to the Hebrews." *Journal of Biblical Literature* 89 (1970): 204–14.

Bruce, F. F. "'To the Hebrews' or 'To the Essenes'?" *New Testament Studies* 9 (1963): 217–32.

———. "The Kerygma of Hebrews." *Interpretation* 23 (1969): 3–19.

———. "The Structure and Argument of Hebrews." *Southwestern Journal of Theology* 28 (1985): 6–12.

———. "'To the Hebrews': A Document of Roman Christianity?" In *Aufstieg und Niedergang der römischen Welt: Geschichte und Kultur Roms im Spiegel der neueren Forschung,* ed. H. Temporini and W. Haase. Part 2, *Principat,* 25.4. New York: de Gruyter, 1987. Pp. 3496–521.

Campbell, J. C. "In a Son: The Doctrine of the Incarnation in the Epistle to the Hebrews." *Interpretation* 10 (1956): 24–38.

Carlston, C. E. "Eschatology and Repentance in the Epistle to the Hebrews." *Journal of Biblical Literature* 78 (1959): 296–302.

Clements, R. E. "The Use of the Old Testament in Hebrews." *Southwestern Journal of Theology* 28 (1985): 36–45.

Dahms, J. V. "The First Readers of Hebrews." *Journal of the Evangelical Society* 20 (1977): 365–75.

Ellingworth, P. "Jesus and the Universe in Hebrews." *Evangelical Quarterly* 58 (1986): 337–50.

France, R. T. "The Writer of Hebrews as a Biblical Expositor." *Tyndale Bulletin* 47 (1996): 245–76.

Gooding, D. W. *An Unshakable Kingdom: The Letter to the Hebrews for Today.* Leicester: InterVarsity, 1989.

Gordon, R. P. "'Better Promises': Two Passages in Hebrews against the Background of the Old Testament Cultus." In *Templum Amicitiae: Essays on the Second Temple Presented to Ernst Bammel,* ed. W. Horbury. Journal for the Study of the New Testament Supplement Series 48. Sheffield: JSOT Press, 1991. Pp. 434–49.

Guthrie, G. H. *The Structure of Hebrews: A Text-Linguistic Analysis.* Biblical Studies Library. Grand Rapids: Baker, 1994.

Hagner, D. A. "The Son of God as Unique High Priest: The Christology of Hebrews." In *Contours of Christology in the New Testament,* ed. R. N. Longenecker. Grand Rapids: Eerdmans, forthcoming.

Horbury, W. "The Aaronic Priesthood in the Epistle to the Hebrews." *Journal for the Study of the New Testament* 19 (1983): 43–71.

Hughes, G. *Hebrews and Hermeneutics: The Epistle to the Hebrews as a New Testament Example of Biblical Interpretation.* Society for New Testament Studies Monograph Series 36. Cambridge: Cambridge University Press, 1979.

Hughes, P. E. "The Christology of Hebrews." *Southwestern Journal of Theology* 28 (1985): 19–27.

———. "The Epistle to the Hebrews." In *The New Testament and Its Modern Interpreters,* ed. E. J. Epp and G. W. MacRae, 351–70. Philadelphia: Fortress, 1989.

Hurst, L. D. *The Epistle to the Hebrews: Its Background of Thought.* Society for New Testament Studies Monograph Series 65. Cambridge: Cambridge University Press, 1990.

Isaacs, M. E. *Sacred Space: An Approach to the Theology of the Epistle to the Hebrews.* Journal for the Study of the New Testament Supplement Series 73. Sheffield: Sheffield Academic Press, 1992.

Johnsson, W. G. "The Cultus of Hebrews in Twentieth-Century Scholarship." *Expository Times* 89 (1978): 104–8.

————. "The Pilgrimage Motif in the Book of Hebrews." *Journal of Biblical Literature* 97 (1978): 239–51.

Käsemann, E. *The Wandering People of God: An Investigation of the Letter to the Hebrews.* Minneapolis: Augsburg, 1984.

Kistemaker, S. *The Psalm Citations in the Epistle to the Hebrews.* Amsterdam: Van Soest, 1961.

Koester, C. R. "The Epistle to the Hebrews in Recent Study." *Currents in Biblical Study* 2 (1994): 123–45.

Lane, W. L. *Hebrews: A Call to Commitment.* Peabody, Mass.: Hendrickson, 1985.

————. "Hebrews: A Sermon in Search of a Setting." *Southwestern Journal of Theology* 28 (1985): 13–18.

Leschert, D. F. *The Hermeneutical Foundations of Hebrews.* Lewiston, N.Y.: Mellen, 1994.

Lindars, B. "The Rhetorical Structure of Hebrews." *New Testament Studies* 35 (1989): 382–406.

————. *The Theology of the Epistle to the Hebrews.* New Testament Theology. Cambridge: Cambridge University Press, 1991.

Manson, T. W. "The Problem of the Epistle to the Hebrews." *Bulletin of the John Rylands Library* 32 (1949–50): 1–17.

McCown, W. G. "Holiness in Hebrews." *Wesleyan Theological Journal* 16 (1981): 58–78.

Meyer, W. D. "Obedience and Church Authority: The Problem of the Book of Hebrews." *Ashland Theological Journal* 28 (1996): 9–28.

Nairne, A. *The Epistle of Priesthood.* Edinburgh: T & T Clark, 1915.

Olbricht, T. H. "Hebrews as Amplification." In *Rhetoric and the New Testament,* ed. S. E. Porter and T. H. Olbricht. Journal for the Study of the New Testament Supplement Series 90. Sheffield: Sheffield Academic Press, 1993. Pp. 375–87.

Parsons, M. C. "Son and High Priest: A Study in the Christology of Hebrews." *Evangelical Quarterly* 60 (1988): 195–215.

Porter, S. E. "The Date of Composition of Hebrews and Use of the Present Tense Form." In *Crossing the Boundaries: Essays in Biblical Interpretation in Honour of Michael D. Goulder.* Leiden: Brill, 1994. Pp. 295–313.

Pryor, J. W. "Hebrews and Incarnational Christology." *Reformed Theological Review* 40 (1981): 44–50.

Schäfer, J. R. "The Relationship between Priestly and Servant Messianism in the Epistle to the Hebrews." *Catholic Biblical Quarterly* 30 (1968): 359–85.

Schmidt, T. E. "Moral Lethargy and the Epistle to the Hebrews." *Westminster Theological Journal* 54 (1992): 167–73.

Smalley, S. S. "The Atonement in the Epistle to the Hebrews." *Evangelical Quarterly* 33 (1961): 36–43.

Stanley, S. "The Structure of Hebrews from Three Perspectives." *Tyndale Bulletin* 45 (1994): 245–71.

Stewart, R. A. "Creation and Matter in the Epistle to the Hebrews." *New Testament Studies* 12 (1966): 284–93.

Stott, W. "The Concept of 'Offering' in the Epistle to the Hebrews." *New Testament Studies* 9 (1962): 62–67.

Swetnam, J. "Sacrifice and Revelation in the Epistle to the Hebrews." *Catholic Biblical Quarterly* 30 (1968): 227–34.

————. "Form and Content in Hebrews 1–6; 7–13." *Biblica* 53 (1972): 368–85; 55 (1974): 333–48.

————. "Christology and the Eucharist in the Epistle to the Hebrews." *Biblica* 70 (1989): 74–95.

Tasker, R. V. G. *The Gospel in the Epistle to the Hebrews.* London: Tyndale, 1950.

Tetley, J. "The Priesthood of Christ in Hebrews." *Anvil* 5 (1988): 195–206.

Thomas, K. J. "The Old Testament Citations in the Epistle to the Hebrews." *New Testament Studies* 11 (1965): 303–25.

Thompson, J. W. *The Beginnings of Christian Philosophy: The Epistle to the Hebrews.* Catholic Biblical Quarterly Monograph Series 13. Washington, D.C.: Catholic Biblical Association, 1982.

———. "The Hermeneutics of the Epistle to the Hebrews." *Restoration Quarterly* 38 (1996): 229–37.

Trotter, A. H., Jr. *Interpreting the Epistle to the Hebrews.* Guides to New Testament Exegesis 6. Grand Rapids: Baker, 1997. An excellent book, providing much helpful information and sage advice.

Vanhoye, A. *Our Priest Is Christ: The Doctrine of the Epistle to the Hebrews.* Rome: Pontifical Biblical Institute, 1977.

———. *Structure and Message of the Epistle to the Hebrews.* Rome: Pontifical Biblical Institute, 1989.

Vos, G. *The Teaching of the Epistle to the Hebrews.* Grand Rapids: Eerdmans, 1956.

Wikgren, A. "Patterns of Perfection in the Epistle to the Hebrews." *New Testament Studies* 6 (1960): 159–67.

Williamson, R. "Hebrews and Doctrine." *Expository Times* 81 (1969–70): 371–76.

———. "The Eucharist and the Epistle to the Hebrews." *New Testament Studies* 21 (1974–75): 300–312.

———. "The Background of the Epistle to the Hebrews." *Expository Times* 87 (1975–76): 232–37.

———. "The Incarnation of the Logos in Hebrews." *Expository Times* 95 (1983–84): 4–8.

Witherington, B., III. "The Influence of Galatians on Hebrews." *New Testament Studies* 37 (1991): 146–52.

Glossary

admonition
A warning or exhortation given in the love of Christ, meant to affect the behavior of those to whom it is given.

adoptionist
A view that maintains that Jesus Christ is the Son of God by adoption only, as, for example, at the resurrection.

Akedah
The binding of Isaac just prior to the near sacrifice of Isaac by Abraham (Genesis 22), notable for its parallel to the offering of God's Son on the cross.

allusion
An indirect reference, short of quotation, to a passage of Scripture.

anachronism
The erroneous reference of an event, circumstance, or custom to a wrong date; anything done or existing out of date.

anchor
A fixed point that provides stability and security.

apostasy
Abandonment or renunciation of one's religious faith.

archetype
The original pattern or model from which copies are made; a prototype.

atonement
The death of Jesus on the cross as the reestablishment, reconciliation, or restoration of the ruptured relationship between God and sinners.

benediction
A blessing that is stated, often at the end of a letter or sermon.

camp, the
The community of Israel, alluding to the wilderness experience. The author of Hebrews uses this term to draw a parallel between the suffering of Jesus "outside the camp" and the suffering of his readers, whose Christian faith has put them outside the camp of Israel and subjected them to abuse.

Christology
That branch of theology relating specifically to the person of Christ; a doctrine or theory concerning Christ.

codex
An ancient book form that replaced the scroll with pages; made from papyrus, parchment, or vellum.

cognate
Something akin in origin, nature, quality; kindred, related, connected, having affinity.

confession
In the objective sense, common in the New Testament, this term refers to what is believed and what is confessed at the time of baptism.

continuity
Substantial connection of present realities with past realities; e.g., the new covenant as the realization of the promises of the old covenant.

corpus (pl., corpora)
A collection of writings grouped together, usually because of common or similar origin.

covenant
A formal agreement between two parties establishing a relationship with mutual obligations and responsibilities.

covenant/will
The double meaning of the Greek word *diathēkē*. Both words involve death. A will is enacted only upon someone's death; a covenant is established by the death of an animal.

Day, the
The time of eschatological judgment.

discipline
Subjection to temporary and painful experience for one's ultimate good.

discontinuity
The way that present realities bring a degree of newness that moves one beyond the realities of the past; e.g., the new covenant brings one to a level of experience that could not be experienced earlier.

docetic
Used of an early sect of heretics who held that Christ was not genuinely human but only "seemed" or "appeared" (*dokeō*) to have a human body and to be a human person.

doxology
A form of praise to God, and in the case of Hebrews, also to Jesus, as in 13:21, "through Jesus Christ, to whom be glory for ever and ever."

dualism
A viewpoint that regards reality as divided into two irreducible elements or modes. In Hellenistic thought this often took the form of a division between matter and spirit, as in Plato's concept of heavenly ideas corresponding to earthly realities.

eschatological
Of or relating to eschatology, the study of the last things.

eschatology
That branch of systematic theology dealing with the doctrines of the last things (*ta eschata*).

exegesis
Literally, "a drawing out." In biblical studies it is the act of interpreting or explaining the meaning of a passage of Scripture.

exhortation
The act of warning or advising in regard to desirable conduct.

expiation
The act of making atonement; the means by which atonement is made in the removal of sin and guilt.

faith
Belief, trust, and obedience to God as revealed in Jesus Christ.

forgiveness
The pardoning or remitting of an offense, which restores right relationship with God.

functional Christology
Refers to the nature of Christ in terms of the salvific function performed by Jesus; "the work of Christ." (See *ontological Christology*.)

Gnosticism
A viewpoint that developed into a cult in the second century of the Christian era, distinguished by the conviction that matter is evil and that emancipation comes through *gnosis* ("knowledge").

grammatico-historical interpretation
The interpretation of biblical texts by focusing on their syntactical constructions and cultural and historical contexts in order to arrive at the author's intended meaning.

guarantee
Surety or confirmation; e.g., Jesus is the guarantee of a better covenant.

heavenly Jerusalem
A symbol in Jewish literature for ultimate salvation and the experience of eschatological *shalom*.

hermeneutic
Belonging to or concerned with the underlying rationale of interpretation, especially as distinguished from exegesis or practical exposition.

hope
Confident expectation based on God's reliability and faithfulness.

house
In Hebrews this term refers to those who confess faith in Jesus as their apostle and high priest, those who acknowledge Jesus as the unique Son of God. The distinction between "house" and "builder of the house" is important.

imperative
Grammatical term for words that express command, request, or exhortation.

incarnation
The doctrine that the second person of the Trinity became a human being.

indicative
Grammatical term for words that point out, state, or declare something.

Levitical priesthood
The traditional priestly line of the Israelites originating with the tribe of Levi. In the argument of Hebrews this is displaced by the emergence of a priest in the line of Melchizedek.

Masoretic Text
Text of the Hebrew Bible compiled by Jewish scholars in the tenth and preceding centuries, constituting the authorized text.

metaphor
Figure of speech in which a name or descriptive term is transferred to some object different from, but analogous to, that to which it is properly applicable. A metaphor is not to be taken literally.

midrash
An ancient Jewish homiletic commentary on some portion of the Hebrew Scriptures involving free use of allegorical interpretation and legendary illustration. Also, the mode of treatment of the text characteristic of this class of commentaries.

Mount Zion
In Hebrews this image is contrasted with Mount Sinai of the old covenant and is a description of the present reality to which Christians have come, the new covenant and its blessings.

oath
Sworn confirmation of one's word; e.g., God took an oath to show more convincingly the unchangeable character of his purpose.

offering
The presentation of one's self or one's possessions to God.

ontological Christology
Refers to the nature of Christ's being; "the person of Christ." (See *functional Christology*.)

papyrus
An ancient writing material made from a plant. Sheets were formed by pasting thin strips in two crosswise layers.

paraenesis
Admonition, usually ethical and eclectic in nature. A text containing paraenesis exhorts readers to appropriate conduct.

perfect
In Hebrews, the end result of the progressive accomplishment of God's will in Jesus' dying on the cross and fulfilling the accomplishment of salvation.

pesher
Hebrew for "commentary." A commentary form using the formula "this means that."

Platonic idealism
The philosophy of Plato that stresses that actual things are copies of transcendent ideas and that these ideas are the objects of true knowledge.

polemic
An aggressive attack on or refutation of the opinions or principles of another.

possession
That which one owns or holds. The author of Hebrews motivates his readers by reminding them of their confidence in a more lasting possession.

prima facie
"At first sight"—initial evidence suggests a particular conclusion.

propitiation
A theological term for making atonement for sin by offering an acceptable sacrifice. Often used to describe the death of Christ and related to the appeasement of God's wrath.

prototype
The original pattern or model from which copies are made; an archetype.

realized eschatology
The view that certain passages in the New Testament do not have an exclusively future reference but are to be understood as being fulfilled in biblical times and especially in the life and ministry of Jesus. This is eschatology in the process of being realized prior to the full coming of future eschatology.

rest
God's rest for the Israelites was thought to be possession of and security in the promised land, but the author of Hebrews stresses that it is more of a transcendental spiritual rest, which involves security, contentment, satisfaction, and peace for God's people.

rhetorical criticism
A form of scriptural analysis that seeks to discover those aspects within a text that demonstrate a reliance on the art of writing or speaking as a means of communication or persuasion.

ritual
A ceremony, usually with religious significance; e.g., the sacrificial ritual of the temple, centering on the sacrifice of animals.

rubric
A title or heading.

sacrifice
Something of value offered as an act of worship or devotion to God by which sins are forgiven and right relationship established.

sanctification
The continuing action of God in making believers holy in their conduct by the power of the Holy Spirit.

sensus plenior
"Fuller sense." The hermeneutical affirmation that the Scriptures contain meanings that go beyond the literal sense or meaning explicitly intended by the original author for the specific cultural-historical audience of the period in which the text was written. This meaning is seen only in retrospect.

Septuagint (LXX)
The Greek version of the Old Testament, deriving its name from the legend that it was made by seventy-two Palestinian Jews (six from each of the twelve tribes) at the request of Ptolemy Philadelphus (284–247 B.C.), being completed in seclusion on the island of Pharos in seventy-two days.

servant
One who is faithful in obedience to God; e.g., Moses was said to be a faithful servant in God's house.

Shekinah
The glorious presence of God in the world as conceived in the Old Testament and Jewish theology.

Son
A unique designation for Jesus in contrast to the title of servant. The title Son implies an unequaled relation to God and rule over God's house.

substance
In Hebrews, refers either to a subjective confidence or, especially in Hebrews 11:1, to an objective reality in the sense of solid evidence.

synonymous parallelism
In poetry, especially Hebrew poetry, the second line of a couplet repeats the thought of the first line in different words.

today
A day set by God for his people to enter his rest. In Hebrews this has both present and eschatological significance.

triumphalism
A view that stresses the victories of the Christian life or church. Often viewed negatively if it does not give a true representation or tries to cover up injustices and oppression against those who are weaker or fewer in number, the vanquished.

type
Forerunner with significant points of comparison; e.g., the priest Melchizedek was a type for Christ.

typology
The study of similarities (or types) found especially in patterns of historical correspondence in the Old Testament and the New Testament. Typology rests on the conviction that since the similarities are divinely intended, the earlier items foreshadow the later, which in turn are regarded as their fulfillment.

uncial
A type of writing in which each letter is printed separately as a capital letter. Also called "majuscule," in contrast to "minuscule" or "cursive" writing, where lowercase letters are written in connected form.

wisdom Christology
Refers to the use of Wisdom (*Sophia*) as a circumlocution for Israel's God and the application of that title to Jesus. Wisdom is one of the basic categories that enrich and inform the early church's Christology.

witness
One who testifies of what is known to be true. In Hebrews the "great cloud of witnesses" are those who are attested to by their faith.

Scripture Index

Genesis

1:3 144
1:26 34
1:28 34
2:2 73
3:19 125
4:1–16 145
4:2–16 144
4:10 145, 165
5:22–24 144, 145
5:24 145
6:1–4 48
6:9–22 144, 145
6:22 145
12:1–3 60
12:1–4 146
12:1–8 144
12:3 116
12:8 146
13:3 146
14 28
14:18–20 98
14:19–20 99
14:22 99
15:6 146
17:15–21 144
18:1 146
18:1–8 171
18:9–15 144
18:11–15 148
18:12 147
18:17–23 99
19:1–3 171
21:1–7 144
21:7 147
21:12 150
22 201
22:1–14 144, 149, 150
22:2 150
22:5 150
22:8 150
22:16 92
22:17 148
23:4 144, 146, 149
25:33–34 161
27:27–29 144, 150
27:30–40 161
27:39–40 144, 150
47:31 151
48:14 151
48:15–20 144, 151
48:20 151

49 151
50:24–25 144, 151

Exodus

2:1–2 144, 151
2:11–15 144, 151
2:16 99
3:6 149
3:14 145
12:12–13 144, 152
12:21–30 144, 152
12:51 152
13:19 151
14:21–29 144, 152
17:1–7 66, 72
19:12 162
19:12–19 162
19:13 162
19:18 166
20:18–21 162
24:3–8 124
24:8 124
25–26 119
25:8 118
25:40 30, 111
28:1 83
40:34–35 120

Leviticus

4:2 120
4:13 120
4:22 120
4:27 120
8:15 124
8:19 124
16 119, 120
16:2 120
16:6–34 105
16:15–16 122
17:11 124

Numbers

12:7 64, 65
14:20–25 66, 72
14:29 67
15:27–29 120
19:9 122
19:17–19 122
19:18–19 124
24:17 102

Deuteronomy

4:11 162
4:24 167
5:22–25 162
9:3 167
9:19 162
17:6 138
19:15 138
29:18 161
31:6 171
31:8 171
32:35–36 138
32:43 47, 48
33:2 163

Joshua

1:5 171
2:1–24 144, 153
6:12–21 144, 152
6:17 144, 153
6:23–25 144, 153
22:4 74
24:32 151

Judges

4:6–5:31 153
6:11–22 171
6:11–8:32 153
11:1–12:7 153
13:2–16:31 153
13:3–21 171
14:6 153

1 Samuel

1–12 153
16–30 153
17:34–35 153

2 Samuel

7 31
7:4–17 47
7:14 31, 47
7:16 47

1 Kings

17:17–24 153, 154
19:1–8 153
19:10 153

2 Kings

4:25–37 153, 154

1 Chronicles

29:15 149

2 Chronicles

24:20–22 153

Job

1:6 48
2:1 48
38:7 48

Psalms

2 46, 47
2:2 46, 47
2:7 28, 31, 46, 47, 83, 84
2:8 47
2:9 47
8 34, 55, 56
8:4–6 34
8:6 55
22 33, 58
22:6–8 58
22:14–17 58
22:18 58
22:22 33, 58
29:1 48
33:6 144
33:9 144
34:14 160
39:12 149
40 129, 131, 132
40:6 129, 130
40:6–8 28, 129, 130
45:6–7 31, 47, 48
51:16 129
68:8 166
78 144
87:1 147
95 66, 77
95:7–8 66
95:7–11 28, 66, 68, 72
95:11 66, 74
102:25–27 32, 47, 49, 166
102:27 172
104:4 27, 47, 48, 50
110 29, 44, 49

110:1 31, 44, 47, 49, 55, 56,
    78, 83, 84, 102, 105, 110,
    131, 159, 180, 183
110:4 28, 44, 49, 83, 84, 85,
    98, 100, 101, 102, 103,
    104, 105, 106, 110, 180,
    183
118:6 171
135:14 138

Proverbs

3:11–12 29, 159, 188
4:26 160
8:27–30 42
8:27–31 42

Isaiah

1:11 129
6:1–5 82
8:11 34
8:13 59
8:17–18 33, 34, 58
26:11 137, 167
33:14 167
35:3 160
42:1 47
42:6 116
49:8 73
53 130
53:12 124
55:3 175

Jeremiah

26:23–24 153
31 132
31:31 114, 115, 174
31:31–34 28, 103, 113, 114,
    123, 131, 165, 182, 183
31:33 114
31:33–34 29, 132, 165
31:34 114, 165
32:40 115, 175

Ezekiel

36:25–26 136
37:26 175

Daniel

3:13–30 153
6:22 153
7:10 163

Hosea

6:6 129

Amos

5:21–22 129

Micah

6:6–8 129

Habakkuk

2:3–4 29, 139
2:4 21, 138

Zephaniah

1:18 167
3:8 167

Haggai

2:6 29, 166
2:21 166

1 Maccabees

2:51–64 144

2 Maccabees

5:27 153
6:11 153
10:6 153

4 Maccabees

13:12 150
16:20 150

Sirach

44–50 144
44:20 150

Tobit

5:4–9 171

Wisdom of Solomon

7:25–26 42, 43
9:2 42
9:9 42
10 144
10:5 150

2 (Syriac) Baruch

4 163

Matthew

1:5 153
2:15 58
3:13–15 58
3:17 47
4:1–11 58

5:8 161
5:9 161
5:17 35
6:24–34 171
17:5 47
18:10 50
21:39 172
22:32 149
22:37–40 170
22:41–46 102
23:35 145, 165
24:2 137
24:29 166
25:35 170
25:38 170
25:44 170
26:28 124
26:36–46 84
26:38 84
26:39 84
27 33
27:51 135

Mark

1:11 47, 150
9:7 47, 150
10:45 124
12:6 150
12:29–31 170
13:1–2 115
14:27 174
15:38 135

Luke

2:32 36
3:22 47
4:25–26 154
9:35 47
10:18 59
10:20 163
12:15 171
18:13 120
21:19 139
22:20 115
23:45 135

John

1:1–18 43
1:3 42
1:14 43, 60
1:18 43, 48
3:16 150
3:18 150
4:22 36
6:45 113
8:56 149
10:11 174

12:31 59
14:9 43
19–20 33
19:20 172

Acts

2:21 59
2:34–35 59
3:15 58, 182
4:25–26 47
4:27 47
4:36 22
5:31 58, 182
6:7 24 n. 6
7 22, 144
7:20 151
7:38 54
7:44 111
7:45 74
7:53 54
12:15 50
13:33 47
18:24–25 23
18:24–28 22
18:26 22

Romans

1:4 47
1:17 21, 138
2:15 113
3:24–26 44
3:25 60, 119, 120
4:11 146
4:16–18 148
4:16–22 147
4:17 150
4:17–21 93
4:19 147
4:20–21 147
5:5 143
5:15 124
5:18 124
5:19 124
6:19 161
6:22 161
7:6 121
7:11–12 113
8:17 163
8:18–25 155
8:26–27 105
8:32 150
8:34 105
8:37–39 154
9:5 36
10:4 121
10:13 59
11:5 114

11:27 113
12:10 170
12:13 170
12:15 171
12:18 161
13:9–10 170
14:17 172
14:19 160
15:33 174
16:20 174
16:22 22

1 Corinthians

1:9 137
1:30 161
2:9 154
3:2 86
5:7 68
6:9 171
8:6 42
8:8 172
9:24 158
10:11 66, 126
10:13 137
11:25 115
12:26 171
13:13 134, 142
14:33 174
15:2 91
15:25 131
15:26 59
15:27 55
15:45 78
15:55 60

2 Corinthians

1:18 137
3:6 115
3:6–18 161
3:7–11 64
4:4 43
4:6 43
4:17 160
5:14–15 124
6:1 91
6:2 73
9:4 143
11:17 143
13:5 91
13:11 161, 174

Galatians

1:12 21, 22
2:2 158
3:9 146
3:11 21, 138
3:15–17 123

3:16 93
3:19 54
3:23–25 121
4:24 115
4:24–31 161
4:26 147, 163
5:7 158

Ephesians

1:22 55
2:6 162
5:5 171

Philippians

1:23 60
2:6–11 43, 57, 183
2:8–9 56–57
2:9–11 59
2:10–11 41
2:12–13 175
2:13 188
2:16 91, 158
3:11 91
3:20 126
4:7 74, 189
4:9 174

Colossians

1:7 22
1:15 43
1:15–20 43
1:16 42
1:17 43
2 25
2:16 172
2:16–17 121
2:17 112, 128
2:18 45
2:21–23 172
3:5 171
4:12–13 22

1 Thessalonians

4:3 161
4:9 170
5:23 174
5:24 137

1 Timothy

2:5 123
2:6 124
3:2 170
4:3 172
5:10 170
6:6–10 171
6:16 152

2 Timothy

1:10 59
2:13 137
2:22 161
4:7 158
4:8 126

Titus

1:8 170

Hebrews

1 27, 28, 66, 175
1:1 40
1:1–2 40
1:1–4 28
1:1–14 26
1:2 33, 40, 42, 46, 47, 48,
  49, 65, 73, 121, 126, 144,
  164
1:2–3 41
1:3 42, 43, 49, 50, 110, 131,
  143
1:4 45, 46
1:4–14 50
1:5 31, 46, 47, 83
1:5–8 27
1:5–13 46, 47
1:5–14 25, 28
1:6 33, 47, 48, 58
1:7 27, 47, 48, 50
1:8 48
1:8–9 31, 47, 48
1:9 32
1:10 65
1:10–12 32, 47, 49, 58, 166
1:12 48, 172
1:13 31, 44, 47, 49, 55, 56,
  83, 110
1:13–2:3 27
1:14 27, 48, 50
1:17 60
2 61, 62
2:1 66, 135, 173
2:1–3 136, 137, 138, 165
2:1–4 26, 27, 28, 54, 158
2:3 21, 22, 25, 137
2:5 56
2:5–9 25, 27, 28, 54
2:5–3:6 26
2:6–8 28, 34
2:7 105
2:8 34, 55, 56, 164
2:9 40, 56, 60, 78, 90, 124,
  130, 183
2:10 57, 65, 84, 105, 123,
  136, 158, 182
2:10–18 28, 57

2:11 57
2:12 60
2:12–13 33
2:13 33
2:14 48, 60, 130, 183
2:14–18 58
2:16 60
2:17 61, 64, 78, 104, 105,
  120, 130, 187
2:17–18 77, 159, 186
2:18 78, 82, 92, 104
3–4 66
3:1 27, 61, 65, 66, 78, 123,
  135, 136
3:1–6 28, 64
3:1–4:13 27
3:2 61
3:5 65, 151
3:6 61, 65
3:7 76
3:7–11 66, 67
3:7–19 26, 28, 66
3:7–4:11 27, 72
3:7–4:13 174
3:12 23, 67, 135, 138, 173
3:12–14 136, 137
3:12–4:10 27
3:12–4:11 28
3:13 67, 135
3:14 67, 91, 92, 143
3:15 66, 67, 76
3:16 67, 76
3:17 67
3:18 67
3:18–19 67
4:1 135, 136, 137
4:1–11 72
4:1–13 28
4:1–16 26
4:2 67, 76
4:3 66, 73, 75, 84, 164, 184
4:4 73, 74
4:5 66, 73
4:6 72
4:7 66, 76
4:7–9 72
4:8 74
4:9 74
4:10 74, 75
4:11 73, 75, 76, 135, 136,
  173
4:12 76
4:12–13 76
4:14 27, 49, 65, 104, 105,
  110, 122, 135, 136
4:14–15 61
4:14–16 28, 77, 92, 172

4:15 60, 61, 82, 104, 105, 123, 186
4:15–16 159
4:16 77, 78, 135, 136, 164, 187
5 82
5–9 78
5:1–4 60, 82
5:1–10 26, 28
5:3 120
5:5 47, 61, 104
5:5–6 28, 84, 98, 105
5:5–10 83
5:6 49, 85, 100, 101, 122
5:7 84, 85
5:7–8 92
5:8 65, 160
5:8–9 85
5:9 57, 83, 86, 105, 122, 158
5:9–12 92
5:10 49, 61, 85, 94, 98, 100
5:11 98
5:11–6:3 28, 85
5:11–6:12 26, 28, 82
5:11–6:19 98
5:12 86
5:12–14 24
5:14 57
6 77, 94
6:1 23, 57, 135
6:1–2 86
6:2 86
6:4 65, 90, 137, 139
6:4–5 91
6:4–6 91, 92, 135, 137, 161, 173
6:4–8 134, 191
6:4–12 28, 90, 132
6:5 41, 73, 164
6:6 65
6:9 46, 139
6:10 25, 137, 139, 170, 171
6:11 92, 135, 143, 164
6:11–12 92
6:12 144
6:13–15 146
6:13–18 103
6:13–20 28, 92
6:13–10:18 26
6:14 92, 93
6:15 93, 149
6:17 93
6:18 93, 95, 135
6:19 77, 93, 95, 103, 164
6:19–20 93
6:20 49, 61, 65, 78, 93, 100, 104, 122, 182
7 28, 85, 106

7–10 85
7:1 82, 98, 100
7:1–10 28, 98
7:1–22 44
7:2 98, 100
7:3 49, 65, 99, 100
7:4 100
7:5 100
7:6 99, 100
7:7 46, 101
7:10 100
7:11 49, 57, 100, 101, 103
7:11–22 101
7:11–28 27, 28
7:12 101
7:14 65, 102
7:15 49, 100
7:16 102, 104, 186
7:17 49, 100, 101, 122
7:18 101, 103
7:18–19 130
7:19 46, 57, 77, 103
7:20–21 106
7:21 49, 103, 122
7:22 46, 65, 103, 104, 107, 112, 165, 174
7:23–27 118
7:23–28 104
7:24 49, 104, 122, 172, 175
7:24–25 187
7:25 77, 104, 105, 125, 159, 164, 172
7:25–26 107
7:26 49, 61, 78, 104, 105, 122
7:27 82, 105, 111, 120, 122, 128
7:28 47, 49, 57, 65, 82, 104, 105, 122
8 28, 132, 182
8–10 61, 107
8:1 30, 49, 61, 104, 131
8:1–2 78
8:1–6 28, 110
8:1–7 128
8:2 65, 104, 110, 112, 121
8:2–5 112
8:3 60, 111
8:4 111
8:5 30, 65, 110, 111, 121, 122, 124, 125, 128, 167
8:6 46, 65, 104, 112, 116, 123, 164, 174, 183
8:6–12 165
8:7 101, 104, 113, 130
8:7–13 28, 113
8:8 104, 114, 115
8:8–10 114

8:8–12 103, 123, 175
8:9 104, 114
8:10 104, 114
8:11 114
8:12 114, 123, 165
8:13 25, 35, 101, 104, 114, 115, 130
9 28
9–10 44, 105, 111, 114, 172, 174, 187
9:1 104, 122, 167
9:1–10 28, 111, 118
9:3 135
9:4 104
9:4–5 119
9:5 60, 119, 120, 176
9:6 120, 167
9:7 60, 61, 82, 93, 120, 122
9:8 120, 135
9:9 57, 120, 121, 122, 167
9:9–10 101
9:10 25, 121, 122
9:11 30, 57, 61, 104, 121, 122, 124, 128, 164
9:11–12 78, 110
9:11–14 121
9:11–10:18 28
9:12 86, 104, 105, 112, 121, 122, 124, 172, 175
9:12–14 174
9:13 122
9:13–14 165
9:14 23, 82, 86, 122, 136, 138, 167, 187
9:14–15 122
9:15 65, 86, 104, 105, 112, 114, 115, 122, 123, 136, 164, 165, 174, 183
9:15–22 123
9:16–17 123
9:18 104
9:18–22 122
9:19 124, 165
9:20 124, 174
9:21 124, 165
9:22 124
9:23 46, 65, 101, 122, 125
9:23–24 30, 122
9:23–25 112
9:23–26 128
9:23–28 124
9:24 112, 121, 122, 124, 125
9:25 82, 125
9:25–26 124
9:25–28 122
9:26 41, 105, 122, 125
9:27 125, 164

9:28 82, 105, 124, 139, 164
10 28
10:1 30, 57, 77, 101, 112, 122, 124, 164
10:1–3 122
10:1–4 128
10:2 122, 167
10:4 101
10:4–10 122
10:5 57, 130
10:5–9 183
10:5–10 128, 129
10:5–14 27
10:8–10 129, 130
10:8–18 27
10:9 101, 130
10:10 105, 130, 131, 172
10:10–14 122
10:11 111, 122, 131
10:11–12 82
10:11–18 131
10:12 105, 131
10:12–13 49
10:13 131, 164
10:14 57, 122, 131
10:16 104
10:16–17 114, 165
10:17 132, 165
10:17–18 123
10:18 132
10:19 77, 134, 174, 187
10:19–21 164
10:19–25 28, 134
10:19–39 26, 90, 91
10:20 135
10:21 61, 65, 66, 136
10:22 77, 134, 135, 136, 164, 187
10:22–24 136, 139, 142
10:23 66, 92, 134, 135, 136, 187
10:24 134, 135, 140, 170, 187
10:24–25 161
10:25 164
10:26–27 161
10:26–29 137
10:26–31 28, 136, 137
10:26–36 134
10:27 137, 164, 167
10:27–31 139
10:28–29 138, 165
10:29 78, 104, 137, 165, 174
10:30 138, 164
10:30–31 167
10:31 164
10:32 25, 90, 135

10:32–34 25, 92, 159
10:32–39 28, 138
10:33–34 171
10:34 46, 137, 139, 170, 171
10:35 135, 137, 139, 140, 173
10:36 136, 137, 138, 139
10:37 137, 138, 164
10:38 21
10:39 136, 139, 149
11 20, 29, 143, 144, 146, 158, 161, 172, 182, 185, 187, 188, 191
11:1 30, 143, 145, 146, 147, 149, 152, 204
11:1–3 142
11:1–40 26, 28
11:2 143, 154, 158
11:3 30, 142, 144, 146
11:4 144, 172
11:4–7 144
11:5 144, 145
11:6 77, 145, 146, 152
11:7 144, 145, 146
11:8 146
11:8–9 146
11:8–10 144, 146, 149
11:8–12 92
11:9 146
11:10 137, 146, 149, 163, 173
11:11 137, 146, 148
11:11–12 144, 147
11:12 147, 148
11:13 146, 149
11:13–16 147, 149
11:14 146, 149
11:14–16 137, 173
11:15 149
11:16 46, 65, 146, 149, 163
11:17 146, 149, 150
11:17–19 92, 144, 149, 150
11:18 150
11:19 150
11:20 144
11:20–22 150
11:21 144, 151
11:22 144, 151
11:23 144, 151
11:23–28 151
11:24–26 151

11:24–28 144
11:25 152
11:25–26 161
11:26 137, 146, 151, 152
11:27 145, 146, 152
11:29–30 144, 152
11:29–38 152
11:31 144, 152
11:32 22, 23 n. 3, 153, 176
11:32–38 153
11:33–34 153
11:35 46, 137, 153, 154
11:35–38 145, 153, 154
11:38 154
11:39 143, 149, 154, 158
11:39–40 154
11:40 46, 57, 137, 149, 155, 164
12 25, 29
12:1 135, 158, 187
12:1–3 158
12:1–17 26, 28
12:2 49, 57, 58, 65, 123, 131, 158, 159, 182, 187
12:3 135, 159, 173
12:3–11 136
12:4 25, 139
12:4–11 159
12:5–6 159
12:5–11 27
12:7 159, 172
12:7–8 160
12:7–11 159
12:8 159, 172
12:9 159, 160
12:10 159, 160
12:11 160, 188
12:12 160
12:12–13 135
12:12–17 160
12:13 160
12:14 160, 188
12:15 78, 135
12:16–17 161
12:17 172
12:18 162
12:18–24 26, 28, 54, 121, 161, 182
12:20 162
12:21 162
12:22 41, 65, 138, 147, 162, 163, 176
12:22–24 73, 164, 184, 185

12:23 57, 163, 164, 176
12:24 46, 65, 104, 112, 115, 123, 145, 164, 165, 172, 174, 183
12:25 54, 135, 138, 166
12:25–29 165
12:25–13:6 26
12:25–13:17 28
12:26 166
12:27 166
12:28 135, 164, 166, 173, 185, 187
12:29 138, 164
13 29, 29 n. 14, 135, 170
13:1–9 170
13:1–19 170
13:2 170
13:3 171
13:4 60, 171
13:5 171
13:7 173
13:7–21 26
13:8 43, 48, 49, 122
13:9 25, 60, 78, 171, 172
13:10 167, 172
13:10–15 29
13:10–16 172
13:12 172, 174
13:13 136, 152, 159, 173, 185
13:14 137, 147, 163, 173
13:15–16 173
13:17 173
13:18–19 173
13:18–21 28
13:20 65, 86, 104, 115, 122, 165
13:20–21 170, 174
13:21 173, 175, 188, 202
13:22 22, 26, 29
13:22–23 176
13:22–24 170
13:22–25 28
13:23 22, 173
13:24–25 176
13:25 78, 170
32:43 33

James

2:21–22 146
2:21–23 150

2:24 145
2:25 153
2:26 145

1 Peter

1:1 149
1:2 164
1:6–7 160
1:15 161
1:22 170
2:2 86
2:5 173
2:11 149
3:11 160–161
3:15–16 59
4:9 170
4:11 175
4:12–14 160
5:4 174
5:12 22

2 Peter

2:21 138
3:18 175

1 John

1:1 60
2:1 105
4:2 60

3 John

5–8 170

Revelation

1:6 175
1:17–18 172
2:26 47
2:27 47
5:11 163
7:11 163
12:5 47
19:6 163
19:15 47
19:16 59
21:2 147, 163
21:10 147, 163
21:14 147
21:19 147
22:4 161

Subject Index

Aaron, 83, 99, 102
Abel, 144–45, 162, 165, 185
Abraham, 28, 92–93, 98–101, 103, 144, 146–50
Adam, 130
Akedah, 150
Alexandria, 112
altar, 172
Ambrose, 193
Ambrosiaster, 193
Amos, 153
analogy, historical, 67
anchor, metaphorical use of, 93
angels, 46, 48–51, 54–56, 163, 170–71
  as God's servants, 48
  as intermediaries, 45
  superiority of Christ to, 45–46, 48, 50, 57, 64, 184
  worship of, 45
anointing, 48
Antiochus, 153
apocalyptic literature, 164
Apollos, 22
apostasy, 54, 77, 89–95, 133–40, 167
Apostolic Fathers, 191
Aquinas, Thomas, 191
Ark of the Covenant, 119
Arminian, 91
ascension, 46, 49–50, 55, 83, 174
asceticism, 171–72
Athanasius, 193
atonement, 43, 58, 60, 78, 92, 103, 107, 118, 120–21, 138, 184
Augustine, 193

baptism, 136
Barak, 153
Barnabas, 22
benediction, 169–77
Beza, 195
blessing, eschatological, 145, 189
blood, 118–24, 128, 164–65, 174, 182–83, 185, 189
Boaz, 153
Bruce, F. F., 121, 163, 185, 193
Buchanan, George W., 29, 44

Cain, 144–45
Cajetan, 194
Calvin, John, 21, 85, 194
Calvinist, 91
Carthage, Third Council of, 194
Christianity, 86, 90, 110, 128, 159, 184–85
Christology, 31, 33, 57, 59–60, 175, 180, 182–83
  doctrine of, 86
  functional, 49
  logos, 76
  ontological, 49
  wisdom, 42–43
church, 75, 120, 123, 131, 163, 184–86
  early, 44, 47, 83, 182
  leaders, 172–73
Claudius, 139
Clement of Alexandria, 191
Clement of Rome, 22, 191
Codex Claromontanus, 192
comfort, 136
confession, 136, 171
confidence, 136, 139, 142–43
courage, 136, 159
covenant
  Abrahamic, 60, 93, 116
  better, 104, 109–16, 123, 174
  contrast of old and new, 122, 162, 182–83
  Davidic, 47–48
  eternal, 86, 104, 115, 122, 174–75, 189
  in Hebrews, 104
  new, 103–4, 109–16, 123–24, 128, 131–32, 156, 162, 164–67, 173–75, 177, 182, 188
  old, 111, 113–16, 119–20, 122, 125, 128–29, 131, 156, 162, 164, 182
  second, 113
cross, 61, 82, 84, 90, 105, 110, 122, 125–26, 128, 158–59, 182
crucifixion, 58, 135, 172
Cyprian, 192, 194

Daniel, 153
David, 74, 102, 153
Dead Sea Scrolls, 24, 31, 48, 98
death, 59–60, 125, 162
devil, 59
discipline, 136, 159–60, 188
discontinuity, motif of, 35–36, 101, 113
docetic, 60
Dodd, C. H., 119
doxology, 170, 188
dualism, 30, 65, 112, 171
  eschatological, 30
  metaphysical, 111–12
  Platonic, 65, 111–12, 182
  temporal, 111–12

election/predestination, 91
Elijah, 98, 145, 153
Elisha, 153
encouragement, 137–39
endurance, 133–40, 158
Enoch, 144–45
Epaphras, 22
Ephraim, 151
Erasmus, 194
Esau, 144, 161
eschatology, 40, 54, 56, 65, 72, 73, 121, 126, 137, 161–62, 164, 166, 180, 183–86, 189
eschaton, 75, 128, 154
Essenes, 24
ethics
  Hellenistic, 86
  New Testament, 132
Eusebius, 191–92
exodus, 68, 151–52
expectation, 46, 142, 145, 184
expiation, 119

faith, 86, 92, 134, 138, 141–56, 182, 188
  according to Hebrews 11:1, 143
  Christian, 128
  examples of, 141–56, 153, 172
  James' view of, 145
  Paul's view of, 145–46, 148

faithfulness, 133–40, 157–67, 185, 187, 189
fellowship, 137
firstborn, assembly of, 163
food prohibitions, 172
forgiveness, 82, 105, 114, 120, 123, 128, 165, 187–89

Gethsemane, garden of, 84, 85
Gideon, 153
glory, 42, 56–57, 175
Gnosticism, 25, 45, 171–72
Gobarus, Stephen, 191
God
  character of, 167
  faithfulness of, 89–95, 137, 143
  as helper, 171
  holiness of, 118, 159, 162
  house of, 64, 66
  Jesus as essence of, 43
  as judge, 164
  kingdom of, 50, 166
  people of, 75, 113, 151–52
  power and authority of, 162
  presence of, 77, 79, 93, 134–36, 164, 167, 187
  provision of, 174
  reward of, 145–46
  sovereignty of, 44, 91
  will of, 84, 105, 139–40, 175, 188
  word of, 144
gospel, the, 72, 103
grace, 177
Guthrie, George, 29

Harnack, Adolf von, 85
heaven, 125, 163, 166
Hebrews
  audience, 23–25, 46, 72, 90, 92, 161, 170, 176–77, 191
  anti-gnostic elements in, 60
  archetypes in, 26
  argument of, 26, 165
  authorship, 20–23, 112, 173, 176, 191–95
  "better" in, 46

canonicity of, 180, 191–95
"city" in, 163
date, 25, 111
"eternal" in, 86, 122
exhortations in, 26, 54, 135, 169–77, 184–86
genre, 29–30
"grace" in, 78
"heavenly" in, 65
"many" in, 124
"offer" in, 82
"once for all" in, 105
outline, 28
and Pauline Epistles, 21
place in New Testament, 179–89
purpose of, 25–26, structure of, 26–29, 135, 170, 176
theology of, 134, 180–84
"today" in, 73–74
unseen in, 145–46
"Word of God" in, 76
hermeneutic, 23
holiness, 160–61
Holy of Holies, 118–20, 122, 134, 135, 180, 183
Holy Spirit, 54, 67, 90, 120, 123, 131
hope, 93, 134, 142–43, 149, 152, 186–87
Hosea, 153
hospitality, 170–71

idealism, Platonic, 23, 30
imitation, 142, 144, 172
imperative, 73, 75
incarnation, 48, 54, 57–62, 77, 183
indicative, 73, 75
inheritance, 122–23, 137, 156, 163, 188
interpretation
    christocentric, 31, 34, 46, 58, 129–30, 183
    grammatico-historical, 20
    Jewish, 100
    Midrashic, 27–29, 55, 58, 67, 73, 75, 98, 129–30, 139, 166, 183
    of Old Testament, 30–35, 46–50, 66, 74, 86
    Pesher, 31, 33
Irenaeus, 191
Isaac, 144, 146–47, 149–51
Isaiah, 153
Israel
    election of, 116

people of, 92, 144, 146, 152
remnant of, 114

Jacob, 144, 146, 150–51
Jephthah, 153
Jeremiah, 153, 165
Jerome, 193
Jerusalem, 99, 114, 115, 118, 137, 146, 162–64, 185
Jesus Christ
    as Anointed One, 184
    as apostle, 64, 65
    as author of faith, 158, 182
    coming of, 131
    as creator, 33, 42, 49
    death of, 54, 57–59, 62, 85, 90, 114, 120–25, 134, 164, 180–81
    deity of, 48, 50, 54, 62, 123, 183, 186
    exaltation of, 50, 56
    final truth of, 40
    flesh of, 135
    as forerunner, 65, 93
    as fulfillment of Old Testament, 31
    as God, 183
    as God's eschatological Word, 184
    as guarantee of covenant, 103–4, 107
    as heir of all things, 41, 65
    "historical," 45
    humanity of, 54, 57, 62, 78, 123, 130, 183, 186
    humility of, 57
    identification with YHWH, 48, 59
    as king, 45
    as kyrios (Lord), 33–34, 49, 58, 65
    as mediator of new covenant, 65, 112, 123–24, 136, 183, 185
    as Messiah, 31–33, 46, 48, 102, 120, 125, 183
    as minister, 65
    as model, 158, 187
    as perfecter of faith, 65, 158
    as pioneer of salvation, 57, 58, 65, 123, 136, 182
    prayer of, 85
    as priest/high priest, 44–45, 60–62, 65, 77–79, 81–87, 92–

94, 97–107, 110–12, 122–23, 125, 130, 136, 139, 159, 164, 172, 175, 180–83, 186–88
    prophecy of, 137
    as prophet, 34, 45, 123
    as representative of Israel, 34, 58
    as sacrifice, 82, 105, 110, 117–26, 128, 131, 135, 150, 172–74, 177, 180–82, 185, 187–88
    as second Adam, 33 n. 22, 78
    as shepherd, 65, 174, 188–89
    sinlessness of, 77–78, 105, 123
    as Son, 34, 40–51, 55, 64, 65, 83, 100, 105, 120, 122, 124, 126, 138, 177, 182–84, 186, 188
    as source of salvation, 183
    teaching of, 48
    as telos, 31, 35
    titles of, 20, 65
    truth of, 40
    as wisdom personified, 42
Jethro, 99
Joseph, 144, 151
Josephus, 98
Joshua, 74, 152–53
Judah, 114
Judaism, 35–37, 86, 90, 110, 115, 145, 151, 159, 162, 172
Judas Maccabeus, 153
judgment, 86, 92, 98, 126, 137–39, 145, 165–67
Justin Martyr, 191

land, 92
Last Supper, 124
law, the, 35, 101–3, 106, 112–13, 119–21, 138, 182
love, 134, 137, 142, 170
Luke, 22
Luther, Martin, 194

Manasseh, 151
Manson, T. W., 25
marriage, 170–71
martyrdom, 139, 145, 153, 159, 163, 171
Masoretic Text, 30
maturity, 85–87

Melchizedek, 28, 44, 46, 61, 94, 97–107, 180, 183, 188
mercy, 114
Mercy Seat, 120
Michael, the archangel, 98
money, love of, 170–71
Morris, Leon, 119
Moses, 54, 63–69, 99, 102, 110, 144, 151–52, 161–62, 184
Muratorian Canon, 191, 194

Nag Hammadi, 98
Nero, 139
Noah, 144–45

oath, 92, 95, 103, 106, 180
obedience, 73, 77, 84, 85, 142–43, 145, 150, 170, 173
oral tradition, 84, 115
Origen, 21, 192

Papyrus 46, 191
paraenesis, 137
Passover, 68, 152
Pelagius, 193
Pentateuch, 102
perfect/perfection, 57, 84, 86, 101, 121, 127–32, 154–55, 164, 182
persecution, 86, 139, 154, 159, 171
perseverance, 75, 92, 139–40, 187, 189
Pharisees, 86
Philaster, 193
Philo, 30, 34, 98, 100, 112, 146, 159
Plato, 112
preparation and fulfillment, 54
priesthood, 82, 86, 100–103, 106, 118, 120, 152, 165, 172, 180, 182
Priscilla, 22
prison, 170–71
promise(s), 46, 56, 92, 95, 100, 137, 142
propitiation, 119

Qumran, 24, 31, 33

Rahab, 144, 152–53
reconciliation, 128
redemption, 86, 105, 114, 122
repentance, 86, 94
rest, 66, 71–76, 188–89
resurrection, 46–47, 50, 85, 86, 154, 164, 174

rhetoric, 26–27
righteousness, 48, 86, 160
Rome, 177
Ruth, 153

Sabbath, the, 76, 112, 189
sacrifice(s), 44, 46, 82, 105, 111, 114, 118, 123–25, 129, 131, 145, 173
    cessation of, 132
    insufficiency of, 128–29
    ritual of, 77, 103, 111, 118–21, 164, 173, 181, 183, 185, 188
    true, 172–73
saints, 155–56, 163–64
salvation, 40, 46, 54, 57, 84–86, 90–92, 101, 103–5, 107, 121–23, 125, 128, 130, 136, 138, 152, 156, 162–

63, 177, 180, 183, 186, 188
Samson, 153
Samuel, 153
sanctification, 58, 131–32, 161, 187
Sarah, 144, 147–48
Sensus Plenior, 27, 31–34, 46, 55–56, 183
Septuagint, 30, 33–34, 48, 130
servant, 64–65
sexual immorality, 171
Shadrach, Meshach, and Abednego, 153
shalom, 72, 76, 160, 163, 174, 189
Shekinah, 120
Silas, 22
sin, 43, 59–60, 82, 92, 120, 124–26, 128, 137, 158

Sinai, Mount, 111, 120, 162–64, 182
solidarity, 92
Solomon, 47, 111, 153
Spirit, eternal, 86, 122–23
strength, 136
suffering, 33, 57, 61, 92, 125, 139, 154, 158–60, 170–71, 173, 188
synonymous parallelism, 55
Synoptic Gospels, 115, 135

tabernacle, 110–12, 118–20, 124, 181, 183
Talmud, Babylonian, 98
temple, 77, 86, 93, 110–11, 115, 118–20, 125, 167, 181
temptation/testing, 61–62, 78–79
Tertullian, 191

throne, 48
Timothy, 176
Torah, 121
trinity, doctrine of, 49
triumphalism, 185
Tyndale, William, 195
typology, 34, 67–68, 72, 100, 172–73

unbelief, 66–69, 84
uncial manuscripts, 191

victory/triumph, 154, 159

witnesses, cloud of, 158
works, 74, 75, 137
worship, 167

Yom Kippur, 61, 119

Zechariah, 153
Zion, Mount, 161–65, 182, 184–86